Shakespeare's Sonnets:

A Record of 20th-Century Criticism

by

Tetsumaro Hayashi

The Scarecrow Press, Inc.
Metuchen, N.J.   1972

Other books by the same author:

1. Sketches of American Culture (1960)
2. Steinbeck: A Concise Bibliography (1930-1965) (1967)
3. Arthur Miller Criticism (1969)
4. A Looking Glasse for London and England by Thomas Lodge and Robert Greene, an Elizabethan Text   ed. (1970)
5. Robert Greene Criticism (1971)
6. Steinbeck: The Man and His Work ed. with Richard Astro (1971)

Monographs by the same author:

1. A Textual Study of A Looking Glasse for London and England (1969)
2. John Steinbeck: A Guide to the Doctoral Dissertations (1946-1969)   ed. (1971)

Journals edited by the same author:

1. Steinbeck Quarterly (1968-   )
2. Steinbeck Monograph Series (1970-   )

Dedicated to Louis Marder,

A Distinguished Editor of the Shakespeare Newsletter,

Teacher, Scholar, and Educator

Table of Contents

Page

Preface vi

Key to Abbreviations xi

Chronology: The Principal Dates in Shakespeare's Life xii

Chapter One: Primary Sources (Sequence numbers 1-154)
A. Facsimile Editions (1-9) 15
B. Modern Editions (10-154) 15

Chapter Two: Secondary Sources (Criticism of the Sonnets) (155-1974)
A. Books (155-272) 23
B. Discussions in Books (273-755) 31
C. Articles and Book Reviews: (756-1580)
   (1) Articles: (756-1426) 55
   (2) Book Reviews: (1427-1514) 86
   (3) Book Reviews ("See References" only): (1515-1580) .. 90
D. Individual Sonnet Criticism (1581-1922) 93
   "See References" 110
E. Biography (1923-1974) 112

Chapter Three: Background Sources (1975-2503)
A. Life in Shakespeare's England (1975-2043) 115
B. English Renaissance (2044-2107) 118
C. Pre-Shakespearean English Drama (2108-2159) 121
D. Shakespeare in the Theatre (2160-2267) 124
E. Shakespeare's Drama: (2268-2355)
   (1) Comedies (2268-2294) 129
   (2) Histories (2295-2311) 130
   (3) Problem Plays (2312-2318) 131
   (4) Tragedies (2319-2346) 132
   (5) Tragicomic Romances (2347-2355) 133
F. Language and Style (2356-2383) 134
G. Textual Problems (2384-2422) 135
H. Reference Books (2423-2503) 137

Appendix A. A List of Reference Guides Consulted 141

Appendix B. A List of Annuals, Newspapers, and Periodicals Indexed 143

Author Index 149

Preface

I. PURPOSE

No teacher of Shakespeare's Sonnets can be unaware of one of the frustrating paradoxes of contemporary criticism: while the uninterrupted flow of scholarship attests both to Shakespeare's perpetual appeal and to his richness, this same criticism serves to set back the student and scholar alike, so vast, so dazzling, and so chaotic does it sometimes seem to be. Consequently, scholars have long felt the need of a clear and functional bibliography for the sonnets, a guide which might provide a sense of order and cohesiveness to this fascinating aspect of Shakespearean criticism. For although many of the materials herein have been recorded, indexed, reviewed, and catalogued before, they have never had the shelter of a single roof. And so, when the Modern Language Association, through the good offices of Professor W. R. Elton's Shakespeare Research and Opportunities, set before me this interesting challenge, I unhesitatingly accepted it. My objectives, which are largely self-evident, are to save the student of the sonnets time, energy, and frustration, as well as to effect a more efficient dissemination and use of scholarly materials.

II. SCOPE AND LIMITATIONS

Admittedly, this bibliography is selective rather than exhaustive. My controlling principle was to include all worthy critical materials published on the sonnets and/or reprinted in English since 1900. Most of these materials, primary and secondary alike, were published in the United States and England; yet, where I thought entries from other countries might be of particular interest to the student and scholar, I included those materials as well. My only hope is that I have successfully wedded a close and informed selection with a broad enough scope, so that no significant item has been omitted.

III. RESEARCH METHODS AND ACKNOWLEDGMENTS

To complete my work, I have entered the debt of many individuals and institutions. I have had access to some of the finest libraries in the country either by direct visit, by interlibrary loan, or by correspondence. Especially cooperative have been the Ball State University Library, the Cleveland Public Library, the Folger Shakespeare Library, the Indiana University Library, the Kent State University Library, the University of California Library (Berkeley), and the University of Chicago Library.

Mr. Donald L. Siefker, head of the Reference Division at the Ball State University Library, and his staff were extremely helpful in obtaining critical research materials through their interlibrary loan service. Both Professor Hyman Kritzer, director of the Kent State University Libraries, and Dr. Ronald Roskens, vice president of Kent State University, kindly permitted me access to that excellent graduate research library and extended me the privilege of visiting research scholar, both in the summer of 1970 and in the spring of 1971. To these individuals and their staffs, and to the respective libraries I am indebted.

Of course, no scholarly idea can be conceived without funding. The Office of Research at Ball State University under the direction of Dr. Charles E. Smith, Jr., and the Office of Vice President Dr. Richard W. Burkhardt, provided a special research grant during the 1970-1971 academic year. This grant made it possible for me to visit the Kent-Cleveland area to examine the holdings of various libraries, as well as to cover the inevitable expenses of manuscript preparation.

Thirdly, a number of publishers allowed me to examine very late editions, which I have here indexed. These publishers are Appleton-Century-Crofts, Barnes and Noble, Blaisdell Publishing Co., Dent (London), Dutton, Funk and Wagnalls, Harper and Row, D. C. Heath, McGraw-Hill, New American Library, Penguin Books, Peter Pauper Press, F. H. Revell Co., Schocken Books, the University of California Press (Berkeley), and Washington Square Press.

Fourthly, Dr. Louis Marder, the eminent Shakespeare scholar and editor of the Shakespeare Newsletter, has given me valuable and constant advice on research methods, sources, the organization of the bibliography, and other pertinent matters connected with the project from its inception. Dr. Reloy Garcia, associate professor of English at Creighton University and senior contributing editor of the Steinbeck Quarterly, has advised me on the manuscript and generously helped me improve its contents and organization.

To these scholars, administrators, librarians, publishers, friends, and to many other generous and helpful people I owe my sincere and grateful thanks.

IV. A SURVEY OF THE BIBLIOGRAPHIES
     OF SHAKESPEARE'S SONNETS

There are at least five major bibliographies which at various lengths treat the sonnets: (1) William Jaggard's Shakespeare Bibliography (Stratford-upon-Avon: Shakespeare Press, 1911), which includes five pages of material on the sonnets (pp. 452-456); (2) Walter Ebisch and Levin L. Schucking's A Shakespeare Bibliography (Oxford: Clarendon Press, 1931), which devotes seven pages to the sonnets (pp. 263-269), together with its supplement (London: Oxford University Press, 1936), reprinted by Benjamin Blom (New York, 1964), which indexes two pages of material; (3) Samuel A. Tannenbaum's Shakespeare's Sonnets: A Concise Bibliography (New York: S.A. Tannenbaum, 1940; Elizabethan Bibliographies No. 10), which devotes 88 pages to the sonnets; (4) Joseph M. Kuntz's Poetry Exposition (Chicago: Swallow Press, 1962), which indexes 75 items in eight pages (pp. 220-227) on 43 of the sonnets; (5) and, lastly, Professor Gordon Ross Smith's impressive A Classified Shakespeare Bibliography, 1936-1958 (University Park: Pennsylvania State University Press, 1963), which devotes nine pages to sonnet criticism (pp. 764-772). Although these bibliographies are of unquestioned value, each has its own particular strengths and limitations. My intention is to counter their weaknesses and buttress their strengths. Yet, my own book, having its defining weaknesses and strengths, is best seen as a guide and complement to other works on the sonnets.

I also urge beginning students of Shakespeare's sonnets to read two concise and excellent essays on the sonnet scholarship: Louis B. Wright and Virginia A. LaMar's "Introduction" to Shakespeare's Sonnets (New York: Washington Square Press, 1967) and Irving Ribner's "Preface" to The New Kittredge Shakespeare: The Sonnets (Waltham, Mass.: Blaisdell, 1968). Beginning students will find these essays sensible and sound; it is my own belief that students and scholars should avoid the pitfalls of extreme and fanciful interpretation, a belief these essays reinforce, for, the sonnets, after all, are better served by judicious and measured analysis.

V. SPECIAL FEATURES OF THIS BOOK

Every bibliography is defined by its bibliographical intent and informed by the identity of its topic, genre, or author. Yet, I feel that this bibliography has several distinctive features. First, in Part II, it contains the largest index to date of critical materials on the sonnets, functionally classified by individual sonnet. It indexes all known worthy materials since 1900, and especially since 1958, the closing date of Professor Smith's fine bibliography. Secondly, my work not only attempts to give a clear and comprehensive picture of 20th-century sonnet criticism, it also maps out directions that future criticism might take. Thirdly, given that Shakespeare employed the sonnet form in other works, as in Love's Labor's Lost and Romeo and Juliet, Part III, "The Background Sources," places the sonnets in the larger context of the poet's total creative activities. Lastly, Part IV, "A List of Annuals, Newspapers, and Periodicals Indexes," provides the means by which the user of this bibliography can piece together and update his own criticism long after the publication of this work.

VI. CONCLUSION

Should this bibliography achieve its primary objectives, then the expenditure of my own time and effort shall have been worthwhile. In the final analysis, my larger hope was to discover a sense of historical perspective in the works of scholars who, working independently in many lands, find a community of purpose in elucidating the sonnets.

In principle I have followed Kate L. Turabian's Manual, which is more descriptive than the MLA Style Sheet, but I have simplified this bibliographical system when I thought it beneficial to the user of this book.

Tetsumaro Hayashi

April, 1971

Key to Abbreviations

CHEL = Cambridge History of English Literature.
EIC = Essays in Criticism.
ELN = English Language Notes.
ES = English Studies.
(F) = Facsimile edition.
JEGP = Journal of English and Germanic Philology.
JELH = Journal of English Literary History.
MLN = Modern Language Notes.
MLQ = Modern Language Quarterly.
MLR = Modern Language Review.
MP = Modern Philology.
N & Q = Notes & Queries.
n. p. = No publisher identified.
n. v. = No volume number known.
PMLA = Publication of the Modern Language Association of America.
PQ = Philological Quarterly.
(R) = Review or Reviewer.
RES = Review of English Studies.
S = Shakespeare.
SJ = Shakespeare Jahrbuch (Germany).
SNL = Shakespeare Newsletter.
SQ = Shakespeare Quarterly.
SR = Saturday Review.
SS = Shakespeare Survey.
TLS = Times (London) Literary Supplement
YWES = Year's Work in English Studies

xi

Chronology: The Principal Dates in Shakespeare's Life

1557   Marriage of John Shakespeare of Stratford-on-Avon
        to Mary Arden.

1558   Accession of Queen Elizabeth.

1564   (April 26) Baptism of William Shakespeare, third
        child of John and Mary Shakespeare. (Stratford
        Parish Register).

1568   John Shakespeare became bailiff of Stratford.

1576   The Theatre, the first permanent public theater in
        London, was erected by James Burbage, leader of
        the Leicester's Men.

1577   The Curtain was built.

1577-80 John Shakespeare was in financial difficulties.

1582   (November) Marriage of William Shakespeare and
        Anne Hathaway (Episcopal Register, Diocese of
        Worcester).

1583   (May 26) Baptism of Susanna, daughter of William
        and Anne Shakespeare, at Stratford (Stratford Parish
        Register).

1585   (February 2) Baptism of Hamnet and Judith, twin
        children of William and Anne Shakespeare, at Strat-
        ford (Stratford Parish Register).

1587   The Rose was built by the Lord Admiral's Men.

1588   Shakespeare was in London (?).

1588   Defeat of the Spanish Armada.

1592   Shakespeare was referred to in Robert Greene's
        Groatsworth of Wit as actor and playwright in
        London.

1593   Venus and Adonis was published, with dedication to
        the Earl of Southampton.

1594	The Rape of Lucrece was published, with dedication to the Earl of Southampton.
1594	(December 28) Performance of A Comedy of Errors at Gray's Inn "by the players" (Gesta Grayorum).
1594	Shakespeare a member and sharer of the Lord Chamberlain's company of actors.
1596	Death of Hamnet Shakespeare (Stratford Parish Register).
1596	(October 20) Grant of arms to John Shakespeare in consideration of the faithful and valiant service rendered by his antecedent to Henry VII (College of Arms MSS.).
1597	Shakespeare purchased New Place, the largest house in Stratford (Public Record Office).
1598	Shakespeare was referred to by Francis Meres in Palladis Tamia as the author of sonnets and twelve successful plays.
1598	(Before September 20) Acted in Ben Jonson's Every Man in His Humour.
1599	The Globe Theater (I) was built and opened by Shakespeare's company.
1600	(August 23) Shakespeare was first mentioned by name in the Stationers' Register in connection with Much Ado and Henry IV Pt. 2.
1601	Death of John Shakespeare (Stratford Parish Register).
1603	Acted in Ben Jonson's Sejanus (Note appended to the text of the play in Jonson's Works, 1616).
1603	Death of Queen Elizabeth; accession of King James I; the Chamberlain's Men became the King's Men.
1604-5	Othello, The Merry Wives of Windsor, Measure for Measure, A Comedy of Errors, Love's Labor's Lost, Henry V, and The Merchant of Venice were acted at Court during the Christmas season by the King's Men.
1607	Susanna Shakespeare married Dr. John Hall.
1608	(August 9) Shakespeare became a housekeeper of the Blackfriars Theatre with a seventh share.
1608	(September 9) Burial of Mary Shakespeare, widow

(Stratford Parish Register).

1609   Shakespeare's Sonnets entered at Stationers' Hall.

1610   Probable retirement of Shakespeare.

1611   King James' Version of the Holy Bible published.

1613   The Globe playhouse burned to the ground during a performance of Henry VIII.

1613   The Hope was built.

1614   The Globe theatre (II) was rebuilt after the 1613 fire.

1616   Ben Jonson's First Folio.

1616   (February 10) Marriage of Judith Shakespeare, aged 32, to Thomas Quincy in Lent without license. (Stratford Parish Register).

1616   (April 23) Death of William Shakespeare at Stratford. (April 25) Burial of Shakespeare, Gentleman (Stratford Parish Register).

1623   Publication of Shakespeare's collected plays (The First Folio) edited by John Heminges and Henry Condell.

1640   Second printing of the sonnets in John Benson's edition of Shakespeare's Poems.

Cf.   Gerald Eades Bentley, Shakespeare, A Biographical Handbook. New Haven: Yale University Press, 1961.

Cf.   Karl J. Holzknecht, The Backgrounds of Shakespeare's Plays. New York: American Book Co., 1950. pp. 3-20.

Cf.   Hyder E. Rollins, William Shakespeare Sonnets. New York: Appleton-Century-Crofts, 1951. pp. xv-xvi.

Chapter One

PRIMARY SOURCES

A. Facsimile Editions
   Based on the 1609 Quarto

1. Alden, Raymond Mac-
   donald (ed.)
   The Sonnets of S.* (From
the Quarto of 1609 with variorum
readings and commentary.) Boston: Houghton Mifflin, 1916.
(1906) (F).**

2. Eagle, Roderick L.
   The Secrets of S's
Sonnets. London: Mitre Press,
1965 (Criticism and the Sonnets
Facsimile, 1609) (F).

3. Elizabethan Club
   S's Poems: A Facsimile
of the Earliest Editions. New
Haven: Yale University Press,
1964. "Sonnets, pp. 239-307."
(F).

4. Hadow, W. H. (ed.)
   S's Sonnets and A Lover's
Complaint (Facsimile ed. of the
1609 edition). London: Oxford
University Press, 1907 (F).

5. Lee, Sidney (ed.)
   S's Sonnets: Being a Re-
production in Facsimile of the
First Edition, 1609, from the
Copy in the Malone Collection
in the Bodlean Library. Oxford:
Clarendon Pr. , 1905 (F).

6. S's Sonnets. A Facsimile

(of the first edition of 1609).
London: Jonathan Cape, 1925
(F).

7. S's Sonnets. Lexington:
Anvil Press, 1956 (F).

8. Sonnets. (A Facsimile
of the 1609 Edition). London:
[n. p.], 1926 (F).

9. William S: Sonnets, 1609.
Menston, England: Scolar Press,
1968 (F).

B. Modern Editions Published
   or Reprinted Since 1900

10. Alden, Raymond Mac-
    donald (ed.)
    "Six Sonnets" in Poems
of the English Race. New York:
Scribner's, 1921. pp. 228-230.

11. The Alfred Dodd Edition
    of S's Sonnets
    See Dodd, Alfred.

12. Auden, W. H.
    See Burto, William (ed.).

13. Auslander, Joseph (ed.)
    S's Sonnets. New York:
Printed by R. Ellis for Cheshire
House, 1931.

14. Ballou, Robert O. (ed.)
    The Sonnets, with the
Famous Temple Notes and Intro-

*S = Shakespeare. **F = Facsimile.

15

duction. N. Y.: Crown, 1961.

15. Barber, Cesar Lombardi
See Sisson, Charles J. (ed.).

16. Barton, A. T.
The Sonnets of William
S with a Latin Translation by
Alfred Thomas Barton, ed. by
John Harrower. London: [n. p.],
1923. (1st edition, Latin only,
1913).

17. Beaty, John Owen and
Bowyer, John W. (eds.)
Famous Editions of Eng-
lish Poets. New York: Dial
Press, 1935. pp. 5-58.

18. Beeching, Henry Charles
(ed.)
The Sonnets of S. Bos-
ton, London: Ginn, 1904.

19. Black, Matthew W. (ed.)
"S's Sonnets" in Elizabe-
than and 17th Century Lyrics.
Philadelphia: Lippincott, 1938.

20. No entry.

21. Blind, Mathilde (ed.)
S's Sonnets. London:
The De La Mere Press, 1902.

22. Bock, Vera (illustrator)
The Love Poems and Son-
nets of William S. Garden City,
New York: Hanover House,
1957. "Sonnets, pp. 7-86."

23. Bower, John W. (ed.)
See Beaty, John Owen.

24. Bray, Sir Denys (ed.)
The Original Order of
S's Sonnets. London: Methuen,
1925.

25. .
S's Sonnet-Sequence. (The
test of the Sonnets with introductory chapters). London: Martin Secker, 1938.

26. Brett-Smith, H. F. B.
See Bullen, Arthur H. (ed.).

27. Brooke, C. F. Tucker (ed.)
The S Apocrypha. Oxford:
Clarendon Press, 1908; New York:
Oxford University Press, 1936.

28. .
S's Sonnets edited with
Introduction and Notes. New
Haven: Yale University; Lon-
don: Oxford University Press,
1936.

29. Bullen, Arthur H. (ed.)
S's Sonnets. Stratford-
on-Avon: S Head Press, 1905
[A Foreword by H. F. B. Brett-
Smith] (1921).

30. (ed.)
"S's Sonnets" in The
Works of William S. Stratford-
on-Avon: S Head Press, 1934
(1938). pp. 1225-1244.

31. (ed.)
S's Sonnets in The Works
of S. New York: Oxford Univ.
Press, 1907 (1938), X, 177-
230 (S Head Press Edition).

32. (ed.)
The Sonnets of William
S. Oxford: S Head Press, 1945.

33. Burto, William (ed.)
William S: The Sonnets.
Introduction by W. H. Auden.
New York: New Amsterdam
Library, 1964.

34. Bush, Douglas and Har-
bage, Alfred (eds.)
S's Sonnets. Baltimore:
Penguin Books, 1961.

35. (ed.)
S's Sonnets in William S:
The Complete Works, ed. by
Alfred Harbage. Baltimore:
Penguin Books, 1969. pp. 1449-
1479.

36. Butler, Samuel
S's Sonnets Reconsidered.
London: Jonathan Cape, 1899
(1925, 1927).

37. Cameo Classics
See Hudson, Henry Norman, et al. (eds.).

38. Campbell, Oscar James
(ed.)
The Living S: Twenty-Two Plays and The Sonnets. New York: Macmillan, 1949.

39. _____ (ed.)
S's Sonnets. New York: Bantam Books, 1964.

40. _____ (ed.)
The Sonnets, Songs, and Poems of S. New York: Bantam, 1964; New York: Schocken Books, 1964 (1967).

41. The Complete Sonnets of William S. London: Sylvan Press, 1955 (Sylvanus Editions).

42. Corman House Series
See Fox, Levi (ed.).

43. Craig, W. J. (ed.)
The Complete Works of William S. London: Oxford University Press, 1904 (1936). p. 1281-1305.

44. Crofts Classics Edition
See Rollins, Hyder E. (ed.).

45. De Chambrun, Clara Longworth (ed.)
See Pineton, Clara Longworth (Countess de Chambrun).

46. De Selincourt, E.
See Wordsworth, William.

47. Dodd, Alfred
The Personal Poems of
Francis Bacon. Liverpool: Daily Post Printers, 1931 (The Alfred Dodd Edition of S's Sonnets).

48. _____ .
The Secret History of Francis Bacon, Our S, The Son of Queen Elizabeth. London: C. W. Daniel, 1936 (1941).

49. Donner, H. W. (ed.)
See Beddoes, Thomas Lovell.

50. Douglas, Lord Alfred
(ed.)
The True History of S's Sonnets (The text of the sonnets with a discussion and commentary). London: Martin Secker, 1933.

51. Dowden, Edward (ed.)
The Sonnets of William S. London: Dryden Library, 1905.

52. Ferguson, Francis (ed.)
See Sisson, Charles J. (ed.).

53. _____ and Sisson, Charles Jasper (eds.)
Sonnets. New York: Dell, 1960.

54. Flower, Margaret (ed.)
The Sonnets of William S. London: Cassell, 1933.

55. The Folger Library General Reader's S.
See Wright, Louis B. and LaMar, Virginia A. (eds.).

56. Fontana Series
See Maine, G. T. (ed.).

57. Fort, James A. (ed.)
A Time Scheme for S's

Sonnets, with a text of short
notes. London: Mitre Press,
1929.

58. Fox, Levi (ed.)
     The Sonnets. London:
Jarrold, 1958; Norwich: Jarrold,
1963 [Corman House Series].

59. Frankenberg, Lloyd (ed.)
     Poems of William S.
Etching by Nonny Hogrogian. New
York: Thomas Y. Crowell, 1966.
(Sonnets, p. 101-158).

60. Godwin, Parke (ed.)
     Study of the Sonnets of S
[with "The Original Sonnets" as
newly arranged]. New York and
London: Putnam's, 1900.

61. Gollancz, Sir Israel (ed.)
     S's Sonnets. London:
[n.p.], 1919.

62. Gorton, Mary Jane (ed.
     & illustrator)
     William S's Sonnets. New
York: Peter Pauper Press,
[n.d.].

63. Harbage, Alfred (ed.)
     See Bush, Douglas (ed.).

64. Harrison, George B. (ed.)
     S, The Complete Works.
New York: Harcourt, Brace and
World, 1948. p. 1592-1623.

65. _____ (ed.)
     S's Sonnets. London:
Penguin Books, 1938 (Penguin
Edition).

66. _____ (ed.)
     Sonnets. New York: S
Society, [1960?].

67. _____ (ed.)
     The Sonnets and a Lover's
Complaint. London: Penguin
Books, 1949.

68. _____ (ed.)
     William S: The Sonnets
and a Lover's Complaint.
Harmondsworth, Eng.: Penguin
Books, 1949 (The Penguin S).

69. Harrower, John (ed.)
     See Barton, A.T.

70. Herrnstein, Barbara
     (ed.)
     S's Sonnets. Boston:
Heath, 1964; London: Hanap,
1964

71. Hill, Charles J. (ed.)
     See Neilson, William A.
     (ed.).

72. Hogrogian, Nonny
     See Frankenberg, Lloyd
     (ed.).

73. Holzapfel, Rudolf Meland-
     er
     S's Secret: A New and
Correct Interpretation of S's
Sonnets. Dublin: Melander S
Society, 1961.

74. Hubler, Edward (ed.)
     See Parrott, Thomas
     Marc (ed.).

75. _____ (ed.)
     The Riddle of S's Son-
nets. New York: Basic Books,
1962. p. 256-336.

76. _____ (ed.)
     S's Songs and Poems.
New York: McGraw-Hill, 1959
(1964). p. 1-166.

77. Hudson, Henry Norman,
     et al. (eds.)
     The Aldus S: Sonnets.
New York: Funk and Wagnalls,
1968.

78. _____ (eds.)
     Sonnets. New York:

Grossett, 1936 (Cameo Classics).

79. Ibbs, Edith A. (illustrator)
Sonnets by S (a selection).
London: Constable, 1913.

80. Ingram, W. G. and Redpath,
Theodore (eds.)
Sonnets. London: University of London Press, 1964; New
York: Barnes & Noble, 1964
(1965).

81. _____ (eds.)
Sixty-five Sonnets of S.
London: London University Press,
1967.

82. Iorio, Adrian J. (illustrator)
S's Sonnets. London:
George G. Harrap, 1912.

83. Jennett, Sean (ed.)
The Sonnets. London:
Grey Walls Press, 1948.

84. Jones, Gwyn (ed.)
The Poems and Sonnets of
William S. London: Golden
Cockerell Press, 1960.

85. Kittredge, George Lyman
(ed.)
The Complete Works of S.
Boston: Ginn, 1936. p. 1493-
1519.

86. _____ (ed.)
William S: The Sonnets,
revised by Irving Ribner. Waltham, Mass.: Blaisdell, 1968.

87. Krämer, Ilse (tr.)
William S: Sonette [Both in
English and in German]. Klosterberg, Basel (Switzerland): Verlag
Benno Schwabe, 1945.

88. LaMar, Virginia A. (ed.)
See Wright, Louis B. (ed.)

1*
89. Langham Booklets
S's Sonnets. London:
The Langham Booklets, 1906.

90. The Laurel S
See Sisson, Charles
Jasper (ed.).

16
91. Love: A Sonnet (Sonnet
XVI). London: Ernest Nister,
1902 (Printed in Bavaria).

92. Mabie, H. W. (ed.)
Sonnets of S. Outlook,
92 (1909), 1025-1030.

93. Mackenzie, Barbara A.
(ed.)
S's Sonnets. Cape Town:
Maskew Miller, 1946.

94. Maine, G. T. (ed.)
A S Anthology, Selections from Comedies, Histories,
Tragedies, Songs, and Sonnets.
London: Collins, [n.d.] (Fontana Series).

95. Morley, Christopher (ed.)
The Complete Works of
S, illustrated by Rockwell Kent.
New York: [n.p.], 1936.

96. Neilson, William Allan
and Hill, Charles Jarvis
(eds.)
The Complete Plays and
Poems of William S. Boston:
Houghton Mifflin, 1942. p.
1369-1396.

97. The New S.
See Wilson, John Dover
(ed.).

98. The New Temple S.
See Ridley, M. R. (ed.).

99. Parrott, Thomas Marc

*1 = Sonnet 1. Hereafter, an Arabic number above an author's or
editor's last name indicates that a specific sonnet is discussed.

19

(ed.)
S. New York: [n.p.],
1938.

100. _____ and Hubler, Edward (eds.)
S; Six Plays and the Son-
nets. New York: Scribner's,
1956.

101. _____, et al. (eds.)
S's Twenty-Three Plays
and the Sonnets. New York:
Scribner's, 1938 (1958). p. 1085-
1116.

102. Penguin Edition
See Harrison, George B.
(ed.).

103. The Penguin S.
See Harrison, George B.
(ed.).

104. Peter Pauper Press
Sonnets. Mt. Vernon,
N.Y.: Peter Pauper Press, 1936.

105. Phillips, G.W. (ed.)
S's Sonnets. Oxford: B.
Blackwell, 1934.

106. _____ (ed.)
Sunlight on S's Sonnets (A
Rearrangement of the Text with a
Commentary). London: Thornton
Butterworth, 1935.

107. Pineton, Clara Longworth
(Countess de Chambrun)
(ed.)
An Explanatory Introduction
to Thorpe's Edition of S's "Sonnets
1609," with text transcription.
Aldington, Kent: Hand & Flower
Press, 1950.

108. Pooler, C. Knox (ed.)
The Works of S: Sonnets.
3rd ed. London: Methuen, 1918
(1931, 1943) (The Arden S.).

109. Redpath, Theodore (ed.)

See Ingram, W.G. (ed.).

110. Reed, Edward B. (ed.)
S's Sonnets. New Ha-
ven: Yale University Press,
1923 (The Yale S).

111. Reed, Victor B. (ed.)
See Willen, Gerald (ed.).

112. Ribner, Irving (ed.)
See Kittredge, G.L.
(ed.).

113. _____ and Kittredge,
George Lyman (eds.)
The Complete Works of
S. Waltham, Mass.: Ginn,
1939 (1971). p. 1685-1729.

114. Ridley, M.R. (ed.)
Sonnets. London: J.M.
Dent, 1934 (1935) (The New
Temple S).

115. Rollins, Hyder E. (ed.)
A New Variorum Edition
of S: The Sonnets. 2v. Philadelphia: Lippincott, 1944.

116. _____ (ed.)
Sonnets. New York:
Appleton-Century-Crofts, 1951
(Crofts Classics Edition).

117. Rowse, A.L. (ed.)
S's Sonnets. New York:
Harper & Row, 1964; London:
Macmillan, 1964.

118. Seymour-Smith, Martin
(ed.)
S's Sonnets. London:
Heinemann, 1963.

119. _____ (ed.)
Sonnets. New York:
Barnes & Noble, 1963 (1966).

120. S Head Press
The Sonnets of William
S. Oxford: S Head Press,
1945.

20

121. S's Sonnets
Hammersmith: Doves Press,
1909 (Tercentenary Edition).

122. S's Sonnets, 1609
London: L. C. C. Central School
of Arts & Crafts, 1930.

123. S's Sonnets
New York & London: Harper,
1933

124. Simon, Henry W. (ed.)
Sonnets, Songs and Poems.
New York: Pocket Books, 1954.

125. Sisson, Charles Jasper
(ed.)
See Fergusson, Francis
(ed.).

126. _____ (ed.)
The Sonnets by William S.
Introduction by C. L. Barber.
New York: Dell, 1958 (1960).
[The Laurel S, ed. by Francis
Fergusson].

127. _____ (ed.)
William S: The Complete
Works. New York: Harper and
Row, 1953. p. 1299-1318.

128. Smith, Barbara H. (ed.)
Sonnets by William S. New
York: New York University
Press, 1969.

129. Sonnets. Garden City,
N. Y.: Dolphin Books, 1960.

130. Sonnets. Lexington, Ky.:
Printed by J. Hammer for the
Anvil Press, 1956.

131. Sonnets
London: Falcon Press, 1948.

132. Sonnets; A Selection
Westwood, N. J.: Revell, 1903.

133. Sonnets, with an Index of
First Lines. London: J. Baker

for the Richard Press, 1904.

134. The Sonnets of S
London: R. Riviere, 1928.

135. Sonnets of S: A Selection. New York: Revell,
1963.

136. The Sonnets of William
S. Mount Vernon, N. Y.:
Peter Pauper Press, [n.d.].

137. Sonnets to a Dark Lady,
and Others. Mount Vernon,
N. Y.: Peter Pauper Press,
[195?].

138. Spurrier, Steven (illus-
trator)
The Sonnets. Leigh-on-
Sea: F. Lewis, 1950.

139. Stone, Reynolds (illus-
trator)
The Sonnets. London:
Cassell, 1948; London: Folio
Society, 1947.

140. Strong, L. A. G.
The Body's Imperfection.
London: Methuen, 1957.

141. Sylvanus Editions
See The Complete Son-
nets of William S.

142. Tercentenary Edition
See S's Sonnets. Doves
Press.

143. Thomson, Walter (ed.)
The Sonnets of William
S and Henry Wriothesley, Third
Earl of Southhampton, together
with A Lover's Complaint and
The Phoenix and Turtle. Ox-
ford: Blackwell, 1938.

144. Titherley, A. W.
S's Earliest Poems in
Approximately Chronological
Order. Winchester, England:

Wykeham Press, 1953.

145.   Tucker, T.G. (ed.)
        The Sonnets of S. (Edited
from the Quarto of 1609) Cambridge: University Press, 1924.

146.   Twenty-Five Sonnets
Stratford-upon-Avon: S Head,
1922; Oxford: Blackwell, 1922.

147.   Twenty-Five Sonnets of S
Oxford: Blackwell, 1930.

148.   The Viking Portable Li-
        brary
        S (Seven Plays, The Songs,
The Sonnets, Selections from the
Other Plays). New York: Viking
Press, 1970 (1944). p. 696-772.

149.   Walsh, C.M. (ed.)
        S's Complete Sonnets.
London: T. Fisher Unwin, 1908.

150.   Willen, Gerald and Reed,
        Victor B. (eds.)
        A Casebook on S's Sonnets.
New York: Thomas Y. Crowell,
1964. p. 3-157.

151.   Wilson, John Dover (ed.)
        The Sonnets. Cambridge:
University Press, 1966 (1967)
(The New S).

152.   Withers, C. (ed.)
        S's Sonnets. Baltimore:
Penguin, 1943.

153.   Wright, Louis B. and
        LaMar, Virginia A. (eds.)
        Sonnets. New York:
Washington Square Press, 1967
(Folger Lib. General Reader's S).

154.   The Yale S
        See Reed, Edward B. (ed.).

Chapter Two

SECONDARY SOURCES
(Criticism of the Sonnets)

A. Books

155. Acheson, Arthur
Mistress Davenant and the
Dark Lady of S's Sonnets. London: B. Quaritch, 1913.

156. .
S and the Rival Poet.
London and New York: John Lane,
1903; AMS Press, 1970 (reprint).

157. .
S's Sonnet Story 1592-1598.
London: B. Quaritch, 1922 (1933).

158. Alden, Raymond M.
The Sonnets of S. Boston:
Houghton Mifflin, 1917.

159. Allen, Percy and Ward,
B. M.
An Enquiry into the Relations between Lord Oxford as S,
Queen Elizabeth and the Fair
Youth of S's Sonnets. London:
Percy Allen, 1936.

160. Anspacher, Louis
S as Poet and Lover and
the Enigma of the Sonnets. New
York: Island Press, 1944.

161. Baldwin, T. W.
On the Literary Genetics
of S's Poems and Sonnets. Urbana:
University of Illinois Press, 1951.

162. Barber, C. L.
The Sonnets of S. (The
Laurel S). New York: Dell,
1960. "The Sonnet as an Action,"

p. 7-33.

163. Barnard, Finch
Science and the Soul.
The Psychology of S as Revealed in the Sonnets. London: Selwyn & Blount, 1918.

164. Barnstoff, D.
Key to S's Sonnets.
New York: AMS Press, 1862
(1970).

165. Blackmur, Richard P.
See Hubler, Edward,
et al.

166. Boaden, J.
On the Sonnets of S.
New York: AMS Press, 1837
(1970).

167. Booth, Stephen
An Essay on S's Sonnets. New Haven: Yale University Press, 1969. Contents:
Preface; 1. The Critical Dilemma; 2. Structures vs. Structure;
3. Multiple Patterns; 4. Unity
& Division, Likeness & Difference; 5. Motion of the Mind;
6. All Forwards Do Contend;
7. Recapitulation & Conclusion.

168. Bray, Denys de Saumariz
(ed.)
The Original Order of
S's Sonnets. London: [n. p.],
1925.

169. (ed.)
S's Sonnet Sequence.

23

London: [n.p.], 1938.

170. Brooke, C. F. Tucker
S's Sonnets. New York:
Oxford Univ. Press, 1936.

171. Brown, Henry
Sonnets of S Solved. New
York: AMS Press, 1870 (1970).

172. Brown, Ivor
Dark Ladies. London:
Collins, 1956. "S's Dark Lady,"
p. 253-309.

173. Butler, Samuel
S's Sonnets Reconsidered.
London: Jonathan Cape, 1899
(1925, 1927). Contents: 1. The
Original Edition and the Partial
Republication of 1640; 2. Gildon,
Swell, Theobald, Tyrwhitt,
Steevens, Capell, Johnson, Bell;
3. Edmond Malone; 4. Mr. George
Chalmers and His Interpretation
of the Word "Begetter" in
Thorpe's Preface; 5. Dr. Drake
& the Lord Southampton Theory;
6. Mr. Sidney Lee's Life of Wil-
liam S; 7. Mr. Sidney Lee's Life
of William S; 8. The Impersonal
and The William Herbert Theories.
On the Social Status of Mr. W.
H.; 9. On the Order in Which the
Sonnets Were Written and on the
Story Which They Reveal; 10. On
the Dates of the Sonnets; 11. On
the Dates of Sonnet 127 (1072) and
the Remaining Sonnets; 12. Mr.
W. H. Conclusion of Introductory
Chapters; S's Sonnets, Facsimile
of the Original Edition of 1609.

174. Cameron, G. M.
See Gittings, Robert (ed.).

175. Campbell, Oscar James
(ed.)
The Sonnets, Songs and
Poems of S. New York: Schocken
Books. 1964 (1967). Contents:
The Sonnets; Songs from the
plays; Venus & Adonis; The Rape

of Lucrece; The Phoenix & the
Turtle; The Passionate Pilgrim;
A Lover's Complaint; Chronol-
ogy of S's Life Bibliography.

176. Chambers, Sir Edmund
K.
Shakespearean Gleanings.
New York: Oxford University
Press, 1944. Contains 3 es-
says on the sonnets: 10. "The
Order of the Sonnets"; 11.
"The 'Youth' of the Sonnets";
and 12. "The 'Mortal Moon'
Sonnet."

177. Cliff's Notes Editors
S's Sonnets Notes. Lin-
coln, Nebraska: Cliff's Notes,
1970.

178. Davies, Randall
Notes upon Some of S's
Sonnets. Kensington, England:
Cayme Press, 1927.

179. De Chambrum, Clara
Longworth
See Pineton, Clara Long-
worth (Countess de
Chambrum).

180. Dodd, Alfred
The Marriage of Eliza-
beth Tudor--an Historical Research Based on One of the
Themes in S's Sonnets. London: Rider, 1940.

181. Douglas, Lord Alfred
The True History of S's
Sonnets. London: M. Secker,
1933; New York: Kennikat,
1970.

182. Eagle, Roderick
New Light on the Enig-
mas of S's Sonnets. London:
Mitre Press, 1916 (1965).

183. .
The Secrets of S's
Sonnets. London: Mitre Press,

1965. Contents: 1. The Dedication; 2. The Problem of the "Friend"; 3. The "Dark Lady"; 4. The Rival Poet; 5. S at Bath!; 6. "A Lover's Complaint"; 7. The Sonnets, p. 69-75.

184. Emerson, John M.
Anagram from the S Sonnets Discovered by J. M. Emerson (purporting to show that Bacon was their author). Liverpool: [n. p.], 1908.

185. _____.
Two Anagrams from the S Sonnets and Francis Bacon's Will. Liverpool: [n. p.], 1912.

186. Fiedler, Leslie
See Hubler, Edward, et al.

187. Forrest, Henry Telford Stonor
The Five Authors of 'S's Sonnets.' London: Chapman & Dodd, 1923.

188. Fort, James A.
A Time Scheme for S's Sonnets. London: Mitre Press, 1929; New York: AMS Press, 1970.

104, 107
189. _____.
The Two Dated Sonnets of S. London: Oxford University Press, 1924.

190. Frye, Northrop
See Hubler, Edward, et al.

191. Garnett, R. M.
Materials for the Study of S's Sonnets. Seattle: [n. p.], 1912 (28-page pamphlet).

192. Gittings, Robert (ed.)
S's Rival. London: Heinemann, 1960.

193. Godwin, Parke

New Study of the Sonnets of S. New York: AMS Press, 1900 (1970).

194. Hadow, W. H.
S's Sonnets & a Lover's Complaint. Folcroft, Pa.: Folcroft, 1907 (1970).

195. Harwood, Henry H.
Two of the Most Remarkable and Interesting of the Sonnets of Francis Bacon, the True S. Richmond, Va.: Ware & Duke, 1908.

196. Herrnstein, Barbara (ed.)
Discussions of S's Sonnets. Boston: D. C. Heath, 1964; Indianapolis: Heath, 1970. Contents: I. Early Commentary: John Benson: A Preface; George Steevens: A Note on S's Sonnets; Samuel Taylor Coleridge: On S's Sonnets; John Keats: from the Letters; Henry Hallam: Sonnets of S; II. Speculations: Leslie Hotson: S's Sonnets Dated; F. W. Bateson: Elementary, My Dear Hotson!; III. Interpretation: Edward Hubler: S and the Unromantic Lady; Patric Cruttwell: S's Sonnets and the 1590's; G. Wilson Knight: Time and Eternity; J. W. Lever: The Poet in Absence [and] The Poet and His Rivals; IV. Evaluation: John Crowe Ransom: S at Sonnets; Yvor Winters: Poetic Style in S's Sonnets; V. Analysis: Robert Graves and Laura Riding: A Study in Original Punctuation and Spelling: Sonnet 129; William Empson: Some Types of Ambiguity in S's Sonnets; Arthur Mizener: The Structure of Figurative Language in S's Sonnets; Winifred M. T. Nowottny: Formal Elements in S's Sonnets: Sonnets 1-6; C. L.

Barber: The Sonnet as an Action.

197. Heuer, Hermann
See Gittings, Robert (ed.).

198. Holland, Vyvyan (ed.)
See Wilde, Oscar.

199. Holzapfel, Rudolf Melander
S's Secret; A New and Correct Interpretation of S's Sonnets.
Dublin: Melander S Society, 1961.

200. Hotson, Leslie
Mr. W.H. London: Hart-Davis, 1964; New York: Knopf, 1964.

201. _____.
S's Sonnets Dated and Other Essays. New York: Oxford University Press, 1949; London: Rupert Hart-Davis, 1949; Toronto: Clarke, Irwin, 1949.

202. Hubler, Edward, et al.
The Riddle of S's Sonnets.
New York: Basic Books, 1962.
Contents: 1. Blackmur, Richard P. "A Poetics for Infatuation," p. 129-161; 2. Fiedler, Leslie. "Some Contexts of S's Sonnets," p. 55-90; 3. Frye, Northrop. "How True a Twain," p. 23-53; 4. Hubler, Edward. "S's Sonnets and the Commentators," p. 1-21; 5. Spender, Stephen. "The Alike and the Other," p. 91-128; 6. Wilde, Oscar. "The Portrait of Mr. W.H.," p. 163-255.

203. _____.
The Sense of S's Sonnets.
Princeton, N.J.: Princeton University Press, 1952; New York: Hill & Wang, 1952. [Princeton Studies in English, No. 33, 1952]; New York: Hill & Wang, 1962 (1970). Contents: Form and Matter; S and the Unromantic Lady; Mutability, Plenitude, and Immortality; The Young Man's Beauty; The Economy of the Closed Heart;

The Natural Pool of Fortune; Reputation and the Knowledge of Good.

204. _____.
S's Songs and Poems.
New York: McGraw Hill, 1959.

205. Jackson, Edith A.
A Consideration of S's Sonnets. Privately Printed. 1904 (16-page pamphlet).

206. Johannes, J.G.
The Mysteries about S's Sonnets Solved? Batavia: G. Kolff, 1928 (28-page pamphlet).

207. _____.
S's Mysterious W.H. and Dark Mistress Revealed (as William Harvey and Elizabeth, Countess of Derby)? Batavia: Kolff, 1928 (39-page pamphlet).

208. Kent, Sydney
The People in S's Sonnets. London: J. Long, 1915; New York: Longmans & Green, 1917.

209. Knight, George Wilson
Gold Dust: A Sequence on the Theme of S's Sonnets with other Poetry. New York: Barnes and Noble, 1968.

210. _____.
The Mutual Flame: An Interpretation of S's Sonnets. London: Methuen, 1955; New York: Barnes & Noble, 1962.

211. Krieger, Murray
A Window to Criticism: S's Sonnets and Modern Poetics. Princeton, N.J.: Princeton University Press, 1964. Contents: Preface; I. The Mirror as Window in Recent Literary Theory; (1) The Resort to "Miracle" in Recent Poetics; (2)

Contextualism and Its Alternatives;
II. The Mirror as Window in S's
Sonnets; Introductory; (1) The
Mirror of Narcissus and the Mag-
ical Mirror of Love; (2) Truth vs.
Troth: The Worms of the Vile,
Wise World; (3) State, Property,
and the Politics of Reason; (4)
The Miracle of Love's Eschatology
and Incarnation; III. The Power
of Poetic Effigy; Index: Index of
Sonnets.

212. Landry, Hilton
        Interpretations in S's Son-
nets. Berkeley & Los Angeles:
University of California Press,
1964; London: Cambridge University Press, 1964. [Perspectives
in Criticism, No. 14, Berkeley
& Los Angeles: University of
California Press, 1963.] Contents: 1. The Unmoved Movers:
Sonnet 94 and the Contexts of
Interpretation; 2. The Canker in
the Rose: Sonnets 69 and 70,
53 and 54; 3. The Civil War:
Sonnets 33-35, 40-42, and 57-58;
4. Their Vile World: Sonnets 66,
121, and 129; 5. Constancy to an
Ideal Object: Sonnets 123, 124,
and 125; 6. Some Tentative Con-
clusions; Notes; Bibliography; Index.

213. Lanier, Sidney
        S and His Forerunners.
New York: Doubleday, Page &
Co., 1902.

214. The Laurel S
        See Barber, C. L.

215. Leishman, J. B.
        Themes and Variations in
S's Sonnets. London: Hutchinson,
1961; New York: Hillary House,
1961, 1962; New York: Hutchinson, 1970. Contents: I. Poetry
as Immortalisation from Pindar
to S; 1. S and the Roman Poets;
2. S and Petrarch; 3. S and Tasso; 4. S and Ronsard; 5. S and

His English Predecessors; II.
Devouring Time and Fading
Beauty from the Greek Anthology to S; 1. Absence of the
Topics carpe diem and carpe
florem from S's Sonnets; 2. S's
Sonnet on Love as the Defier of
Time; 3. The Instinctiveness
and Unphilosophicalness of S's
"Idealism" and "Spirituality":
Contrast with Michelangelo and
other Men of Geist; 4. Person-
ifications of Time, Age and
Youth by Ovid, Horace and S;
5. S and Chaucer: Tragedy and
the Whole Truth; III. "Hyperbole" and "Religiousness" in
S's Expressions of His Love;
1. S's "Un-Platonic Hyperbole";
2. Excursas: Sonnets Written
during Absence; 3. The Theme
of Compensation; 4. The Religiousness of S's Love, S and
Donne; First-line Index of Sonnets Quoted or Mentioned; General Index.

216. Lockwood, Laura Emma
        "The Sonnet," Sonnets.
Boston: Houghton Mifflin, 1916.
p. v-xiv.
217. Lowers, James K.
        S's Sonnets Notes. Lin-
coln, Nebraska: Cliff's Notes,
1965. Contents: Brief Survey
of 16th Century Sonnets: Sir
Thomas Wyatt, Henry Howard
Earl of Surrey, Sir Philip Sidney, Daniel, Drayton and Others; S's Sonnets: Date of Com-
position, Dedication to Mr. W.
H., Order and Arrangement,
Question of Autobiography, The
Fair Young Man, The Dark Lady, The Rival Poet, Dominant
Themes, Other Facets of Interest; Selected Criticism: General; Criticism of Individual
Sonnets; Questions; Bibliography.

218. MacKenzie, Barbara
        S's Sonnets: Their Rela-
tion to His Life. Cape Town:

Maskew Miller, 1946; New York: AMS Press, 1970.

219. MacMahan, Anna B.
S's Love Story as Revealed in the Sonnets, 1580-1609. Chicago: McClury, 1909 (84-page booklet).

220. Malone, Kemp (ed.)
See Lanier, Sidney.

221. Massey, Gerald
Secret Drama of S's Sonnets Unfolded. New York: AMS Press, 1888 (1970).

222. _____.
S's Sonnets Never Before Interpreted. New York: AMS Pr., 1866 (1970).

223. Muir, Kenneth
See Gittings, Robert (ed.).

224. Newbolt, Henry
A New Study of English Poetry: "S." New York: E.P. Dutton & Company, 1919.

225. Nisbet, Ulric
The Onlie Begetter. London: Longmans, Green, 1936.

226. O'Flanagan, J.I.
S's Self-Revelation in His Sonnets. Stratford-on-Avon: Edward Fox, 1902 (38-page pamphlet).

227. O'Neal, Cothburn
The Dark Lady. New York: Crown, 1953.

228. Ord, Hubert
Chaucer and the Rival Poet in S's Sonnets, a New Theory. London: Dutton, 1921; New York: AMS Press, 1970.

229. Palmer, George Herbert
Intimations of Immortality in the Sonnets of S. Boston:

Houghton Mifflin, 1912 (58-page pamphlet).

230. Phillips, Gerald William
S's Sonnets: Addresses to Members of the S Fellowship. Cambridge: privately printed, 1954.

231. _____.
Sunlight on S's Sonnets. London: T. Butterworth, 1935.

232. Pineton, Clara Longworth (Countess de Chambrun)
Explanatory Introduction to Thorpe's Edition of S's Sonnets. Chester Springs, Pa.: Dufour, 1953 [Aldington, Kent: Hand & Flower Press, 1950].

233. _____.
The Sonnets of William S. New York: G. Putnam, 1913.

234. _____.
Two Loves I Have, The Romance of William S. Philadelphia and London: Lippincott, 1934.

235. Pooker, C. Knox
S's Sonnets and A Lover's Complaint. London: Methuen, 1919.

236. Potter, James L.
The Development of Sonnet-patterns in the Sixteenth Century. Washington, D.C.: Howard University, 1954.

237. Pratt, Marjory Bates
Formal Designs from Ten S Sonnets. New Brunswick, New Jersey: Author, 1940.

238. Prince, Frank Templeton
William S: The Poems. London: Longmans Green for the British Council and the Na-

tional Book League, 1963.

239. Ransom, John Crowe
The World's Body. New
York: Scribner's, 1938.

240. Reed, Victor B. (ed.)
See Willen, Gerald (ed.).

241. Rendall, Gerald H.
Personal Clues in S's Poems
and Sonnets. London: John Lane,
1934.

242. _____.
S Sonnets and Edward De
Vere. London: J. Murray,
1930.

243. Riccardi Press Booklets
The Sonnets of Mr. Wil-
liam S. London: The Riccardi
Press Booklets, 1912.

244. Robertson, Jean G.
See Gittings, Robert (ed.).

245. Robertson, John M.
The Problems of the S
Sonnets. London: G. Routledge,
1926.

246. _____.
S and Chapman. London:
T. F. Unwin, 1917.

247. Rollins, Hyder E. (ed.)
A New Variorum Edition of
S: The Sonnets, 2 vols. Phila-
delphia: Lippincott, 1944; New
York: Appleton-Century-Crofts,
1951.

248. Ross, William
The Story of Anne Whateley
and William S as Revealed by
"The Sonnets to Mr. W. H." and
Other Elizabethan Poetry. Glas-
gow: W. & R. Holmes, 1939.

249. Schaar, Claes
An Elizabethan Sonnet
Problem: S's Sonnets, Daniel's

Delia, and Their Literary Back-
ground. Lund: C. W. K.
Gleerup, 1960; New York:
Adler, 1970.

250. _____.
Elizabethan Sonnet
Themes & the Dating of S's
Sonnets. New York: Adler,
1962 (1970).

251. Shaw, George Bernard
"Preface" to The Dark
Lady of the Sonnets, Misalli-
ance, The Dark Lady of the
Sonnets, and Fanny's First
Play. London: Constable,
1914. p. 203-230.

252. Shipley, Joseph T.
S's Sonnets. Analytic
Notes and Critical Commentary
(Study Master). New York:
Amer. R. D. M., 1964.

18
253. Silver, Frederick
Sonnet 18. London:
Williamson Music, 1963.

254. Simpson, Richard
Introduction to the Phi-
losophy of S's Sonnets. New
York: AMS Press, 1868 (1970).

255. Spender, Stephen
See Hubler, Edward,
et al.

256. Stalker, Archibald
The Sonnets of S.
Stirling: Learmonth, 1933
(36-page pamphlet).

257. Stirling, Brents
The S Sonnet Order:
Poems and Groups. Berkeley
and Los Angeles: University
of California Press, 1968;
Cambridge, University Press,
1968, 1969. Contents: 1.
Standards of Coherence: What
the 1609 Text Implies; 2. The

Emended Sonnet Order: Text and
Commentary; 3. Versification.

258.   Strong, J. R.
        Note upon the "Dark Lady"
Series of S's Sonnets. New York
and London: G. P. Putnam's,
1921.

259.   Theobald, B. G.
        S's Sonnets Unmasked.
London: C. Palmer, 1929.

260.   Thomson, Walter (ed.)
        The Sonnets of William S
& Henry Wriothesley Third Earl
of Southampton. Oxford and Liverpool: [n. p.], 1938.

261.   Titherley, Arthur W.
        S's Sonnets as from the
Pen of William Stanley, Sixth
Earl of Derby. [n. p.], 1939.

262.   Tyler, Thomas
        Herbert-Fitton Theory of
S's Sonnets: A Reply. New York:
AMS Press, 1898 (1970).

263.   Violi, Unicio J.
        Monarch Literature Notes
on S's Sonnets. New York:
Monarch, 1970.

264.   Venton, W. B.
        Analyses of S's Sonnets
Using the Cipher Code with Fac-
similes of the Coded Sonnets and
Coded Dedication of the 1609 Edition. London: Mitre, 1968
(1969).

265.   Ward, B. A.
        See Allen, Percy.

266.   Ward, B. R.
        The Mystery of "Mr. W.
H." London: C. Palmer, 1923.

267.   Wilde, Oscar
        See Hubler, Edward, et
al.

268.   .
        The Portrait of Mr. W.
H., ed. with Introduction by
Vyvyan Holland. London:
Methuen, 1901 (1929) (1959).

269.   Wilson, John Dover
        An Introduction to the
Sonnets of S for the Use of
Historians and Others. Cam-
bridge: Cambridge University
Press, 1964. Contents: 1.
The Cave and the Sun; 2. The
Origin and Quality of the Re-
ceived Text; 3. The Friend and
the Poet; 4. The Identity of
Mr. W. H.; 5. Themes and
Sources.

270.   Willen, Gerald and
        Reed, Victor B. (eds.)
        A Casebook on S's Son-
nets. New York: Thomas Y.
Crowell, 1964 (1965). Con-
tents: I. The Sonnets; II. Es-
says: Robert Graves and Laura
Riding, A Study in Original
Punctuation; L. C. Knights, S's
Sonnets; John Crowe Ransom,
S at Sonnets; Arthur Mizener,
The Structure of Figurative
Language in S's Sonnets; Ed-
ward Hubler, Form and Matter;
G. Wilson Knight, Symbolism;
III. Explications: R. M. Lumin-
ansky, S's Sonnet 73; Edward
F. Nolan, S's Sonnet 73; Car-
lisle Moore, S's Sonnets 71-
74; Karl F. Thompson, S's Son-
net 129; C. W. M. Johnson, S's
Sonnet 129; Gordon Ross Smith,
A Note on S's Sonnet 143; Al-
bert S. Gerard, Ironic Organi-
zation in S's Sonnet 146; Hilton
Landry, A Slave to Slavery:
S's Sonnet 57 and 58; Appen-
dices: Bibliography; Authors;
Exercises; Index of Sonnets by
First Lines.

271.   Winny, James
        The Master-mistress:
A Study of S's Sonnets. Lon-

don: Chatto and Windus, 1968;
New York: Barnes & Noble,
1968 (1969).

272. Young, H. McClure
The Sonnets of S: A Psy-
cho-Sexual Analysis. Menasha:
Wisconsin, 1936 (1937).

B. Discussions in Books

273. Adams, Joseph Quincy
"S's Sonnets," A Life of
William S. Boston: Houghton
Mifflin Co., 1923. p. 316-320,
passim.

274. 138,144
"Sonnets 138 and 144 Col-
lated," in his edition The Passionate Pilgrim. New York:
Scribner's Sons, 1939. p. xlvi-
xlvii.

275. Ainslie, Douglas (tr.)
See Croce, Benedetto.

276. Alden, Raymond M.
"The Quarto Arrangement
of the Sonnets," Anniversary Papers by Colleagues and Pupils of
G. L. Kittredge. Boston: 1913.
p. 279-288.

277.
"S's Sonnets," S. New
York: Duffield, 1922. p. 105-
146, passim.

278.
"S's Sonnets" in Anniver-
sary Papers, by colleagues and
pupils of George Lyman Kittredge.
Boston: Ginn, 1913. p. 279-288.

279.
"The Sonnet," An Introduction to Poetry. New York: H.
Holt & Co., 1909. p. 325-332,
passim.

280. Allen, Don Cameron (ed.)

See Winters, Yvor.

281. Allen, Percy
Anne Cecil, Elizabeth
and Oxford. London: D.
Archer, 1934.

282.
The Case for Edward de
Vere, 17th Earl of Oxford as
"S." London: C. Palmer,
1930.

283. Alpers, Paul J. (ed.)
See Barber, C. L.

284. (ed.)
See Knights, L. C.

285. Anders, H. R. D.
S's Books (Schriften der
deutschen S-Gesellschaft, vol.
I). Berlin: [n.p.], 1904.
Passim.

286. 99,12
Anderton, Basil
"Barton's Translation of
Sonnets 99 and 12," Sketches
from a Library Window. Cambridge: W. Heffer, 1922. p.
50, 70.

287. Armstrong, Edward A.
S's Imagination. Lon-
don: Lindsay Drummond, 1946.

288. Atkinson, Charles Francis (tr.)
See Rank, Otto.

289. Auden, W. H.
See Burto, William (ed.).

290. Auden, W. H.
"Introduction," William
S, The Sonnets ed. by William
Burto. New York: New Amer-
ican Library, 1963 (1964). p.
xvii-xxxviii.

291. Babb, Lawrence
The Elizabethan Malady.

31

East Lansing, Mich.: Michigan
State College Press, 1951.

292. Babcock, R.W.
The Genesis of S Idolatry,
1766-1799. Chapel Hill: Univ.
of No. Carolina Press, 1931.

293. Bailey, John
S. London and New York:
Longmans, Green, 1929. p. 58-
65.

294. Bannerjie, S.
"The Sonnets of S," S
Commemoration Volume. Calcut-
ta: Presidency College, 1968.

295. Barber, C.L.
Elizabethan Poetry ed. by
Paul J. Alpers. New York: Oxford University Press, 1967. p.
299-320.

296. _____.
"Introduction," The Son-
nets by William S (The Laurel S)
ed. by Charles Jasper Sisson.
New York: Dell, 1958 (1960). p.
7-33.

297. _____.
See Herrnstein, Barbara
(ed.).

298. Barnard, E.A.B.
New Links with S. Cam-
bridge: The University Press,
1930.

299. Bartlett, Henrietta C.
Mr. William S. New Ha-
ven, Connecticut, 1922.

300. Barton, Sir Dunbar Plunket
See Beck, James M.

301. _____.
Links Between S and the
Law. London: Faber & Gwyer,
1929.

302. Bateson, F.W.

English Poetry and the
English Language. Oxford:
Clarendon Press, 1934.

303. _____.
See Herrnstein, Barbara
(ed.).

304. Bathurst, C.
Remarks on the Differ-
ences in S's Versification in
Different Periods of His Life.
New York: AMS Press, 1857
(1970).

305. Baugh, Albert C. (ed.)
See Brooke, C.F. Tucker.

306. Bayfield, Matthew A.
A Study of S's Versifica-
tion, with an Inquiry into the
Trustworthiness of the Early
Texts. New York: AMS Press,
1920 (1970).

307. Beach, Elizabeth
S and the Tenth Muse.
Hamburg, N.J.: Willoughby
Books, 1969.

308. Beatty, Arthur
See Wisconsin, Univer-
sity of

309. _____.
"S's Sonnets & Plays,"
Wisconsin S Studies by Members of the Department of English of the University of Wisconsin. Madison, Wisconsin:
University of Wisconsin Press,
1916. p. 201-214.

310. Beck, James Montgomery
"Foreword" in Links
between S and the Law by Sir
Dunbar Plunket Barton. London: Faber & Gwyer, 1928.

311. Beeching, Henry Charles
"The Sonnets Discussed"
The Works of William S ed.

32

A. H. Bullen. Stratford-on-Avon: The S Head Press, 1907. X, 363-372.

312. Begley, Walter E.
Is It S? London: J. Murray, 1903. p. 190-250.

313. Belloc, H.
"Milton and S's Sonnets," Milton. London: Cassell, 1935. p. 209-211.

314. Benezet, Louis P.
The Six Loves of S. New York: Pageant, 1958.

315. Bennett, Josephine W. (ed.)
See Taylor, Dick, Jr.

316. Benson, John
See Herrnstein, Barbara (ed.).

317. Bentley, Gerald Eades
S and Jonson: Their Reputations in the Seventeenth Century Compared. 2v. Chicago: Univ. of Chicago Press, 1945.

318. Berry, Francis
Poets' Grammar. London: Routledge and Kegan Paul, 1958.

319. Beza, Marcu
S in Roumania. London: J. M. Dent, 1931.

73
320. Bishop, Henry Rowley
"That Time of Year (Sonnet 73)," Two Gentlemen of Verona. London: Goulding, D'Almaire, Potter, 1821 (1921). p. 11-13.

321. Black, Matthew W. (ed.)
Elizabethan and Seventeenth Century Lyrics. Philadelphia: Lippincott, 1938.

322. Blackmur, R. R.

"A Poetic for Infatuation," The Riddle of S's Sonnets, ed. by Edward Hubler. New York: Basic Books, 1962.

323. Bliven, Bruce
See 1. Conklin, Groff (ed.).
2. Santayana, George.

324. Bloom, Edward A. (ed.)
See Stirling, Brents.

325. Bluertone, Max
In The Riddle of S's Sonnets, by Edward Hubler, et al. New York: Basic Books, 1962.

326. Boas, F. S. (ed.)
See Lee, Sir Sidney.

327. _____.
"S's Sonnets," S and His Predecessors. New York: Scribner's, 1902 (1904). p. 113-121.

328. Bodtker, A. T.
"A Study in the Colour of Eyes," Festskrift til Hjalmar Falk. Oslo: [n.p.], p. 350-368.

329. Booth, Stephen
An Essay on S's Sonnets. New Haven: Yale University Press, 1969. Passim. (This book includes discussions on the following Sonnets: 1, 8, 12, 15, 21, 23, 29, 32-39, 44, 47-48, 53, 60, 63, 71, 73, 77-79, 85-86, 89, 94, 114, 116, 118, 124, 129-130, 141, 145, 153-154.)

330. Booth, William Stone
"The Sonnets" in Some Acrostic Signatures of F. Bacon. Boston: Houghton Mifflin, 1907 (1909). p. 145-149.

331. Borghesi, Pietro

33

Petrarch and His Influence on English Literature. Bologna: N. Zanichelli, 1906.

332. Bradbrook, M. C.
S and Elizabethan Poetry.
London: Chatto and Windus,
1965. "Sonnets, p. 141-146 and
Passim."

333. Bradby, Anne (ed.)
S Criticism, 1919-1935.
London: Oxford University Press,
1936.

334. Bradby, Godfrey Fox
Short Studies in S. London: J. Murray, 1929; New York:
Macmillan, 1929. p. 3-26.

335. Bradley, Andrew Cecil
Oxford Lectures on Poetry.
London: Macmillan, 1909. p.
311-357.

336. _____.
Shakespearean Tragedy.
London and New York: Macmillan,
1904.

337. Bradner, Leicester
"From Petrarch to S,"
The Renaissance: A Symposium,
Feb. 8-10, 1952. New York:
Metropolitan Museum of Art,
1953. p. 63-78.

338. Brewer, Wilmon
"History of the Sonnet,"
Sonnets and Sestinas. Boston:
Cornhill, 1937. p. 91-178.

339. Bridges, H. J.
Our Fellow S. Chicago:
A. C. McClurg, 1916 (1925). p.
270-288.

340. Broadbent, J. B.
Poetic Love. London:
Chatto and Windus, 1964. p. 143-
158.

341. Broadus, Edmund Kemper

"S's Sonnets," The Story
of English Literature. New
York: The Macmillan, 1932.
p. 155-157.

342. Brooke, C. F. Tucker
The Renaissance (1500-
1660) (Vol. II of A Literary
History of England, ed. by Albert C. Baugh). New York:
Appleton-Century-Crofts, 1948.
Passim.

343. Brooks, Alden
Will S, a Factotum and
Agent. New York: Round-Table Press, 1937.

344. Brown, Charles A.
S's Autobiographical
Poems. New York: AMS
Press, 1838 (1970).

345. Brown, George H.
Notes on S's Versification. New York: AMS Press,
1886 (1970).

346. Brown, Harry & Milstead, John (eds.)
What the Poems Mean,
Summaries of 1000 Poems.
Glenview, Illinois: Scott,
Foresman, 1970. "Sonnets,"
p. 195-202.

347. Brown, Henry
"The Singing of the Sonnets," S's Patrons and Other
Essays. London: J. M. Dent,
1912 (W. Herbert, p. 49-84;
H. Wriothesley, p. 87-103).
p. 107-111.

348. Bucke, Richard Maurice
"F. Bacon & the Sonnets," Cosmic Consciousness.
New York: Dutton, 1923 (1935).
p. 153-180.

349. Burto, William (ed.)
See Auden, W. H.

1738038

350. Bush, Douglas and Harbage, Alfred (eds.) "Introduction," S's Sonnets. Baltimore: Penguin Books, 1961. p. 7-20.

351. _____. Mythology and the Renaissance Tradition in English Poetry. Minneapolis: University of Minnesota Press, 1932.

352. Byvanck, Willem Geertrud Cornellis "Reading S's Sonnets," in A Book of Homage to S, ed. by Sir Israel Gollancz. London: H. Milford, 1916. p. 468-472.

353. Campbell, Lily B. S's Tragic Heroes. New York: Barnes and Noble, 1960.

354. Campbell, Oscar James (ed.) "The Sonnets," The Sonnets, Songs & Poems of S. New York: Schocken Books, 1964 (1967). p. 3-20.

355. Cargill, Alexander "The S Sonnets & What They Reveal," S the Player. London: Constable, 1916. p. 109-118.

356. Cargill, Oscar (ed.) See Taylor, Dick, Jr.

357. Carter, Thomas S and Holy Scripture, with the Version He Used. New York: Dutton, 1905.

358. Cazamian, Louis See Legouis, Emile.

359. Chambers, Sir Edmund K. Shakespearean Gleanings. London: Oxford University Press, 1944.

360. _____.

William S, A Study of Facts and Problems, 2 vols. Oxford: Clarendon Press, 1930. I, 555-576.

361. Chambers, R. W. (ed.) See Ker, William Paton.

362. Chapman, J. J. A Glance toward S. Boston: Atlantic Monthly Press, 1922. p. 90-107.

363. Chute, Marchette S of London. New York: Dutton, 1949. p. 339-344, passim.

364. Clark, Cumberland S and Psychology. London: Williams & Norgate, 1936. p. 140-147.

365. _____. S and Science. Birmingham: Cornish Brothers, 1929. Passim.

366. Clarkson, P. S., and Warren, C. T. The Law of Property in S and the Elizabethan Drama. Baltimore: Johns Hopkins Press, 1942.

367. Clemen, Wolfgang H. The Development of S's Imagery. Cambridge, Massachusetts: Harvard University Press, 1951.

368. Clutton-Brock, Arthur "S's Sonnets," Essays on Books. New York: Dutton, 1920. p. 15-26.

369. Coleridge, Samuel Taylor See Herrnstein, Barbara (ed.).

370. _____. See Raysor, Thomas M. (ed.).

35

371. _____.
Biographia Literaria,
(Bohn's Standard Library). Lon-
don: George Bell, 1905.

372. _____.
Miscellaneous Criticism,
ed. by T. M. Raysor. Cambridge,
Massachusetts: Harvard University Press, 1930.

373. Collins, John Churton
"S's Sonnets," Ephemera
Critica. London: [n. p.], 1901.
p. 219-335.

374. _____.
Studies in S. Westminister:
A Constable, 1904.

375. Collison-Morley, Lacy
S in Italy. Stratford-upon-
Avon: S Head Press, 1916.

376. Conklin, Groff (ed.)
See Santayana, George.

377. Conway, Eustace
The Supernatural in S.
Yellow Springs, Ohio: the author,
(Antioch Press), 1932. p. 28-35.

378. Courthope, William John
A History of English Poetry,
(6 vols.). London: Macmillan,
1895-1910. IV, 27-53.

379. Cowling, G. H.
A Preface to S. London:
Methuen, 1925.

380. Craig, Edward Gordon
Books and Theatres. Lon-
don and Toronto: J. M. Dent,
1925. p. 151-158.

381. No entry.

382. Craig, Hardin (ed.)
See Gray, H. D.

383. _____.

S. Chicago: [n. d.],
1931. p. 117-122, Passim.

384. Croce, Benedetto
Ariosto, S and Corneille,
translated by Douglas Ainslie.
New York: H. Holt, 1920. p.
122-123, 192-195.

385. Crosland, Thomas W. H.
The English Sonnet.
London: M. Secker, 1917. p.
190-227.

386. Cruttwell, Patrick
See Herrnstein, Barbara
(ed.).

387. _____.
"S's Sonnets and the
1590's" in Modern Shakespearean
Criticism ed. by Alvin B.
Kernan. New York: Harcourt,
Brace & World, 1970. p. 110-
140.

388. _____.
"S's Sonnets and the
1590's," in his The Shakespearean Moment and Its Place in
the Poetry of the 17th Century.
New York: Columbia University Press, 1955, New York:
Random House, 1960. p. 1-38.

389. Dam, Bastiaan Adriaan
Pieter Van
William S, Prosody and
Text. Leyden: E. J. Brill,
1900.

390. David, Richard
Janus of Poet: Being
an Essay on the Dramatic Value
of S's Poetry Both Good and
Bad. Folcroft, N. Y.: Books
for Libraries, 1935 (1970).

391. Davis, Herbert (ed.)
See Leishman, J. B.

392. Davis, Latham (ed.)
S England's Ulysses, the

36

Masque of Love's Labor's Won or the Enacted Will. (The Text of the Sonnets in a New Order). Seaford, Delaware: M. N. Willey, 1905. p. 26-171.

393. Day, Martin S.
History of English Literature to 1660. Garden City, New York: Doubleday, 1963, "Sonnets," p. 274-297.

393a. Day Lewis, Cecil
The Poetic Image. New York: Oxford University Press, 1947.

394. Dean, Leonard F. (ed.)
S: Modern Essays in Criticism. New York: Oxford Univ. Press, 1957 (1961).

395. De Bruce, Robert
"To Me, Fair Friend," Frankincense. San Francisco: Taylor & Taylor, 1917. p. 23-29.

396. De Chambrun, Clara Longworth
See Pineton, Clara Longworth (Countess de Chambrun).

397. De Sanctis, Francesco
History of Italian Literature, tr. by Joan Redfern, 2 vols. New York: Harcourt, Brace & World, 1931.

398. Dobree, Bonamy (ed.)
See Lewis, C. S.

399. Dodd, Alfred
"S's Sonnets: His Diary," S, Creator of Freemasonry. London: Rider, 1937. p. 174-192.

400. Dodge, R. E. N.
See Wisconsin, University of.

401. _____.

"An Obsolete Elizabethan Mode of Rhyming," in Wisconsin S Studies by Members of the Department of English of the University of Wisconsin. Madison, Wisconsin: University of Wisconsin Press, 1916. p. 174-200.

402. Douglas, Montagu William
"The Evidence of the Sonnets," The Earl of Oxford as S. London: Palmer, 1931. p. 107-132.

403. Downing, Charles
The Messiahship of S, Sung and Expounded. London: Greening, 1901. p. 16-37; 92-101.

404. Dunn, Esther Cloudman
"S's Sonnets," The Literature of S's England. New York: Scribner, 1936. p. 78-89.

405. Eagle, Roderick
"The 'Rival Poet' and the 'Dark Lady'," S: New Views for Old. London: Palmer, 1930. p. 61-84.

406. Eastman, Arthur M. and Harrison, G. B. (eds.)
S Critics from Johnson to Auden: A Medley of Judgments. Ann Arbor: Univ. of Michigan Press, 1964.

407. _____.
A Short History of Shakespearean Criticism. New York: Random House, 1968. p. 314-322.

408. Eliot, T. S.
Selected Essays, 1917-1932. New York: Harcourt, Brace & World, 1932.

37

409.   .
S and the Stoicism of
Seneca. London: Oxford Univer-
sity Press, 1927.

410.   .
The Use of Poetry and the
Use of Criticism. London: Faber
and Faber, 1933.

411.   Elson, L. C.
S in Music. Boston: L.
C. Page, 1901.

412.   Elton, C. I.
William S, His Family and
Friends, ed. by A. H. Thompson.
New York: Dutton, 1904.

413.   Elton, Oliver
Modern Studies. London:
E. Arnold, 1907.

414.   Empson, William
See Herrnstein, Barbara
(ed.).

415.   .
Seven Types of Ambiguity.
London: Chatto and Windus, 1930,
Norfolk, Connecticut: New Direc-
tions, 1947 (See the 2nd, revised
edition, 1947, p. 50-56; 113-138.
A 3rd edition appeared in 1953).

416.   .
Some Versions of Pastoral.
London: Chatto and Windus,
1935; New York: New Directions,
1950, Passim; New York: Norton,
1938.

417.   .
The Structure of Complex
Words. Norfolk, Connecticut:
New Directions, [n. d.].

418.   Erskine, John
"The S Sonnets," The
Elizabethan Lyric. New York:
Macmillan, 1903 (1916). p. 167-
175.

419.   Evans, Willa McClung
Henry Lawes Musician
and Friend of Poets. New
York: MLA, 1941.

420.   Figgis, Darrell
S, A Study. London:
J. M. Dent, 1911.

421.   Finney, Claude Lee
The Evolution of Keats'
Poetry, 2 vols. Cambridge,
Massachusetts: Harvard Uni-
versity Press, 1936.

422.   Fletcher, Charles R. L.
Portraits: The Lives
[Richard II to Henry Wriotheley,
1400-1600]. Oxford: Clarendon
Press, 1909. Passim.

423.   Forbis, John F.
Shakespearean Enigma
& an Elizabethan Mania. New
York: AMS Press, 1924 (1970).
p. 262-270.

424.   Frazer, Robert
The Silent S. Philadel-
phia: W. J. Campbell, 1915.
p. 93-109.

425.   Fripp, Edgar Innes
Master Richard Quyny,
Bailiff of Stratford-upon-Avon
and Friend of William S. London: Oxford University Press,
1924. p. 64-75.

426.   .
"S's Sonnets, " S, Man
and Artist. London: Oxford
Univ. Press, 1938. p. 258-
267; 713-717.

427.   Frye, Northrop
Anatomy of Criticism.
Princeton: Princeton University
Press, 1957.

428.   Frye, Prosser Hall
"The Elizabethan Son-
net. " Literary Reviews and

Criticisms. New York: Putnam, 1908. p. 1-18.

145

429. Fussell, Paul, Jr.
Poetic Meter and Poetic Form. New York: Random House, 1965. p. 130-131.

430. Gardner, Helen (ed.)
See Leishman, J. B.

431. Garnett, Richard and Gosse, Edmund
"S's Sonnets," English Literature. New York: Macmillan, 1904. I, 213-220.

432. Gerard, Albert S.
See Willen and Reed (eds.).

433. Gollancz, Sir Israel
See Byvanck, W. G. C.

434. _____.
"Analysis," The Aldus S-- Sonnets, ed. by Henry Norman Hudson, et al. New York: Funk & Wagnalls, 1968. p. xxxix-L.

435. _____.
"Preface," The Aldus S-- Sonnets, ed. by Henry Norman Hudson, et al. New York: Funk & Wagnalls, 1968. p. ix-xxvii.

436. Gordon, George
Airy Nothings; or, What You Will. New York: Sturgis & Walton, 1917. p. 71-87.

437. Gosse, Edmund
See Garnett, Richard.

438. Graves, Robert
See Riding, Laura.

439. _____.
See Herrnstein, Barbara (ed.).

440. _____.
See Willen and Reed (eds.).

441. _____.
["A Study in Original Punctuation and Spelling, Sonnet 129"] with Laura Riding, The Common Asphodel: Collected Essays on Poetry 1922-1949. London: International Authors N. V., 1949.

442. Gray, Arthur
"The Sonnets," A Chapter in the Early Life of S. London: Macmillan, 1926. p. 97-101.

443. Gray, H. D.
"S, Southampton and Avisa," Stanford Studies in Language and Literature, ed. by Hardin Craig, Stanford, California: Stanford University Press, 1941. p. 143-151.

444. Greene, D. J. (ed.)
See Sherbo, Arthur.

445. Greenwood, Sir Granville George
The S Problem Restated. London: J. Lane, 1908.

446. _____.
"The Sonnets," Is There a S Problem? London: Lane, 1916. Passim.

447. Haines, C. M.
S in France. London: Oxford University Press for the S Association, 1925.

448. Hall, Vernon, Jr.
See Taylor, Dick, Jr.

449. Hallam, Henry
See Herrnstein, Barbara (ed.).

450. Halliday, Frank Ernest
S and his Critics. London: Gerald Duckworth, 1949.

451. Hamer, Enid Hope

39

(Porter) (ed.)
The English Sonnet: an
Anthology. London: Methuen,
1936.

452. _____.
The Metres of English
Poetry. London: Methuen, 1930.
p. 196-198.

453. Hankins, John E.
S's Derived Imagery.
Lawrence: University of Kansas
Press, 1953.

454. Harbage, Alfred
As They Liked It. New
York: Macmillan, 1947.

455. _____ (ed.)
See Bush, Douglas.

456. _____.
Sir William Davenant,
Poet Venturer, 1606-1668. Philadelphia: University of Pennsylvania Press, 1935.

457. Harris, Frank
The Man S and His Tragic
Life-Story. New York: M. Ken-
nerley, 1909.

458. _____.
"S's Love-Story: The Son-
nets," The Man S and His Tragic
Life Story. New York: Kenner-
ley, 1909. p. 199-248.

459. _____.
The Women of S. London:
Methuen, 1911. p. 115-132.

460. Harris, Frederick James
"S's Sonnets and 'W. H.'."
S and the Welsh. London: T. F.
Unwin, 1919. p. 186-194.

461. Harrison, George B. (ed.)
See Eastman, A. M.

462. Harrison, John Smith
"The S Sonnets." Platonism

in English Poetry. New York:
Lemcke, 1908. p. 127-135.

463. Havens, Raymond Dexter
The Influence of Milton
on English Poetry. Cambridge,
Massachusetts: Harvard University Press, 1922.

464. Hazlitt, William Carew
S. London: B. Quar-
itch, 1902. (The 3rd ed.,
1908, and the 4th ed., 1912,
are called S Himself and His
Work). p. 178-227; 280-281.

465. Herford, C. H.
A Sketch of Recent
Shakespearean Investigation
1893-1923. London: Blackie,
1923.

466. Herrnstein, Barbara
(ed.)
Discussions of S's Son-
nets. Boston: Heath, 1964
(1970). See the same entry in
Criticism (Books & Booklets).

467. Highet, Gilbert
"The Autobiography of
S," in People, Places, and
Books. New York: Oxford
University Press, 1953. p.
86-93.

468. _____.
"S in Love," in The
Powers of Poetry. New York:
Oxford University Press, 1960.
p. 39-46.

469. Holzapfel, Rudolph
Melander
S's Secret. Dublin:
Dolmen Press, for the Melander
S Society, 1961.

470. Hosley, Richard (ed.)
See Stirling, Brents.
Taylor, George Coffin.

471. Hotson, Leslie

See Herrnstein, Barbara
(ed.).

472.   .
I, William S Do Appoint
Thomas Russell, Esquire... London: J. Cape, 1937; New York:
Oxford University Press, 1938.

473.   .
S's Motley. London:
Rupert Hart-Davis, 1952.

474.   Hubler, Edward, et al.
See Blackmur, R. R.

475.   , et al.
See Bluertone, Max.

476.   .
See Herrnstein, Barbara
(ed.).

477.   .
See Willen and Reed (eds.).

478.   (ed.)
"Introduction, " S's Songs
and Poems. New York: McGraw-
Hill Book Co., 1959 (1964). p.
xi-Lv.

479.   Hudson, Henry Norman,
et al.
See Gollancz, Sir Israel.

480.   .
"Introduction, " The Aldus
S--Sonnets, ed. by Henry N. Hudson, et al. New York: Funk &
Wagnalls, 1968. p. xxix-xxxviii.

481.   Inge, William Ralph
"Did S Unlock His Heart?"
in Pacifist in Trouble. London:
Putnam, 1939. p. 275-279.

482.   Ingram, W. G. and Redpath, Theodore (eds.)
"Preface, " S's Sonnets.
New York: Barnes & Noble, 1964
(1968). p. ix-xiv.

483.   Irvine, Helen D. (tr.)
See Legonis, Emile.

484.   Jaggard, William
"List of Editions of the
Sonnets from 1609 to 1909."
S Bibliography. Stratford-on-
Avon: The S Press, 1911. p.
452-456.

485.   Jakobson, Roman &
Jones, L. G.
S's Verbal Art in Th'
Expence of Spirit. New York:
Humanities Pr., 1970.

486.   James, George
The Bacon-S. Controversy. Birmingham: Midland
Educational Co., 1894-1901
(40 p.).

487.   Jente, Richard
The Proverbs of S with
Early and Contemporary Parallels. Washington University
Studies, 12 (1926), 391-444.

488.   John, Lisle Cecil
The Elizabethan Sonnet
Sequences: Studies in Conventional Conceits. New York:
Columbia University Press,
1938; New York: Russell &
Russell, 1964.

489.   Johnson, C. F.
S and His Critics. Boston: Houghton Mifflin, 1909.

490.   .
"The Sonnets, " Forms
of English Poetry. New York:
American Book Co., 1904. p.
107-145.

491.   Johnson, C. W. M.
See Willen and Reed
(eds.).

492.   Jones, H. F.
Samuel Butler, Author
of Erewhon (1835-1902), 2 vols.

41

London: Macmillan, 1919.

493. Jones, L. G.
See Jakobson, Roman.

494. Jusserand, Jean Adrian Antoine Jules
A Literary History of the English People. New York and London: G. P. Putnam's, 1906-1909. III, 226-243.

495. Keats, John
See Herrnstein, Barbara (ed.).

496. Keen, Francis
Phoenix: An Inquiry into the Poems of Robert Chester's "Love's Martyr" (1601) and the "Phoenix Nest" (1593) in Relation to S's "Sonnets" and "A Lover's Complaint." London: Author, 1957.

497. Kellett, E. E.
Suggestions. Cambridge: Cambridge University Press, 1923.

67
498. Kellner, Leon
"Sonnet 67, Line 7, Emended," Restoring S. New York: Knopf, 1925. p. 57.

499. Ker, William Paton
Form and Style in Poetry; Lectures and Notes, ed. by R. W. Chambers. London: Macmillan, 1928. p. 173-175.

500. Kermode, John Frank (ed.)
Four Centuries of Shakespearean Criticism. New York: Avon Books, 1965.

501. Kernan, Alvin B. (ed.)
See Cruttwell, Patrick.

502. Kittredge, George Lyman
See Alden, Raymond M.

503. _____ and Ribner, Irving (eds.)
"Preface" and "Introduction," William S, The Sonnets. Waltham, Mass.: Blaisdell, 1968. p. v-xx.

504. _____ .
S An Address. Cambridge, Massachusetts: Harvard University Press, 1916.

505. Knight, G. Wilson
See Herrnstein, Barbara (ed.).

506. _____ .
See Willen and Reed (eds.).

507. _____ .
The Mutual Flame: On S's Sonnets and The Phoenix and The Turtle. New York: Macmillan, 1955; London: Methuen, 1955.

508. _____ .
The Olive and The Sword. New York: Oxford University Press, 1944.

509. _____ .
Shakespeare's Tempest. London: Methuen, 1953.

510. Knights, L. C.
See Willen and Reed (eds.).

511. _____ .
"S's Sonnets," in Elizabethan Poetry: Modern Essays in Criticism, ed. by Paul J. Alpers. New York: Oxford University Press, 1967. p. 274-298. (A Galaxy Book, GB/77).

512. _____ .
Explorations: Essays in Criticism, Mainly on the Lit-

erature of the Seventeenth Century. London: Chatto & Windus, 1946; New York: George W. Stewart, 1947.

513. _____. Elizabethan Poetry, ed. by P.J. Alpers. New York: Oxford University Press, 1967. p. 274-298.

514. _____. Some Shakespearean Themes. London: Chatto & Windus, 1959.

515. Krieger, Murray "The Innocent Insinuations of Wit: The Strategy of Language in S's Sonnets," in The Play and Place of Criticism. Baltimore: Johns Hopkins Press, 1967. p. 19-26.

516. _____. A Window of Criticism. Princeton, New Jersey: Princeton University Press, 1964.

517. Kristeller, Paul O. The Classics and Renaissance Thought. Cambridge, Massachusetts: Harvard University Press, 1955.

518. LaMar, Virginia A. (ed.) See Wright, Louis B. (ed.).

519. Landry, Hilton See Willen and Reed (eds.).

520. Lanier, Sidney S and His Forerunners, 2 vols. New York: Doubleday & Page, 1902 (1908). (Lectures given in 1879-1880. Sonnets lecture 1879). I, 245-270.

521. Lanz, Henry The Physical Basis of Rime. California: Stanford University Press, 1931.

522. The Laurel S See Barber, C.L. Sisson, Charles Jasper

523. Lawrence, Basil Edwin Notes on the Authorship of the S Plays and Poems. London: Gay & Hancock, 1925.

524. Lee, Sir Sidney Elizabethan and Other Essays, ed. by F.S. Boas. Oxford: Clarendon Press, 1929

525. _____. "The Elizabethan Sonnet." Cambridge History of English Literature. III, 247.

526. _____. Elizabethan Sonnets, 2 v. London: Constable, 1904 (For convenience the sonnet sequences of Barnes, Constable, Griffin, R.L. Lodge, and Watson are quoted from this work). I, ix-cx.

527. _____. The French Renaissance in England. Oxford: Clarendon Press, 1910.

528. _____. "Ovid and S's Sonnets," in Elizabethan and Other Essays, ed. by F.S. Boas. Oxford: Clarendon Press, 1929. p. 116-139. 138, 144

529. _____. "Sonnets 138 and 144," in his facsimile edition of The Passionate Pilgrim. Oxford: [n.p.], 1905. p. 22-24.

530. Legouis, Emile and Cazamian, Louis A History of English Lit-

43

erature, 2 v., tr. by Helen D. Irvine. New York: Macmillan, 1926.

531. Leishman, J. B.
The Monarch of Wit, 3rd
ed. London: Hutchinson, 1957.

532. .
"Variations on a Theme in S's Sonnets," in Elizabethan and Jacobean Studies, ed. by Herbert Davis and Helen Gardner. Oxford: Clarendon Press, 1960. p. 112-149.

533. Lever, J. W.
See Herrnstein, Barbara (ed.).

534. .
The Elizabethan Love Sonnet. London: Methuen, (c) 1956 (1966). Contents: 1. The Petrarchan Sonnet; 2. Wyatt; 3. Surrey; 4. Sidney; 5. Spenser; 6. The Late Elizabethan Sonnet; 7. S: Series I: The Mistress, Series II: The Friend, a. The Invitation to Mary, b. The Poet in Absence, c. The Friend's Fault, d. The Poet and His Rivals, e. The Poet's Error, f. The Immortalization; Conclusion; Index.

535. LeWinter, Oswald (ed.)
S in Europe. Cleveland: World Publishing, 1963.

536. Lewis, Cecil Day
See 393a.

537. Lewis, Clive Staple
"S's Sonnets," in English Literature in the 16th Century, Excluding Drama, (Oxford History of English Literature, ed. by F. P. Wilson and Bonamy Dobree, Vol. III). Oxford: Clarendon Press, 1965. III, 502-508.

538. Liddell, Mark H.
"On The Sonnets," An Introduction to the Scientific Study

of Poetry. New York: Doubleday, Page & Co., 1902. Passim.

539. Liggins, E. M. and Piper, H. W.
"Sound and Sense in a S Sonnet," in Langue et Litterature: Actes du VIII Congrès de la Federation Internationale des Langues et Litteratures Modernes (Bibliothèque de la Faculté de Philosophie et Lettres de l'Université de Liège, Fasc. CLXI). Paris: Société d'Edition "Les Belles Lettres," 1961. p. 417 (S's second sonnet).

540. Long, Mason
Poetry and Its Forms.
New York: G. P. Putnam's, 1938. p. 292-313.

541. Looney, J. T.
"S" Identified in Edward de Vere, the 17th Earl of Oxford. London: C. Palmer, 1920. p. 369-389.

542. Lovett, David
S's Characters in Eighteenth Century Criticism. Baltimore: Johns Hopkins Univ. Press, 1935.

543. Luce, Morton
"S's Sonnets" in A Handbook to the Works of S. London: Macmillan, 1906. p. 82-97.

544. .
"Some New Facts About The Sonnets," S: The Man and His Work. Bristol: Arrowsmith, 1913. p. 11-65.

545. Lumiansky, R. M.
See Willen and Reed (eds.).

546. M., J.
Ben Jonson on S's Son-

44

nets: An Exposition of English
(Reprints p. 27-41 of S Self-Re-
vealed; then adds more details.)
London: [n.p.], 1914.

547. _____.
S Self-Revealed. London
and Manchester: [n.p.], 1904.

548. MacCracken, Henry Noble,
et al.
An Introduction to S. New
York: Macmillan, 1910. p. 63-
70.

549. Mackail, John William
The Approach to S. Ox-
ford: Clarendon Press, 1930.
p. 113-119.

550. _____.
Lectures on Poetry. Lon-
don and New York: Longmans,
Green, 1911. p. 179-207.

551. _____.
"S's Sonnets," in Lectures
on Poetry. London: Longmans,
Green, 1911. p. 178-207.

552. Mackenzie, Agnes Mure
The Women in S's Plays.
London: Heinemann, 1924. p.
461-468.

553. MacLeish, Archibald
Poetry and Experience.
Baltimore: Penguin Books, 1960
(1964). p. 38-41, Passim.

554. McMahan, Anna B.
S's Love Story, 1580-1609.
Chicago: A. C. McClurg, 1909.

555. McPeek, J. A. S.
Catullus in Strange and
Distant Britain. Cambridge, Mas-
sachusetts: Harvard University
Press, 1939.

556. Madden, Dodgson Hamilton
"The Sonnets," S and His
Fellows. New York: Dutton,

1916. p. 9-11.

557. Mahood, M. M.
S's Wordplay. London:
Methuen, 1957.

30
558. Main, C. F. and Seng,
Peter J.
Poems, Wadsworth Hand-
book and Anthology. Belmont,
California: Wadsworth, 1961
(1965). p. 246-247.

66
559. _____ and _____.
Poems, Wadsworth Hand-
book and Anthology. Belmont,
California: Wadsworth, 1961
(1965). p. 229-230.

560. Marder, Louis
His Exits and His En-
trances, The Story of S's Reputation. Philadelphia: Lippincott, 1963.

561. Masson, David (ed.)
"The Sonnets," in his
S Personally. New York: Dut-
ton, 1914. p. 191-238.

562. Matthew, Frank
An Image of S. London:
Cape, 1922. p. 93-96; 106-
114.

96
563. A Memorial of the Quater-Centenary Year of William
S, 1564-1964, April 23. Callow End, Eng: Stanbrook Abbey
Press, 1964 (Sonnet 96).

564. Miles, Josephine
Eras and Modes in Eng-
lish Poetry. Berkeley and Los
Angeles: University of California Press, 1957.

565. Mills, Laurens Joseph
One Soul in Bodies
Twain; Friendships in Tudor

45

Literature and Stuart Drama.
Bloomington, Indiana: Principia
Press, 1937. p. 238-244.

566.   Milstead, John (ed.)
        See Brown, Harry (ed.).

567.   Mizener, Arthur
        See Willen and Reed (eds.).

568.   _____.
        See Herrnstein, Barbara
        (ed.).

569.   Monro, John (ed.)
The S Allusion Book: A
Collection of Allusions to S from
1591 to 1700. London: Chatto
and Windus, 1909.

570.   Moore, Carlisle
        See Willen and Reed (eds.).

571.   More, Paul Elmer
        "S's Sonnets," in Shelburne
Essays. New York: Putnam's,
1905. (2nd series) p. 20-45.

572.   Morton, David
        The Sonnet Today and Yes-
terday. New York: Putnam,
1926. 72 p.

573.   Muir, Kenneth
        "Fifty Years of Shakespear-
ian Criticism, 1900-1950." S S,
4. (1951), 1-25.

574.   _____ and O'Loughlin,
        Sean
        The Voyage to Illyria, A
New Study of S. London: Methuen,
1937.

575.   Murry, John Middleton
        Countries of the Mind (1st
series). London: H. Milford,
1922; (2nd series), London: Oxford University Press, 1931. p.
113-125.

                107
576.   _____.

John Clare and Other Studies.
London: Nevill, 1950. p. 246-
252 (Sonnet 107).

577.   _____.
        S. New York: Harcourt,
Brace & World, 1936. p. 71-
93.

                128, 8
578.   Naylor, Edward Woodall
        "Sonnets 128 and 8,"
The Poets and Music. London:
Dutton, 1928. p. 91-92, and
109-110.

579.   Neilson, William Allan
        and Thorndike, Ashley
        Horace
        The Facts about S. New
York: Macmillan, 1931. p.
47-49, Passim.

580.   Nethercot, Arthur H.
        "Mrs. Davenant as the
'Dark Lady'," Sir William
D'Avenant. Chicago: University of Chicago Pr., 1938. p.
427-431.

581.   Nicoll, Josephine C.
        S in Poland. London:
S Association, 1923.

582.   Noble, Richmond
        S's Biblical Knowledge.
London: Society for Promoting
Christian Knowledge, 1935.

583.   Nolan, Edward F.
        See Willen and Reed
        (eds.).

584.   Nowottny, Winifred M. T.
        See Herrnstein, Barbara
        (ed.).

585.   _____.
        The Language Poets Use.
London: Athlone Press, 1962.

586.   Noyes, Alfred
        New Essays and Amer-

46

ican Impressions. New York: H. Holt, 1927. p. 97-116. (Contains an essay first published as "The Origin of S's Sonnets" in the London Bookman 67, (1924), 159-162. Also in his Opalescent Parrot. London: Sheed & Ward, 1929. p. 190-206.)

587. O'Loughlin, Sean
See Muir, Kenneth.

588. Ord, Hubert W.
London Shown by S, and Other Shakespearean Studies including a New Interpretation of the Sonnets. London: Routledge; New York: Dutton, 1916.

589. Owen, D. E.
Relations of the Elizabethan Sonnet Sequences to Earlier English Verse. Philadelphia: [n. p.], 1903.

109
590. Parry, Sir Charles H. H.
"Sonnet 109," English Lyrics. London: [n. p.], 1907. p. 15-18.

591. Pearson, Hesketh (ed.)
See Wilde, Oscar.

592. Pearson, Lu Emily
Elizabethan Love Conversations. New York: Barnes & Noble, 1966; Berkeley: University of California Press, 1933. p. 231-296: IV. S, Petrarchist and Anti-Petrarchist: 1. Social, Religious, and Economic Conditions in S's England; 2. S and Love Conventions; 3. S's Beauteous Youth; 4. The Dark Lady Sonnets; 5. S's Philosophy of Love.

593. Pember, Francis William
Musa Feriata. Oxford: Clarendon Press, 1931.

594. Pemberton, Henry, Jr.
S and Sir Walter Raleigh.

Philadelphia and London: Lippincott, 1914. p. 85-93; 226-235; Passim.

595. Peterson, Douglas L.
"S's Sonnets," in The English Lyric from Hyatt to Donne. Princeton University Press, 1967. p. 212-251.

596. Phillips, Gerald William
"A Table of Similarities Between the Sonnets and Venus and Adonis," Lord Burghley in S. London: T. Butterworth, 1936. p. 245-250.

597. _____.
S's Sonnets. Cambridge: W. Heffer, 1954.

598. _____.
The Tragic Story of "S." London: C. Palmer, 1932. p. 27-146.

599. Pillai, V. K. A.
S Criticism from the Beginnings to 1765. London: Blackie, 1932.

600. Pineton, Clara Longworth (Countess de Chambrun)
S Rediscovered by Means of Public Records, etc. New York and London: Scribner's, 1938.

601. _____.
"Who Mr. W. H. Really Was," Essential Documents--in the S Case. Bordeaux: Delmas, 1934. p. 33-46.

602. Piper, H. W.
See Liggins, E. M.

603. No entry.

604. Pollard, Alfred William
S's Fight with the Pirates

47

and the Problems of the Transmission of His Text. Cambridge: University Press, 1920.

605. Popovic, Vladeta
S in Serbia. London: S Association, 1928.

606. Praz, Mario
The Flaming Heart. Garden City, New Jersey: Doubleday, 1958.

607. Price, Thomas Randall
"The Technic of S's Sonnets," in Studies in Honor of Basil L. Gildersleeve. Baltimore: Johns Hopkins University Press, 1902. p. 363-375.

608. Prince, Frank T.
S: The Poems. New York: London House, 1964.

609. _____.
"The Sonnet from Wyatt to S," in Elizabethan Poetry. Stratford-upon-Avon Studies, 2 (1960). London: Edward Arnold, 1960. p. 11-30.

610. Quiller-Couch, Sir Arthur Thomas
"LLL and The Sonnets," in the New Cambridge edition of Love's Labour's Lost. Cambridge: Macmillan, 1923. p. xxiv-xxvii.

611. Raleigh, Sir Walter
S. London: Macmillan, 1907.

612. Ralli, Augustus
A History of Shakespearean Criticism. 2 v. London: Oxford University Press, 1932; New York: Oxford University Press, 1958.

613. Rank, Otto
Art and Artist, tr. by Charles Francis Atkinson. New York: Alfred A. Knopf, 1932.

p. 55-58.

614. Ransom, John Crowe
See Herrnstein, Barbara (ed.).

615. _____.
The New Criticism. Norfolk, Connecticut: New Directions, 1941.

616. _____.
See Willen and Reed (eds.).

617. _____.
The World's Body. New York: Charles Scribner's, 1938. p. 270-303. ["S at Sonnets" was first printed in the Southern Review, 4, (1938) 531-553.]

618. Raymond, George Lansing
"The Sonnet," Rhythm & Harmony in Poetry & Music. New York: Putnam, 1909. p. 70-73.

619. Raysor, R.M. (ed.)
Coleridge's S Criticism. 2 v. Cambridge, Mass.: Harvard Univ. Press, 1930.

620. Raysor, Thomas Middleton (ed.)
See Coleridge, S.T.

621. _____ (ed.)
Coleridge's Shakespearean Criticism, 2 v. Cambridge, Massachusetts: [n.p.], 1930.

622. Redfern, Joan (tr.)
See De Sanctis, Francesco.

623. Redpath, Theodore (ed.)
See Ingram, W.G. (ed.).

624. Reed, Edward Bliss
"S's Sonnets," English Lyrical Poetry. New Haven: Yale University Press, 1912.

48

p. 169-176.

625. Reed, Victor B. (ed.)
See Riding, Laura.
Willen, Gerald.

65
626. Reeves, James
The Critical Sense. London: Heinemann, 1956. p. 105-107. (Sonnet 65)

627. Ribern, Irving (ed.)
See Kittredge, George Lyman (ed.).

628. Rice, Sir Robert
The Story of Hamlet and Horatio. London: [n.p.], 1924.

629. Richards, I.A.
How to Read a Page. New York: W.W. Norton, 1942.

630. _____.
The Philosophy of Rhetoric. New York: Oxford University Press, 1936.

631. _____.
Practical Criticism. New York: Harcourt, Brace & World, 1929.

632. _____.
Principles of Literary Criticism. New York: Harcourt, Brace & World, 1926.

633. _____.
Speculative Instruments. London: Routledge and Kegan Paul, 1955.

634. Riding, Laura
See Graves, Robert.

635. _____.
See Herrnstein, Barbara (ed.).

636. _____.
See Willen and Reed (eds.).

637. _____ and Graves, Robert
A Survey of Modernist Poetry. New York: Doran, 1928; London: William Heineman, 1929. p. 49-82 (Extensively revised and published as "A Study in Original Punctuation and Spelling," in The Common Asphodel by Robert Graves. London: Hamish Hamilton, 1949. p. 84-95. Reprinted in A Casebook on S's Sonnets, ed. by Gerald Willen and Victor B. Reed. New York: Thomas Y. Crowell, 1964. p. 161-172).

638. Ridler, Anne Bradby (ed.)
S Criticism, 1935-1960. New York: Oxford University Press, 1963.

639. Ridley, Maurice Roy
William S, A Commentary. London: J.M. Dent, 1936.

640. Robertson, J.G.
"S on the Continent," in C.H.E.L., V, 315-343.

641. Robertson, John Mackinnon
The Genuine in S, a Conspectus. London: G. Routledge, 1930.

642. _____.
An Introduction to the Study of the S Canon. London: Routledge; New York: Dutton, 1924.

643. _____.
S and Chapman. London: T.F. Unwin, 1917.

644. Robinson, H.S.
English Shakespearean Criticism in the Eighteenth Century. New York: H.W. Wilson,

49

1932.

645. Roe, J. E.
Sir Francis Bacon's Own
Story. Rochester, New York:
Author (Du Bois Press), 1918.

646. Rollins, Hyder Edward (ed.)
"Introduction," William S
Sonnets. New York: Appleton-
Century-Crofts, 1951. p. v-x.

647. _____ .
"S's Sonnets" in Richard
Tottel's Miscellany. Cambridge:
Harvard Univ. Press, 1929. II,
103-104.

648. Root, R. K.
Classical Mythology in S.
New York: H. Holt, 1903.

649. Ross, William
The Story of Ann Whately
and William S. London: Holmes,
1940.

650. Rouse, William Henry
Denham (ed.)
S's Ovid Being Arthur Gold-
ing's Translation of the Metamorphoses. London: [n.p.], 1904.

651. Rowse, Alfred Leslie (ed.)
"Introduction," S's Sonnets.
New York: Harper and Row,
1964. p. vii-xxxvi.

652. _____ .
"The Problem of S's Son-
nets Solved," in The English
Spirit. New York: Funk & Wagnalls, 1967.

653. _____ .
S's Southampton, Patron of
Virginia. New York: Harper &
Row, 1965.

654. _____ .
William S, A Biography.
New York: Harper & Row, 1964;
London: Macmillan, 1963.

655. Rusden, G. W.
William S; His Life, His
Works, and His Teaching. Mel-
bourne: [n.p.], 1903.

656. Rylands, George
"S The Poet," A Com-
panion to S Studies. Cambridge:
[n.p.], 1934. p. 89-115.

657. Saintsbury, George
"S: Poems," in
C. H. E. L., V, 250-263.

658. Santayana, George
New Republic Anthology,
1915-1935, ed. by Groff Conklin.
New York: Dodge, 1936. [In-
troduction by Bruce Bliven.]

659. _____ .
Reason in Society. New
York: [n.p.], 1905.

660. Schaar, Claes
Elizabethan Sonnet. New
York: Adler's Foreign Books,
1960.

661. _____ .
An Elizabethan Sonnet
Problem: S's Sonnets, Daniel's
Delia, and Their Literary Back-
ground. Lund: C. W. K. Gleerup,
1960 (1962).

662. _____ .
Elizabethan Sonnet
Themes and the Dating of S's
Sonnets, Lund Studies in Eng-
lish, 32. Lund: Gleerup, 1962.

663. Schelling, Felix Em-
manuel
"The Elizabethan Sonnet
& S," The English Lyric. Boston: Houghton Mifflin, 1913.
p. 58-65.

664. Schucking, Levin L.
Character Problems in
S's Plays. London: George
G. Harrap, 1922.

665. Sells, A. L.
The Italian Influence in
English Poetry from Chaucer to
Southwell. Bloomington, Indiana:
Indiana University Press, 1955.

666. Seng, Peter J.
See Main, C. F.

667. Shaaber, Matthias Adam
"T. Thorp as a Purveyor
of 'Copy'," Some Forerunners of
the Newspaper. Philadelphia:
Press of the Univ. of Pa., 1929.
p. 270-272.

668. Shackford, Martha Hale
The Eternities of Poetrie.
Natick, Massachusetts: Suburban
Press, 1950.

669. Shanks, Edward
"Sonnets and Common
Sense," in First Essays on Literature. London: W. Collins,
1923. p. 215-221.

670. Sharp, Frank Chapman
"The Sonnets," S's Por-
trayal of the Moral Life. New
York: Scribner, 1902. Passim.

671. Sharp, (Mrs.) W.
See Sharp, William.

672. Sharp, William
Studies and Appreciations,
ed. by Mrs. William Sharp. New
York: Duffield, 1912. p. 71-105.

673. Sherbo, Arthur
"Johnson as Editor of S:
The Notes," in Samuel Johnson:
A Collection of Critical Essays,
ed. D. J. Greene. Englewood
Cliffs, N. J.: Prentice-Hall, 1965.

674. Shore, William T.
S's Self. London: P.
Allan, 1920. p. 83-89.

675. Siegel, Paul N. (ed.)
His Infinite Variety: Major

Shakespearean Criticism Since
Johnson. Philadelphia: Lippincott, 1964.

676. Simon, Henry William
The Reading of S in
American Schools and Colleges.
New York: Simon & Schuster,
1932.

677. Sipe, Dorothy L.
S's Metrics (Studies in
English No. 167). New Haven,
Conn.: Yale University Press,
1968.

678. Sisson, Charles Jasper
(ed.)
See Barber, C. L.

679. _____.
New Readings in S, 3 v.
Cambridge: Cambridge Univer-
sity Press, 1956. Vol. I.

680. Sitwell, Edith
A Notebook on William
S. New York, London: Mac-
millan, 1948.

681. Smeaton, William Henry
Oliphant
S His Life and Work.
London: J. M. Dent, 1911.

682. Smith, D. Nichol
S in the Eighteenth Cen-
tury. Oxford: Clarendon Press,
1928.

683. _____ (ed.)
S Criticism: A Selection
(1623-1840). New York: Oxford University Press, 1916.

684. Smith, Gordon Ross
See Willen and Reed
(eds.).

685. Smith, Hallett
Elizabethan Poetry.
Cambridge, Massachusetts:
Harvard University Press,

51

1952. p. 131-193.

686. Smith, Logan Pearsall
On Reading S. London:
Constable, 1933.

687. Snider, Denton J.
"The Sonnets," A Biography
of William S. St. Louis: Miner,
1922. Passim.

688. Spencer, Hazelton
The Art and Life of William
S. New York: Harcourt, Brace
& World, 1940. p. 27-35.

689. Spencer, Theodore
S and the Nature of Man.
New York: Macmillan, 1942.

690. Spurgeon, Caroline F. E.
Keats' S. London: H.
Milford; Oxford University Press,
1928.

691. _____.
S's Imagery and What It
Tells Us. New York, Cambridge:
Cambridge University Press,
1935.

692. Squire, John C.
Life and Letters. London:
Heinemann, 1921. p. 182-188.

693. Stalker, Archibald
S, Marlowe and Nashe.
Stirling: A. Learmonth, 1935.

694. Standen, Gilbert
"The Sonnets," S Author-
ship. London: Palmer, 1930.
p. 34-50.

695. Steevens, George
See Herrnstein, Barbara (ed.)

696. Stevenson, Charles L.
Ethics and Language. New
Haven: Yale University Press,
1944.

`97. Stirling, Brents

"More S Sonnet Groups,"
in Essays on S and the Elizabethan Drama in Honor of
Dardin Craig, ed. by Richard
Hosley. Columbia: University
of Missouri Press, 1962. p.
115-135.

698. _____.
"Sonnets 127-154," in
S 1564-1964, ed. by Edward A.
Bloom. Providence, Rhode
Island: Brown University Press,
1964.

699. Stoffel, C. O.
See Van Dam, V. A.

700. Stoll, E. E.
S's Studies. New York:
Macmillan, 1927.

701. Stopes, Charlotte
"The Earl of Southamp-
ton," S's Industry. London:
Macmillan, 1916. p. 227-236.

702. _____.
S's Environment. Lon-
don: G. Bell, 1914.

703. _____.
The Life of Henry, Third
Earl of Southampton, S's Patron.
Cambridge: University Press,
1922.

704. Stotsenburg, John Hawley
An Impartial Study of
the S Title. Louisville, Ken-
tucky: J. P. Morton, 1904.
p. 212-231.

705. Strachey, Giles Lytton
Spectatorial Essays.
New York: Harcourt, 1964.
p. 71-75.

706. Strachey, John St. Loe
"S & The Sonnets," The
River of Life. London: Hodder
& Stoughton, 1924. p. 28-31.

52

707. Strong, L. A. G.
The Body's Imperfection.
London: Methuen, 1957.

59, 60, 61
708. Suddard, Sarah Julle Mary
"Sonnets 59, 60, and 61,"
Keats, Shelley, and S Studies.
Broadway, Press, 1912. p. 177-181.

709. Taylor, Dick, Jr.
"Clarendon and Ben Jonson as Witness for the Earl of Pembroke's Character," in Studies in the English Renaissance Drama: (In Memory of Karl Julius Holzknecht), eds. by Josephine W. Bennett, Oscar Cargill, and Vernon Hall, Jr. New York: New York University Press, 1959. p. 322-344.

710. Taylor, George Coffin
"Two Notes on S," in Renaissance Studies in Honor of Hardin Craig. California: Stanford University Press, 1941. p. 179-184.

711. Taylor, Henry Osborn
Thought and Expression in the Sixteenth Century, 2 vols. New York: Macmillan, 1920.

712. Terry, Ellen
Four Lectures on S. London: Martin Hopkinson, 1932.

713. Thaler, Alwin
S's Silences. Cambridge, Massachusetts: Harvard University Press, 1929.

714. Thompson, A. H. (ed.)
See Elton, C. I.

715. Thompson, Karl F.
See Willen and Reed (eds.).

716. Thomson, James Alexander Ken
S and the Classics. London: Allen & Unwin, 1952.

717. Thomson, Patricia
Sir Thomas Wyatt and His Background. Stanford: University Press, 1964. Passim.

718. Thorn-Drury, George
More Seventeenth Century Allusions to S and His Works Not Hitherto Collected. London: P. J. and A. E. Dobell, 1924.

719. Thornton, Gregory
Sonnets of S's Ghost. Sydney: Angus and Robertson, 1920.

720. Traversi, D. A.
An Approach to S. London: Sands, Poladin Press, 1938; 2nd ed. Garden City, New York: Doubleday, 1956. p. 39-48.

721. Van Dam, V. A. & Stoffel, C. O.
William S, Prosody and Text. New York: AMS Press, 1900 (1970).

722. Van Doren, Mark
S. New York: Henry Holt, 1939 (1953). p. 4-9.

723. Vizetelly, Ernest Alfred
"The Dark Lady," Loves of the Poets. London: Holden & Hardingham, 1915. p. 62-70.

724. Ward, Bernard Rowland
The Mystery of "Mr. W. H, " London: Palmer, 1923. p. 132.

725. Warren, Clyde T.
See Clarkson, P. S.

65
726. Wassal, G.

"Since Brass Nor Stone
(Sonnet 65)," A S Song Cycle.
Cincinnati: [n.p.], 1904. p. 34-
37.

727.   90, 91
                 .
"Some Glory in Their Birth
(Sonnet 91)," A S Song Cycle.
Cincinnati: [n.p.], 1904. p. 25-
27.

728.   Watkins, W. B. C.
        S and Spencer. Princeton,
New Jersey: Princeton University Press, 1950.

729.   Watson, Curtis Brown
        S and the Renaissance Con-
cept of Honor. Princeton, New
Jersey: Princeton University
Press, 1960.

730.   Weinberger, J.
        "The Dark Lady" in Under
the Spreading Chestnut Tree. New
York: [n.p.], 1939.

731.   Wells, Henry Willis
        Poetic Imagery Illustrated
from Elizabethan Literature. New
York: Columbia University Press,
1924. [Columbia University
Studies in English and Comparative Literature].

732.   Wendell, Barrett
        "S's Sonnets," William S.
New York: Addison J. Selections,
1902. p. 221-231.

733.   .
        The Traditions of European
Literature, from Homer to Dante.
London and New York: J. Murray,
1921.

734.   Westfall, Alfred van
        Rensselaer
        American Shakespearean
Criticism, 1607-1865. New York:
H. W. Wilson, 1939.

735.   Whitaker, Virgil K.
        S's Use of Learning.
San Marino, California: Huntington Library, 1953.

736.   White, Edward Joseph
        Commentaries on the
Law in S. St. Louis: F. H.
Thomas Law Book Co., 1911.
p. 506-512.

737.   White, Henry Kelsey
        An Index to the Songs,
Snatches, & Passages in S
Which Have Been Set to Music.
Great Fencote, Yorkshire: J.
R. Tutin, 1900.

738.   Wilde, Oscar
        "Portrait of Mr. W. H.,"
in Essays, ed. with an introduction by Hesketh Pearson.
London: Methuen, 1950. p.
189-226.

739.   Willen, Gerald and Reed,
        Victor B. (eds.)
        A Casebook on S's Son-
nets. New York: Thomas Y.
Crowell, 1964. Contents: See
Criticism (Books and Booklets).

740.   Williams, Frayne
        Mr. S of the Globe.
New York: Dutton, 1941.

741.   Wilson, F. P. (ed.)
        See Lewis, C. S.

742.   .
        S and the Diction of
Common Life. (British Acade-
my Lecture) London: Oxford
University Press, 1941.

743.   Wilson, John Dover (ed.)
        Life in S's England.
Harmondsworth, England: Penguin Books, 1944.

744.   .
        The Essential S. Cam-
bridge: University Press, 1932.

745. Winters, Yvor
See Herrnstein, Barbara
(ed.).

746. _____.
"Poetic Style in S's Son-
nets," in Four Poets on Poetry,
ed. by Don Cameron Allen. Baltimore: Johns Hopkins University Press, 1959.

747. Wisconsin, University of
S Studies by Members of
the Department of English of the
University of Wisconsin. Madison:
University of Wisconsin Press,
1916. [Contains R. E. N. Dodge's
"An Obsolete Elizabethan Mode of
Rhyming," p. 174-200, and Arthur
Beatty's "S's Sonnets and Plays,"
p. 201-214.]

748. Wright, Louis B. and La-
Mar, Virginia A. (eds.)
"Supreme Poetry of Love--
Beguiling Mystery," S's Sonnets
(The Folger Library General
Reader's S). New York: Wash-
ington Square Press, 1967. p.
vii-xxxiii.

749. Wright, W. Aldis (ed.)
See Bacon, Francis.

750. Wyndham, George (ed.)
"Poems of S," in Essays
in Romantic Literature. London:
Macmillan, 1919. p. 237-388.

751. Yates, Frances A.
A Study of Love's Labour's
Lost. Cambridge: University
Press, 1936.

752. Yeatman, John P.
"The Authorship of the
Sonnets," The Gentle S. London:
Roxburghe Press, 1896 (1911).
p. 295-301.

753. Young, Frances Berkeley
Mary Sidney, Countess of
Pembroke. London: David Nutt,
1912.

754. Young, Sir George
An English Prosody on
Inductive Lines. Cambridge:
University Press, 1928.

755. The Youth
See Brown, Henry.

C. Articles and Book Reviews

(1) Articles

756. Abend, Murray
"Two Unique Gender
Forms in the S Sonnets," N &
Q, 195 (1950), 325.

757. Acheson, Arthur
"Mistress Davenant: The
Dark Lady of S's Sonnets,"
Spectator, 110 (1913), 1019-
1020.

758. _____.
"S and the Rival Poet,"
Athenaeum. June 30, 1904.
139-140.

759. _____.
"S's Lost Years," TLS,
January 6, 1921. p. 9.

760. _____.
"Trailing the Dark Lady
of the Sonnets," New York
Times Book Review, March 20,
1921, p. 4, 27.

761. Adams, J. Q.
"Hamlet and the Sonnets,"
MLN, 29 (1914), 1-3.

30
702. Aiken, Ralph
"A Note on S's Sonnet
30," SQ, 14 (1963), 93-94.

763. Ainger, A.
" 'Beget' and 'Begetter'
in Elizabethan England," Athenaeum, March 17, 1900. p. 346.

764. Akrigg, G. P. V.
"The S of the Sonnets,"
Queen's Quarterly, 72 (1965), 78-
90.

765. Alden, Raymond M.
"J. Strong's Note upon The
Dark Lady," Literary Review.
July 23, 1921.

766.   .
"The 1710 and 1714 Texts
of S's Poems," MLN, 31 (1916),
268-274.

767.   .
"1640 Text of S's Sonnets,"
Modern Philology, 14 (1916), 17-
30.

768.   .
"The Lyrical Conceit of the
Elizabethans," Studies in Philology,
14 (1917), 129-152.

769.   .
"The 1640 Text of S's Sonnets," Modern Philology, 14
(1917), 17.

770.   .
"The Punctuation of S's
Printers," in PMLA, 39 (1924),
557-580.

771. Alexander, P.
"Fort's Time Scheme,"
RES, 6 (1930), 467-469.

772. All for Love
See Davies, Neville H.

773. Allen, Ned B.
"Publisher of the Sonnets,"
SNL, 12 (September 1962), 34.
[Leona Rostenberg, "Thomas
Thorpe, Publisher of S's Sonnets,"
Papers of the Bibliographical So-
ciety of America, 54 (1960), 16-
38.]

774.   .
"S's Sonnet Artistry," SNL,

12 (1962), 26. [M. Albert S.
Gerard, "Iconic Organization in
S's Sonnet 146," ES, 42 (1961),
157-159.]

106
775.   and Brussels,
Robert T.
" 'Still' or 'Skill,' A
Note on S's Sonnet 106," SJ,
97 (1961), 203-207; SNL, 13
(1963), 10.

776. Allen P.
"The Rhyme-Linked Or-
der of S's Sonnets," Christian
Science Monitor, January 18,
1929. p. 9.

777.   .
"The 'Mortal Moon,' "
TLS, March 8, 1934. p. 162.

778. Alter, Jean V.
"Apollinaire and Two
Shakespearean Sonnets, 147-
148," Comparative Literature,
14 (1962), 377-385.

779. Angell, Pauline K.
"Light on the Dark Lady:
A study of some Elizabethan
libels." (PMLA) 52 (1937),
652-674.

780.   and Baldwin, T. W.
"Light on the Dark La-
dy," PMLA, 55 (1940), 598-
602.

781. Antony & Cleopatra
See Madariaga, S. de.

782. Archer, C.
" 'Thou' and 'You' in
the Sonnets," TLS, June 27,
1936, p. 544.

783. Archer, W.
"Sonnets of S," Living
Age, 244 (1905), 313-316.

784. Aretino

See Steadman, J. M.

785. Aring, Charles D.
"Perception As a Moral
Test," Journal of Nervous and
Mental Diseases, 144 (1968), 539-
545.

786. Auden, W. H.
"S's Sonnets," Listener,
72 (1964), 7-9; 45-47.

787. Bagg, R.
"Some Versions of Lyric
Impasse in S and Catullus," Arion,
4 (1965), 65-95.

788. Baldwin, T. W.
See Angell, Pauline K.

8
789. Banks, Theodore H.
"S's Sonnet No. 8," MLN,
63 (1948), 541-542.

790. Barber, C. L.
"S in His Sonnets," Mas-
sachusetts Review, 1 (1960), 648-
672.

791. Barker, G. A.
"Themes and Variations in
S's Pericles," ES, 44 (1963), 401-
414.

109
792. Barrell, Charles Wisner
"The Wayward Water-
Bearer Who Wrote 'S's Sonnet
109," S Fellowship Quarterly, 6
(1945), 37-39.

793. Bartlett, Henrietta C.
"First Editions of S's
Quartos," Library, 16 (1935),
166-172.

794. Basdekis, P.
"Death in the Sonnets of S
and Camões," Hispania, 46 (1963),
102-105.

795. Bates, E. S.

"The Sincerity of S's
Sonnets," MP, 8 (1910), 87-
106; 129-152.

796. Bates, Paul A.
"A New Key to S's Son-
nets," SNL, 11 (1961), 2.

797. .
"S's Sonnets and Pastoral
Poetry," SJ, 103 (1967), 81-96.
[Virgil's Second Eclogue of
Richard Barnfield's The Affec-
tionate Shepherd (1594)].

798. Bateson, F. W.
"Elementary My Dear
Hotson! A Caveat for Literary
Detectives," EIC, 1 (1951), 81-
88.

799. .
See Empson, William.

800. .
"The Function of Criti-
cism at the Present Time,"
EIC, 3 (1953), 1-27.

801. .
See Wheeler, Charles B.

802. Baym, Max I.
"Recurrent Poetic
Theme," S Association Bulletin,
12 (1937), 155-158.

803. Beckwith, Elizabeth
"On the Chronology of
S's Sonnets," JEGP, 25 (1926),
227-242.

804. Beeching, H. C.
"The Sonnets," Corn-
hill Magazine, 12 (1902),
244.

804a. Begetter
See Ainger, A.; Brown,
Ivor; Dowden, E.; Lee,
Sir Sidney; Lynch, Ar-
thur.

805. Bennett, Josephine A. W.
"Benson's Alleged Piracy
of S's Sonnets and of Some of
Jonson's Works," Studies in Bibliography, 21 (1968), 235-248.

806. _____.
"Remembrance of Things
Past," N & Q, 9 (1962), 151-152.

807. Benson, John
See Smith, Hallett.

124
808. Bercovitch, Sacvan
"S's 'Sonnet 124,' " Ex-
plicator, 27 (1968), Item 22.

809. Berkelman, Robert G.
"The Drama in S's Son-
nets," College English, 10 (1948),
138-141.

810. Berry, Francis
" 'Thou' and 'You' in S's
Sonnets," EIC, 8 (1958), 138-146.

12
811. Berry, J. Wilkes
"S's Sonnet 12," Explicator,
27 (1968), 13.

812. Berryman, John Wilkes
"S at Thirty," Hudson Re-
view, 6 (1953), 175-203.

813. Best, C.
See Nickalls, B.

814. Biggs, Alan J.
"Carew and S," N & Q,
3 (1956), 225.

815. Birchenough, Josephine and
Goodacre, Edward B.
"Fair Youth and Dark Lady,"
TLS, September 17, 1964.

816. Birdwood, G.
"Canker-blooms," Athenae-
um, July 30, 1904. p. 156.
August 13, 1904. p. 219-220.

1-18,126,127,152
817. Blackmur, R. P.
"Poetics for Infatuation,"
Venture, 3 (1963), 38-59. Also
in Kenyon Review, 23 (1961),
647-670.

818. Blatt, William M.
"New Light on the Son-
nets," MP, 11 (1913), 135-140.

819. Boas, F. S.
"The Date of S's Son-
nets," TLS, July 7, 1950. p.
421.

820. Bowen, Gwynneth
"Oxford's Letter to Bed-
ingfield and 'S's Sonnets,' "
Shakespearean Authorship Review, 17 (1967), 6-12.

85, 86
821. Bradbrook, M. C.
"A New Reading of Son-
nets 85 and 86," Filoloski
Pregled 1-2 (1965), 155-157.

822. Bradley, Haldeen
"S's Sonnet Plan and the
Effect of Folk Belief," Midwest
Folklore, 12 (1962), 235-240.

823. Bray, Sir Denys
"The Art-form of the
Elizabethan Sonnet Sequence and
S's Sonnets," SJ, 63 (1927),
159-182.

824. _____.
"Difficult Passages in
the Sonnet Reexamined," N & Q,
190 (1946), 200-202; 191 (1947),
92-95.

149
825. _____.
"Sonnet 149," TLS, July
4, 1942, p. 331.

826. Brooke, Arthur
See Law, Robert A.

827. Brooks, C.
"S as a Symbolist Poet,"
Yale Review, 34 (1945), 642-665.

828. _____ and Mizener, A.
"Equality of Poetry," Po-
etry, 71 (1948), 318-324.

829. Brooks, H. F.
"S and the Governour, Bk.
II, Ch xiii, Parallels with Richard
II and the More Addition," SQ,
14 (1963), 195-199.

128
830. Brophy, James
"S's 'Saucy Jacks,' " ELN,
1 (1963), 11-13.

831. Brown, Ivor
"Cavendish the 'Begetter'
of the S," Baconiana, 13 (1905),
68.

832. _____ .
"A Performance of Shaw's
Dark Lady," SR, 149 (March 1,
1930), 263.

833. _____ .
See SNL.

106
834. Brussels, Robert Thornon.
See Allen, Ned B.

835. Bullock, W. L.
"The Genesis of the Eng-
lish Sonnet Form," PMLA, 38
(1923), 729-744.

836. Burckhardt, Sigurd
"The Poet as Fool and
Priest," JELH, 23 (1956), 289-
298.

837. Buxton, John, et al.
"S's Sonnets," TLS, Jan-
uary 2, 1964. p. 9.

838. Byars, W. V.
"The Dark Lady," Reedy's
Mirror, 22 (1913), 4-6.

839. Cabaniss, Allen
"S and The Holy Rosa-
ry," Univ. of Mississippi
Studies in English, 1 (1960),
118-128.

840. Caldwell, James R.
"States of Mind: States
of Consciousness," EIC, 4
(1954), 168-179.

841. Calvin, I.
"S Unlocked His Heart,"
Atlantic, 144 (1929), 55-62.

842. Camden, C.
See Johnston, G. B.

843. Carew, T.
See Biggs, Alan J.

844. Carpenter, B. F.
"S's Sonnets: To Whom
Dedicated?" Catholic World,
106 (1918), 496-507.

845. Carter, Albert
"The Punctuation of S's
Sonnets of 1609," Gaya College
Journal, 2 (1961), 10-16.

846. Cavendish, G.
See Brown, Ivor.

847. Chambers, Sir Edmund K.
"The Date of the 'Mortal
Moon,' " TLS, January 25,
1934. p. 6.

848. _____ .
"The 'Mortal Moon,' "
Year's Work in English Studies,
9 (1930), 148.

20
849. _____ .
"The Youth of S's Son-
nets; Significance of Hews in
Sonnet 20," RES, 21 (1945),
331.

850. Chapman, G.
See Douglas, Lord Alfred.

851. .
See Lever, J. W.

852. .
See Murry, J. M.

853. Chapman, J. A.
"Marching Song," Essays
and Studies, 28 (1942), 13-21.

854. Chaucer, Geoffrey
See Ord, H.

855. Chronology
See Dating.

116
856. Clark, W. R.
"Poems for Study: Sonnet
116," Clearing House, 34 (1960),
316.

146
857. Clarke, Robert F.
"An Emendation of Sonnet
146," SNL, 8 (1958), 11.

858. Clarkson, Paul S.
"Mr. W. H. ?" Saturday Review of Literature, 12 (1935), 13.

46
859. and Warren, Clyde T.
"Pleading and Practice in
S's Sonnet 46," MLN, 62 (1947),
102-110.

860. Cohen, H. L.
"Poetry Corner," Scholastic,
36 (1940), 20.

861. Colvin, I.
"S Unlocked His Heart,"
Atlantic, 144 (1929), 56-62.

862. Cook, I. R. W.
"William Harvey and S's
Sonnets," SS, 21 (1968), 97-105.

863. Coriolanus
See Eccles, C. M.

864. Cormican, L. A.

"Medieval Idiom in S:
(I) S and the Liturgy," Scrutiny,
17 (1950), 186-202.

865. Craig, Harding
"A Woman Colour'd Ill,"
SNL, 15 (1965), 24.

866. Cranefield, P. F. and
Federn, W.
"Possible Source of a
Passage in The Tempest," SQ,
14 (1963), 90-92.

85
867. Creighton, Charles
"A New Reading in Son-
net 85," TLS. January 23,
1919. p. 46.

868. .
"S and the Earl of
Pembroke," Blackwood's, 149
(1901), 668-683, 829-845.

869. Cripps, A. R.
See Douglas, A.

870. Cruttwell, Patrick
"A Reading of the Son-
nets," Hudson Review, 5 (1952/
53), 554-570.

871. D., A.
"S's Sonnets," N & Q,
(1951), 5-6.

872. Daniel, Samuel
See Maxwell, J. C.

873. Dannenfeldt, Karl H.
"Egypt and Egyptian
Antiquities in the Renaissance,"
Studies in the Renaissance, 6
(1959), 7-27.

874. Darby, Robert H.
"The Date of S Sonnets,"
SJ, 85 (1939), 135-138.

874a. "The Dark Lady"
See Acheson, Arthur;
Alden, Raymond M. ;

Angell, Pauline K.;
Baldwin, T.W.;
Birchenough, Josephine and
Goodacre, E.B.;
Brown, Ivor;
Byars, W.V.;
Craig, Harding;
Eagle, Robert L.;
Greenwood, G.G.;
Harris, F.;
Munro, John;
Scott, David;
Shaw, G.B.;
Watson, Wilfred.

874b. Dating
See Beckwith, Elizabeth;
Boas, F.S.;
Chambers, Sir E.K.;
Darby, Robert H.;
Fort, James A.;
Garnett, R.;
Gray, Henry David;
Harbage, Alfred;
Hotson, Leslie;
Knight, G. Wilson;
Lewis, M. and Scotland,
C.W.;
Mattingly, Garrett;
Perrett, Arthur J.;
Thomson, Patricia.

875. Davenport, A.
"Seed of a S Sonnet,"
N & Q, 182 (1942), 242-244.

51
876. .
"S's Sonnet 51 Again,"
N & Q, 198 (1953), 15-16.

66
877. Davies, H. Neville
"S's Sonnet 66 Echoed in
All for Love," N & Q, 15 (1968),
262-263.

71
878. Davis, Jack M. and Grant,
J.E.
"A Critical Dialogue on S's
Sonnet 71," Texas Studies in Lit-
erature and Language, 1 (1959),

214-232.

879. De Chambrun, Clara
Longworth
See Pineton, Clara Long-
worth (Countess de
Chambrun).

880. Dellinger, J. Howard
"An 1890 Identification
of S," S Authorship Review, 5
(1961), 1-2.

881. De Montmorency, J.E.G.
"The Mystery of S's Son-
nets," Contemporary Review,
101 (1912), 737-742.

882. .
"The Other Poet," Con-
temporary Review, 101 (1912),
885-889.

883. Denning, W.H.
"Who Wrote the Son-
nets?" English Record, 11
(1925), 766-768.

884. Disher, M. Wilson
"The Trend of S's
Thought," TLS, Oct. 20, 27,
Nov. 3, 1950, p. 668, 684,
700. See the letters "The Ri-
val Poet" by J.M. Murry,
Ibid., Nov. 17, 1950. p. 727
(See Murry, J.M.).

885. Doctor Faustus (by
Thomas Mann)
See Puknut, S.B.

116
886. Doebler, John
"A Submerged Emblem
in Sonnet 116," SQ, 15 (1964),
109-110.

887. Douglas, Lord Alfred
See Kingsmile, H.;
Murry, John Middleton;
Palmer, H.E.;
Wells, Henry W.

888. _____ .
"S and Will Hughes," TLS,
May 21, 1938. p. 353.

889. _____, et al.
"Chapman & the Rival Po-
et," TLS, June 11, 1938. p.
402.

890. _____ and Cripps, A. R.
"S and Will Hughes," TLS,
May 28, 1938. p. 370.

891. Douse, T. L. M.
"S's Sonnets," Literature,
6 (1900), 229.

892. Dowden, E.
" 'Beget' and 'Begetter' in
Elizabethan England," Athenaeum.
March 10, 1900, p. 315-316;
March 24, p. 379-380.

893. Downer, Alan S.
"S Preserv'd," Kenyon Re-
view, 26 (1964), 554-556.

894. Dryden, John
See Davies, H. Neville.

895. Durrell, Lawrence
"The Rival Poet," TLS,
Jan. 5, 1951, p. 5.

896. Eagle, Robert L.
"The Dark Lady," Baco-
niana, 22 (1914), 218-226.

897. _____ .
"The Headpiece on S's Sonnets, 1609," N & Q, 192 (1947),
38.

898. _____ .
"The 'Master Mistress'
Identified," Baconiana, 22 (1914),
159-164.

899. _____ .
"The Problem of S's Son-
nets," Quest, 16 (1925), 508-516.

900. _____ .

"The Rival Poet,"
Baconiana, 22 (1914), 227-230.

55
901. Eccles, C. M.
"S and Jacques Amyot:
Sonnet 55 and Coriolanus,"
N & Q, 12 (1965), 100-102.

902. Eccles, Mark
"The 'Mortal Moon' Son-
net," TLS, Feb. 15, 1934, p.
108.

903. Echhoff, Lorentz
"S's Sonnets in a New
Light," Studia Neophilologia,
39 (1967), 1-14.

904. Edward III
See Osterberg, V.

905. _____ .
See Platt, Arthur.

111
906. Edwards, H. L. R.
"Emending Sonnet 111,
Line 12," TLS. October 25,
1934. p. 735.

907. Eliot, T. S.
"On the Nature of Po-
etry," Theatre Arts, 27 (1943),
327-328.

5
908. Elman, Paul
"S's Gentle Hours (Son-
net 5)," SQ, 4 (1953), 301-309.

909. Elonen, Paul
"S's Gentle Hours," SQ,
4 (1953), 301-309.

910. Emerson, Oliver Farrar
"S's Sonneteering,"
Studies in Philology, 20 (1923),
111-136.

911. Empson, William
See Ransom, John Crowe.

912. .
"Mr. W.H.," New States-
man, 67 (1964), 642.

913. .
"S's Angel," New States-
man, 66 (1963), 447-448.

914. .
"They That Have Power,"
Studies in English Literature,
(Tokyo Imperial University), 13
(1933), 451-469. (This essay was
reprinted in his Some Versions of
Pastoral (London, 1935), p. 89-
115.)

915. ____ and Bateson, F.W.
" 'Bare Ruined Choirs,' "
EIC, 3 (1953), 357-363.

916. Enright, D.J.
"Mr. W.H.," New States-
man, 62 (1964), 642-644.

917. Erasmus, D.
See Reichert, John F.

918. Ervine, St. J.
"Did S Despise the Stage?"
Observer (London). August 17,
1930. p. 9.

919. Essex, Robert Devereaux
See Scott, David.

920. Evans, E.C.
See Levin, Richard.

97
921. .
"S's Sonnet 97," RES, 14,
(1963), 379-380. Reply. R.
Leven, RES, 15 (1964), 408-409.

116
922. Evans, Willa McClung
"Lawes' Version of S's
Sonnet 116," PMLA, 51 (1936),
120-122.

923. Every Man Out of His
Humor

See McNeal, T.H.

924. "Fair Youth and Dark
Lady," TLS, Sept. 10, 1964,
p. 840.

925. Falstaff, John
See Viswanathan, K.

926. Farr, Henry
"Notes on S's Printers
and Publishers," Library, 3
(1923), 225-260.

927. Federn, W.
See Cranenfield, P.F.

928. Feldman, A. Bronson
"The Confessions of
William S," American Imago,
10 (1953), 113-116.

929. Ficino, M.
See Steadman, J.M.

930. Finkenstaldt, Thomas
See Berry, Francis.

930a. Fitton, Mary
See Gray, Cecil G.;
Strachey, C.

931. Flatter, Richard
"Sigmund Freud on S,"
SQ, 2 (1951), 368-369.

932. Foakes, R.A.
"Much Ado About the
Sonnets," English, 15 (1964),
50-52.

107
933. Fort, James A.
"The Date of S's 107th
Sonnet," Library, 9 (1929),
381-384.

934. .
"Further Notes on S's
Sonnets," Library, 9 (1928),
305-325.

935. ____ .

63

"The 'Mortal Moon' Sonnet,"
TLS, February 15, 1934. p. 108;
February 22, 1934. p. 126;
March 22, 1934. p. 214.

936. _____ .
"The Order and Chronology
of the Sonnets," RES, 9 (1933),
19-23.

937. _____ .
"The Story Contained in
the Second Series of S's Sonnets,"
RES, 3 (1927), 406-414.

938. _____ .
"Thorpe's Test for S's
Sonnets," RES, 2 (1926), 439-445.

939. _____ .
"Time-Scheme of the First
Series of S's Sonnets," 19th Cen-
tury, 100 (1926), 272-279.

940. Fox, Charles O.
"Early Echoes of S's Son-
nets and The Passionate Pilgrim,"
N & Q, 198 (1953), 370.

941. _____ .
"Shakespearean Allusion,"
N & Q, (1951), 412.

126
942. _____ .
"S's Sonnet 126, Lines 1
and 2," N & Q, 197 (1952), 134-
135.

146
943. _____ .
"S's Sonnet 146," N & Q,
199 (1954), 83.

944. _____ .
"Thomas Lodge and S,"
N & Q, 3 (1956), 190.

945. Freeman, A.
"Richard II, I. iii, 294-
95," SQ, 14 (1963), 89-90.

946. Freud, Sigmund

See Flatter, Richard.

947. Furnivall, F. J.
"Eroticism as Displayed
in Literature," International
Journal of Psychoanalysis,
[n. v. n.], (1920), 396-413.

948. Gahan, C. J.
"Mr. W. H.," Observer
(London). April 8, 1923. p.
17.

949. Garnett, R.
"The Date of the Son-
nets," Literature, 6 (1900), 212.

950. Garwood, H. P.; Leigh, M.
"Rhyme-links in the Son-
nets," Observer. April 17,
1938. p. 5; April 24, p. 10.

951. Gerard, Albert S.
See Rolle, Dietrich.

952. Gerard, M. Albert
See Allen, Ned B.

146
953. _____ .
"Iconic Organization in
S's Sonnet 146," ES, 42 (1961),
157-159.

94
954. _____ .
"The Stone as Lily: A
Discussion of S's Sonnet 94,"
SJ, 96 (1960), 155-160.

955. Gerritsen, Johan
"S Conference," ES, 42
(1961), 369-370.

956. Gilbank, P. E.
" 'S's' Sonnets: A New
Interpretation," Culture, 24
(1963), 107-115.

957. Gleeson, J. F.
"Introducing S," English
Journal, 56 (1967), 1293-1294.

958. Godwin, P.
"New Study of Sonnets of S," Nation, 79 (1904), 273-274.

959. Goldsmith, Ulrich K.
"Words Out of a Hat? Alliteration and Assonance in S's Sonnets," JEGP, 49 (1950), 33-48.

960. Goldstein, Neal L.
"Money and Love in S's Sonnets," Bucknell Review, 17 (1969), 91-106.

961. Goodacre, Edward B.
See Birchenough, Josephine.

962. Gosse, E.
"Elizabethan Dedications of Books," Harper's, 105 (1902), 165-172.

963. The Governour
See Brooks, H. F.

964. Gower, John
See Hussey, R.

965. Grant, J. E.
See Davis, Jack M.

966. Graves, Robert
See Riding, Laura.

967. Gray, Cecil G.
"Mary Fitton and Sir Richard Leveson," N & Q, 197 (1952), 74-75.

968. Gray, Henry David
"The Arrangement and Date of S's Sonnets," PMLA, 30 (1915), 629-644.

969. .
"S's Last Sonnets," MLN, 32 (1917), 17-21.

970. .
"S's Rival Poet," JEGP, 47 (1948), 365-373.

971. Grebanies, B.
"Rest Is Still Silence," SR, 47 (1964), 56-57.

972. Green, A. Wigfall
"Echoes of S's Sonnets, Epitaph, and Elegiac Poems of the First Folio in Milton's 'On S, 1630,' " University of Mississippi Studies in English, 4 (1963), 41-47.

973. .
"Significant Words in S's Sonnets," University of Mississippi Studies in English, 3 (1962), 95-113 [A selective concordance.]

974. Greene, Robert
See McNeal, Thomas H.

975. Greenwood, G. G.
"The Dark Lady," Observer. February 1, 1920. p. 18.

976. Groos, K.; Netto, I.
"Visual Sense Impressions in S's Poems: A Psychological and Statistical Study," Englische Studien, 43 (1910-11), 27-51.

977. Gundolf, F.
"S's Sonnets and Poems," S, 1 (1928), 163-180; 450-467.

978. Grundy, Joan
"S's Sonnets and the Elizabethan Sonneteers," SS, 15 (1962), 41-49 [YWES, 43 (1962), 125].

979. Gundry, W. G. C.
"The Sonnets Interpreted," Baconiana, 37 (1929), 48-51.

980. Haines, C. R.
"Recent Shakespearean Research," Quarterly Review, 236 (1921), 225-243; 237 (1922), 1-17.

981. Hall, A.
"Mr. W. H.," Literature,
6 (1900), 248, 320.

143
982. Hamer, D.
"S: Sonnet 143," N & Q,
16 (1969), 129-130.

983. Hamlet
See Adams, J. Q.

984. _____.
See Madariaga, S. de.

985. _____.
See Tonog, Lanua, F. G.

107,123
986. Harbage, Alfred
"Dating S's Sonnets," SQ,
1 (1950), 57-63 (Interprets the
imagery of sonnets 107 and 123
as referring to the events of
1603).

107
987. Harrison, G. B.
"On Sonnet 107," TLS.
November 29, 1928. p. 938.

988. Harvey, Gabriel
See Moore, H.

989. Harvey, William
See Cook, I. R. W.

138
990. Hax, Samuel
"S's Sonnet 138," Explicator,
25 (1967), Item 45.

991. Hayashi, Tetsumaro
"The Sonnet Mystery,"
SNL, 13 (1963), 42.

992. Hayes, Ann L.
"The Sonnets," Carnegie
Series in English, 10 (1966), 1-15.

8
993. Hemingway, S. B.
"Sonnet 8 and Mr. William

Hughes, Musician," MLN, 25
(1910), 210.

30
994. Hendricks, W. O.
"Sonnet 30," Language,
42 (1966), 3.

995. Henry IV (Pt. 1)
See Johnston, G. B.

996. _____.
See King, Arthur H.

997. Henry VI (Pts. 1, 2, &
3)
See Kirov, Todor T.

142
998. Herbert, T. Walter
"S's Sonnet 142," Ex-
plicator, 13 (1955), 38 (An ex-
plication with special reference
to the "scarlet ornaments" of
1. 6.).

999. _____.
"S's Word-Play on
Tombe," MLN, 64 (1949), 235-
241.

1000. _____.
"Sound and Sense in Two
S Sonnets, (12 and 30)," Tennessee Studies in Literature,
3 (1958), 43-52.

1001. Herbert, William
See Newcomer, A. G.
and Porter, C.

1002. _____.
See Porter, C.

1003. Herford, C. H.
"A Sketch of the History
of S's Influence on the Continent," John Rylands Library
Bulletin, 9 (1925), 20-62.

1004. Hews, Will
See Rattray, R. F.

1005. Holgate, W.
See "New Light on S: W.
Holgate as 'W. H.' "

1006. Hinman, C.
"The Pronunciation of
'Wriothesly,' " TLS, Oct. 2,
1937, p. 715. Comment by A. F.
Pollard, TLS, Oct. 9, 1937, p.
735.

1007. Hoffman, Banesh
"Sherlock, S and the
Bomb," Baker Street Journal, 10
(1960), 69-79.

1008. Holzapfel, Rudolf Melander
See Hubler, Edward.

68
1009. Holzer, G.
"The Grave's Tiring-room
and Sonnet 68," Baconiana, 15
(1907), 201-209.

1010. Hope-Wallace, Philip
"In the Basket," Listener,
(1955), 569. See Hope-Wallace's
similar notice in Time and Tide,
36 (1955), 968.

1011. Horace
See Wilkinson, L. P.

1012. Hotson, Leslie
See Michael, Laurence.

1013. _____.
See Nosworthy, J. M.

1014. _____.
See SNL.

1015. _____.
"The Date of S's Sonnets,"
TLS, June 2, 1950, p. 348.

1016. _____.
"More Light on S's Son-
nets," SQ, 2 (1951), 111-118.

1017. _____.
"The S Mystery Solved,"

Sunday Times Magazine, April
12, 1964, p. 6-24.

1018. _____.
"When S Wrote the Son-
nets," Atlantic, 184, (1949),
61-67.

1019. Hubler, Edward
"S's Secret by Rudolf
Melander Holzapfel, Dublin:
Dolmen Press for the Melander
S Society, Dublin, 1961," SNL,
12 (1962), 21.

1020. _____.
"Three Shakespearean
Myths: Mutability, Plenitude,
and Reputation," English Institute Essays, (1948), 95-119.

1020a. Hughes, Will
See Douglas, Lord Alfred;
Hemingway, S. B.;
Wells, H. W.

1021. Hunt, F. C.
"Cupid in the Sonnets,"
Baconiana, 10 (1902), 66-75.

1022. _____, et al.
"Eclipse Endured,"
Baconiana, 14 (1906), 134-137.

1023. _____.
"The Unspeakable Son-
nets: 294 Years of Their Criticism," New Shakespeareana,
2 (1903), 9-22.

1024. Hunt, T. W.
"English Sonnets--the
Sonnets of S," Bibliotheca
Sacra, 67 (1910), 611-624.

1025. Hunter, G. K.
"The Dramatic Technique
of S's Sonnets," EIC, 3 (1953),
152-164.

1026. Hussey, R.
"S and Gower," N & Q,
180 (1941), 386.

67

1027. Hutchinson, J.
"A New View of the S Sonnets," Baconiana, 20 (1912), 82-94.

1028. _____ .
"On the Sonnets," Baconiana, 20 (1912), 221-230.

146
1029. Huttar, Charles A.
"The Christian Basis of S's Sonnet 146," SQ, 19 (1968), 355-365.

153, 154
1030. Hutton, James
"Analogues of S's Sonnets 153-154: Contributions to the History of a Theme," MP, 38 (1941), 385-403.

138
1031. Hux, Samuel
"S's Sonnet 138," Explicator, 25 (1967), 45.

129
1032. Johnson, Charles M. W.
"S's Sonnet 129," Explicator, 7 (1949), 41.

1033. Johnston, G. B.
"Camden, S, and Young Henry Percy," PMLA, 76 (1961), 298. Reply with rejoinder L. Michel, 77 (1962), 510-512.

1034. Jonson, Ben
See McNeal, Thomas H.

1035. Jonson, G. C. A.
"S's Sonnets," Poetry Review, 22 (1931), 274-292.

1036. _____ .
"The Sonnets of S," Poetry Review, 17 (1926), 201-206.

1037. _____ .
"S's Sonnets," Poetry Review, 22 (1931), 274-292.

90
1038. Jorgensen, Virginia
"Of Love and Hate," English Journal, 53 (1964), 459-461.

1039. Joyce, James
See Loughlin, R. C.

1040. Julius Caesar
See Sanders, Norman.

34
1041. Kallsen, T. J.
"S's Sonnet 34," Explicator, 27 (1969), Item 63.

1042. Kaplin, Milton
"Regarding S," Harper's, (1956), 37-38.

1043. Kastner, L. E.
"The Elizabethan Sonneteers and the French Poets," MLR, 3 (1908), 268-277.

1044. Kaula, David
" 'In War with Time': Temporal Perspectives in S's Sonnets," Studies in English Literature, 1500-1900, 3 (1963), 45-47.

1045. Keats, John
See Salle, J. C.

111
1046. Kenyon, J. S.
"An Emendation in Sonnet 111, Line 12," TLS. October 18, 1934. p. 715.

111
1047. Kenyon, John
"S, Sonnet 111," MLN, 60 (1945), 357-358.

73
1048. Keogh, J. G.
"S's Sonnet 73," Explicator, 28 (1969), Item 6.

1049. Kermode, Frank

"The Banquet of Sense,"
John Rylands Library Bulletin, 44
(1961), 68-99.

1050. Kern, F.A.
"Friendship as a S Theme,"
University of Virginia Magazine,
66 (1905), 42-48.

1051. King, Arthur H.
"Some Notes on Ambiguity
in Henry IV Part I," Studia
Neophilologica, 14 (1941-1942),
161-183.

1052. Kirov, Todor T.
"The First Step of a
Giant," SJ, 103 (1967, Supple-
ment), 109-140 [H VI, Titus
Andronicus, and The Sonnets].

1053. Klein, David
"Foreign Influence on S's
Sonnets," Sewanee Review, 13
(1905), 454-474.

1054. Knight, G. Wilson
"The Date of S's Sonnets,"
TLS, July 14, 1950. p. 437.

1055.   .
"New Light on S's Sonnets,"
Listener, 71 (1964), 715-717.

1056.   .
"Romantic Friendship in
S," Holborn Review, 71 (1929),
450-460.

1057.   .
"S's Sonnets," TLS, Jan-
uary 30, 1964, p. 93.

1058.   .
"S's Sonnets," TLS, De-
cember, 1963, p. 1072.

1059.   .
See SNL.

1060. Knights, Lionel Charles
"S's Sonnets," Scrutiny, 3
(1934), 133-160. [Reprinted in

Explorations, London: Chatto
& Windus, 1946; p. 40-65.]

1061.   .
"Review of The Mutual
Flame by G. Wilson Knight,"
RES, 8 (1958), 302-304.

1062. Kobayashi, Minoru
"A Note on the Inverted
Platonism of S's Sonnets," S
Studies, 242 (1963), 31-48.

30
1063. Kock, E.A.
"On Sonnet 30, Lines 1-
4," Anglia, 31 (1908), 134.

1064. Krieger, Murray
"The Strategy of Lan-
guage in S's Sonnets," SNL,
18 (1964), 80.

1065. Landry, Hilton
"Malone as Editor of S's
Sonnets," Bulletin of the New
York Public Library, 67 (1963),
435-442.

116
1066.   .
"The Marriage of True
Minds: Truth and Error in
Sonnet 116," S Studies, 3 (1968),
98-110.

1067.   .
"The Use and Abuse of
Poetry: John Crowe Ransom
on S's Sonnets," Paunch, 23
(1965), 18-35.

110
1068. Larbaud, V.
" 'Motley' in Sonnet
110," TLS. June 24, 1926, p.
432.

18, 33
1069. Law, Robert A.
"Two Notes on Shake-
spearean Parallels," Studies in
English, 9 (1929), 82-85 [Paral-

lel between Sonnets 18 and 33 and Arthur Brooke's Romeo and Juliet].

1070. Lee, Sir Sidney
" 'Beget' and 'Begetter' in Elizabethan England," Athenaeum, Feb. 24, 1900. p. 260-261. March 17, 1900. p. 345-346.

1071. _____ .
"Fire Out," Athenaeum. January 19, 1901. p. 80-81.

1072. _____ .
"Ovid and S's Sonnets," Quarterly Review, 210 (1909), 455-476 [Reprinted in his Elizabethan and Other Essays, Oxford: Clarendon Press, 1929, p. 116-139].

1073. Leigh, M.
See Garwood, H. P.

146
1074. Leisi, Ernest
"A Possible Emendation of S's Sonnet 146," ES, 47 (1966), 271-285.

144
1075. Leith, A. A.
"Sonnet 144," Baconiana, 23 (1915), 85-87.

1076. Leven, R.
See Evans, E. C.

1077. Lever, J. W.
"Chapman and S," N & Q, 5 (1958), 99-100.

130
1078. _____ .
"S's French Fruits (Sonnet 130)," SS, 6 (1953), 83-84.

1079. Leveson, Sir Richard
See Gray, Cecil G.

1080. Levin, Richard
"Correspondence," RES,

15 (1964), 408-409.

64
1081. _____ .
"S's "Sonnet 64,' " Explicator, 24 (1965), 39.

66
1082. _____ .
"S's Sonnet 66," Explicator, 22 (1964), 36.

97
1083. _____ .
"Sonnet 97," RES, 15 (1964), 408-409. [Reply to art. by E. C. Evans, Ibid., 14 (1963), 370-380.]

129
1084. _____ .
"Sonnet 129 as a Dramatic Poem," SQ, 16 (1965), 175-181.

1085. _____ .
See Evans, E. C.

1086. Lewis, Michael and Scotland, Catherine W.
"The Date of S's Sonnets," TLS, June 23, 1950. p. 389.

1087. Liddell, M. H.
"Three S Sonnets in Manuscript," Nation, 75 (1902), 10-11.

1088. Lloyd, Roger
"Love and Charity and S," Manchester Guardian Weekly, Feb. 16, 1956, p. 6.

1089. Loane, G. G.
See Murry, John Middleton.

77,105,140
1090. _____ .
"Sonnets 77, 105, and 140," TLS. March 19, 1925. p. 200.

1091. Lodge, Thomas
See Fox, Charles O.

1092. Loewenberg, J.
"The Idea of Mutability in Literature," Univ. of California Chronicle, 24 (1922), 129-131.

1093. Long, P. W.
"S's Sonnets as Published," MLR, 6 (1911), 390-397.

1094. Loughlin, Richard L.
"Time Out," English Record, 16 (1966), 2-8. [Sonnets and Milton's On Time, J. Joyce's Finnegans Wake, etc.]

113
1095. Louthan, Doniphan
"Sonnet 113," TLS, July 6, 1951, p. 421.

1096. _____.
"The 'Tome-Tomb' Pun in Renaissance England," PQ, 29 (1950), 375-380.

1097. Love's Labour's Lost
See McClumpha, C. F.

1098. _____.
See Stroup, Thomas B.

73
1099. Lumiansky, R. M.
"S's Sonnet 73," Explicator, 6 (1948), 55.

66
1100. Lundquist, Carole
"Sonnet 66," Kerygma, 4 (1964), 22-23.

1101. Lynch, A.
"The Authorship of S's Sonnets," Review of Reviews, 80 (1930), 307-312.

1102. _____.
"The 'Onlie Begetter' of S's Sonnets," Review of Reviews, 80 (1930), 307-312.

1103. _____.
"S Found Out! (The Patron Identified)," Book Monthly, 14 (1919), 543-546.

1104. McClumpha, C. F.
"Parallels between S's Sonnets and Love's Labour's Lost," MLN, 15 (1900), 168-174.

1105. _____.
"Parallels between S's Sonnets and A Midsummer Night's Dream," MLN, 16 (1901), 164-168.

1106. _____.
"Parallels between S's Sonnets and Romeo and Juliet," SJ, 40 (1904), 187-203.

1107. McGuinness, Kevin
"S and the Sonnets," Revue des Langues Vivantes, 31 (1965), 287-301.

1108. Mackail, John William
"A Lover's Complaint," Essays and Studies by Members of the English Association, 3 (1912), 51-70.

99
1109. MacKenzie, A. C.
"The Forward Violet (Sonnet 99)," Monthly Musical Record, 46 (1916), 113-116.

116
1110. MacLeish, Archibald
"The Proper Pose of Poetry," SR, March 5, 1955, p. 11-12; 47-49.

1111. McNeal, Thomas H.
"Studies in the Greene-S Relationship," S Association Bulletin, 15 (1940), 210-218.

128
1112. McNeal, Thomas H.
"Every Man out of His Humor and S's Sonnets," N & Q,

197 (1952), 376. [On a possible borrowing in Sonnet 128.]

1113. Macphail, A.
"Two Sonnets," University Magazine, 18 (1919), 358.

1114. Madariaga, Salvadore de
"The Impact of S," (1964), 83-91. [Hamlet, A & C, & Othello and the Sonnets.]

18, 20
1115. Mahony, P.
"Aptness & Two Shakespearean Sonnets," Etudes Anglaises et Americaines, 2 (1964), 67-78. [Formerly Travaux du Centre d' Etudes Anglaises et Americaines.]

1116. Mahood, M. M.
"Love's Confined Doom," SS, 15 (1962), 50-61. [YWES, 43 (1962), 125.]

1117. Malone, Edmund
See Landry, Hilton.

1118. Malue, H. W.
"Sonnets of S," Outlook, 92 (1909), 1025-1028.

1119. Marder, Louis
"A. L. Rowse's Reply to TLS and The Rejoinder," SNL, 14 (1964), 4.

1120. .
"The Secret of S's Sonnets?," SNL, 12 (1962), 21.

1121. Marlowe, Phil
"Mr. W. H.--A Contribution to Shakespearean Scholarship," Cambridge Review, (1964), 357-359.

1122. Martin, Philip
"S's Sonnets," Twentieth Century, 19 (1965), 131-141.

1123. Masson, David I.
"Free Phonetic Patterns in

S's Sonnets," Neophilologus, 38 (1954), 277-289.

1124. Matthews, G. M.
See SNL.

1125. .
"Sex and the Sonnet," EIC, 2 (1952), 119-137. [See comment by Paul Siegel, Ibid., p. 465-468.]

107
1126. Mattingly, Garrett
"The Date of S's Sonnet 107," PMLA, 48 (1933), 705-721.

146
1127. Maxwell, J. C.
"Rebel Powers: S and Daniel," N & Q, 14 (1967), 119-127. [Daniel's Cleopatra (1594).]

106
1128. May, Louis F., Jr.
"The Figure in Sonnet 106," SQ, 11 (1960), 93-94.

1129. May, Thomas
See Smith, Hallett.

1130. Meeks, L. H.
"The Human S of the Sonnets," Teachers College Journal, 2 (1931), 71-72.

1131. Meller, Margrit
"S's Sonnets," TLS, April 9, 1964. p. 291.

1132. The Merchant of Venice
See Sanders, Norman.

107
1133. Michel, Laurence
"S's Sonnet 107," JEGP, 54 (1955), 301-305. [Criticizes Hotson's dating.]

1134. .
See Johnson, G. B.

1135. Mid-summer Night's Dream
See McClumpha, C. F.

1136. Milton, John
See Green, A. Wigfall.

1137. _____.
See Loughlin, R. L.

1138. Mr. W. H.
See Clarkson, Paul S.;
Empson, William; En-
right, D. J.; Gahan, C. J.;
Hall, A.; Kingsmile, H.;
Marlowe, Phil; "New Light
on the Identity of W. H.";
Nosworthy, J. M.; Pohl,
F. J.; Stopes, C. C.;
Thurston, Herbert; Turner,
L. M.; Ward, B. R.

1139. "Mistress Fitton"
Blackwood's Magazine, 169
(1901), 829-845.

1140. Mizener, Arthur
See Brooks, C.

1141. _____.
"The Structure of Figura-
tive Language in S's Sonnets,"
Southern Review, 5 (1940), 730-
747.

1142. _____.
"What Meres Knew about
S's Sonnets," Catholic World, 107
(1918), 235-246.

1143. Montgomery, Robert L.
"Donne's 'Ecstasy,' Philos-
ophy, and the Renaissance Lyric,"
Kerygma, 4 (1964), 3-14.

71-74
1144. Moore, Carlisle
"S's Sonnets 71-74," Ex-
plicator, 8 (1949), 2.

1145. Moore, H.
"G. Harvey the Rival Po-
et," SP, 23 (1926), 337-357.

1146. Morgan, A.
"What Meres Knew about
S's Sonnets," Catholic World,
107 (1918), 235-246.

1147. Morgan, Paul
" 'Our Will S' and Lope
de Vega: An Unrecorded Contemporary Document," SS, 16
(1963), 118-120.

1148. Morley, Christopher
"Sonnets: When in the
Chronicle of Wasted Time;
Like as the Waves Make towards
the Pebbled Shore," Golden
Book, 16 (1932), 146-147.

1148a. The Mortal Moon
See Allen, P.; Chambers,
Sir Edmund K.; Eccles,
Mark; Fort, James A.;
Hunt, F. C.; Mutschmann,
M.; Rendall, G. H.

1149. Muir, Kenneth
"Biographical Red Her-
rings and S's Sonnets," Literary
Half Yearly, 6 (1966), 61-69.

1150. _____.
"Blundeville, Wyatt and
S," N & Q, 8 (1961), 293-294.

1150a. _____.
"S: Prose and Verse,"
(Review Article), MLQ, 29
(1968), 467-475.

1151. _____.
"Troilus & Cressida,"
SS, 8 (1955), 28-29.

1152. Munro, John
"Dark Ladies of Litera-
ture," Contemporary Review,
1060 (1954), 227-231.

1153. Murray, Howard
"The Trend of S's
Thought," TLS, 5 (1951), 7.

1154. Murry, John Middleton

See Disher, M. Wilson.

1155. _____.
"Chapman the Rival Poet,"
TLS, June 4, 1938, p. 385-386.
(See letters by G.G. Loane and
Alfred Douglas, TLS, June 11,
1938, p. 402.)

107
1156. _____.
"Concerning Sonnet 107,"
New Adelphi, 2 (1929), 251-254.

1157. _____.
"S's Dedication," New
Adelphi, 2 (1931), 199-213.

123
1158. _____.
"The Meaning of Sonnet
123," Wanderer, 1 (1934), 64.

1159. Mutschmann, M.
"The 'Mortal Moon' Sonnet,"
TLS. March 1, 1934. p. 144.

29
1160. Nearing, Homer, Jr.
"S as a Nondramatic Poet;
Sonnet 29," SQ, 13 (1962), 15-20.

1161. "The Necessity of Reflect-
ing on a S Sonnet," The Fifties, 3 (1959), 20-21.

1162. Needham, F.
"The Rival Poet," TLS.
October 12, 1933. p. 691.

1163. Nejgebauer, A.
"The Sonnets," SS, 15
(1962), 10-18.

1164. _____.
"Twentieth-Century Studies
in S's Sonnets, Songs, and Poems.
2. The Sonnets," SS, 15 (1962),
10-18.

1165. Netto, I.
See Gross, K.

1166. No entry

1167. Nevinson, J.L.
"Show of the Nine
Worthies," SQ, 14 (1963),
103-107.

1168. Newcomer, A.G.;
Porter, C.
"S and Herbert," Na-
tion, 96 (1913), 55 and 80.

1169. Newdigate, B.H.
"The Rival Poet and the
Youth," TLS. November 9,
1933. p. 774; November 16,
1933. p. 795.

1170. "A New Facsimile of
S's Sonnets," TLS, December
3, 1925. p. 831.

1171. "New Light on the Identity of W.H.," Australasian,
March 24, 1928. p. 6.

1172. "New Light on S: W.
Holgate as 'W.H.,'" Daily
Telegraph (London). February
3, 1928.

1173. Nicholson, F.C.
"Minnesong & Elizabethan
Sonnets," MLQ, 4 (1901), 180-
184.

1174. Nickalls, B.
"C. Best, the Youth of
the Sonnets," TLS. September
13, 1934. p. 620.

1175. Nicoll, Allardyce
See S Survey, 15.

73
1176. Nolan, Edward F.
"S's Sonnet 73," Ex-
plicator, 7 (1948), 13.

107,108,123,124
1177. Nosworthy, J. M.
"All Too Short a Date:
Internal Evidence in S's Sonnets,"
EIC, 2 (1952), 311-324. [Questions the early dates given by
Dr. Hotson to sonnets 108, 123,
and 124; finds evidence in parallels in vocabulary between the
sonnets and plays for later dates,
1600-1606.]

1178. _____.
"S and Mr. W. H.," Library, 18 (1963), 294-298.

1179. Nowottny, M. T.
See SNL.

1180. Nowottny, Winifred
"Conventional & Unconventional in the Descriptions of Scenery in S's Sonnets," ES, 45
(1964), 142-149.

1-6
1181. _____.
"Formal Elements in S's
Sonnets 1-6," EIC, 2 (1952), 76-84.

1182. Noyes, Alfred
"Origin of S's Sonnets,"
Bookman, 67 (1924), 159-162.

1183. O'Dea, Raymond
"The King of Men in S's
Early Work: Time," Discourse,
11 (1968), 141-144.

1184. Ogle, M. B.
"The Classical Origin and
Tradition of Literary Conceits,"
American Journal of Philology,
34 (1913), 125-152.

1185. _____.
"The 'White Hand' as a
Literary Conceit," Sewanee Review, 20 (1912), 452-469.

1186. Olfson, L.
"O Mistress Mine, Poem,"

Good Housekeeping, 136 (1953),
4.

1187. _____.
"Shall I Compare Thee
to A Summer's Day?, Poem,"
Good Housekeeping, 136 (1953),
4.

1188. Oliphant, E. H. C.
"Sonnet Structure: An
Analysis," PQ, 11 (1932), 135-148.

1189. Ong, Walter J.
"Historical Backgrounds
of Elizabethan and Jacobean
Punctuation Theory," PMLA,
59 (1944), 349-360.

24
1190. Orange, Linwood E.
"S's Sonnet 24," Southern
Quarterly, 4 (1966), 409-410.

1191. Ord, H.
"Chaucer & the Rival
Poet," TLS. May 18, 1922.
p. 324.

1192. _____, et al.
"Chaucer & S's Sonnets,"
TLS. June 22, 1916. p. 297-298; June 29, 1916. p. 310.

1193. Order
See Fort, James A.

1194. _____.
See Gray, Henry David.

1195. Osterberg, V.
"The 'Countess Scenes'
of 'Edward III,' " SJ, 65 (1929),
49-91.

1196. Othello
See Madariaga, S. de.

1197. Ovid
See Lee, Sir Sidney.

1198. Palk, R.

75

"A Solution for the Puzzle of the S Sonnets," TLS, April 20, 1916. p. 189.

1199. _____ .
"W. Raleigh the Author of the Sonnets," TLS, October 24, 1918. p. 512.

1200. Parish, Verna N.
"S's Sonnets and The French Academie," Satire News-letter, 10 (1960), 25.

1201. Parker, David
"Verbal Moods in S's Sonnets." MLQ, 30 (1969), 331-339.

146
1202. Parsons, Howard
"S's Sonnet 146," N & Q, 11 (1955), 97.

1203. The Passionate Pilgrim
See Fox, Charles O.

1204. Pastoral Poetry
See Bates, Paul A.

1205. Pemberton, H., Jr.
"Topical Allusions in the Sonnets," New Shakespeareana, 8 (1909), 61-67.

1206. Pembroke, Earl of
See Creighton, Charles.

1207. Percy, Henry
See Johnston, G. B.

1208. Pericles
See Barker, G. A.

1209. Perrett, Arthur J.
"The Date of S's Sonnets," TLS, June 16, 1950. p. 373.

1210. Perrine, Laurence
"When form and content kiss/intention made the bliss: the Sonnet in Romeo and Juliet," English Journal, 55 (1966), 874+.

129
1211. Peterson, Douglas L.
"A Probable Source for S's Sonnet 129," SQ, 5 (1954), 381-384. [Wilson's Arte of Rhetorique.]

1212. Pettett, E. C.
"S's Conception of Poetry," Essays and Studies, 3 (1950), 29-46.

1213. Phelps, W. L.
"Notes on S," Proceedings of the American Philosophical Society, 81 (1939), 573-579.

1214. Pineton, Clara Long-worth (Countess de Chambrun)
"Inspirers of S's Sonnets," North American Review, 198 (1913), 131-134.

1215. Piper, H. W.
"S's Thirty-first Sonnet," TLS, April 13, 1951, p. 229.

1216. _____ .
See Liggins, E. M.

1-27
1217. Pirkhofer, Anton M.
" 'A Pretty Pleasing Pricket'--On The Use of Alliteration in S's Sonnets," SQ, 14 (1963), 3-14.

1218. Platonism
See Kobayashi, Minoru.

1219. Platt, Arthur
" 'Edward III' and S's Sonnets," MLR, 6 (1911), 511-513.

1220. Pohl, Frederick J.
"On the Identity of 'Mr. W. H.,' " SNL, 8 (1958), 43.

1221. _____ .
"Where S Saw Moun-

tains," SNL, 8 (1958), 37.

1222. Pollard, A. F.
See Hinman, C.

1223. Porter, C.
See Newcomer, A. G.

1224. .
"S & Herbert," Nation, 95
(1912), 533; 96 (1913), 80.

1225. Pott, C. M.
"F. Bacon's Fair Lady,"
Baconiana, 15 (1907), 178-196.

1226. Prince, Frank Templeton
"The Sonnet from Wyatt to
S," Elizabethan Poetry, 338 (1961),
11-29.

1227. "The Problem of the Sonnets: Fresh Interpretations,"
TLS. May 14, 1938. p. 334.

1228. Publishers
See Allen, Ned B.

1229. .
See Farr, Henry.

1230. Puknat, E. M.
See Puknat, S. B.

1231. Puknat, S. B. and Puknat,
E. M.
"Mann's Doctor Faustus
and S," Research Studies, 35
(1967), 148-154.

128
1232. Purdum, R.
"S's Sonnet 128," JEGP,
63 (1964), 235-239.

1233. Raby, F. J. E.
"S's Sonnets," TLS, March
26, 1964, p. 255; April 16, 1964,
p. 317.

110
1234. Radley, Virginia L. and
Redding, David C.

"S: Sonnet 110, A New
Look," SQ, 12 (1961), 462-463.

1235. Raleigh, Walter
See Palk, R.

1236. Ransom, John Crowe
See Landry, Hilton.

1237. .
"Mr. Empson's Muddles,"
Southern Review, 4 (1938), 322-
339.

1238. .
"A Postscript on S's
Sonnets," Kenyon Review, 30
(1968), 523-531.

1239. .
"S at Sonnets," Southern
Review, 3 (1938), 531-553.
[Reprinted in The World's Body,
New York: Charles Scribner's
Sons, 1938; p. 270-303.]

1240. Rattray, R. F.
"Will Hews," TLS.
April 12, 1928. p. 272.

1241. Redding, David C.
See Radley, V. L.

1242. Redin, Mats
"The Friend in S's Son-
nets," ES, 56 (1922), 390-407.

1243. Redpath, Theodore
"S's Sonnets," Archiv
(Archiv für das Studium der
Neueren Sprachen und Lite-
raturen), 204 (1968), 401-413.
[Lecture at Heidelberg Univer-
sity.]

20
1244. Reichert, John F.
"Sonnet 20 and Erasmus'
'Epistle to Perswade a Young
Gentleman to Marriage,'" SQ,
16 (1965), 238-240.

1245. Rendall, G. H.

"The 'Mortal Moon' Sonnet,"
TLS. March 15, 1934. p. 194.

1246. Rewcastle, G.
"That S Mystery," Book
Monthly, 14 (1919), 704.

1247. Richard II
See Brooks, H. F.; Free-
man, A.

130
1248. Richmond, H. M.
"Tradition and Lyric: An
Historical Approach to Value,"
Comparative Literature Studies,
1 (1964), 119-132.

85
1249. Richmond, O. et al.
"A Reading in Sonnet 85,"
TLS, December 26, 1918, p. 657.
January 2, 1919, p. 10. January
9, p. 21. January 16, p. 34.
January 23, p. 46.

1250. Rinaker, Clarissa
"Some Unconscious Factors
in the Sonnet as a Poetic Form,"
International Journal of Psycho-
Analysis, 12 (1931), 167-187.

1251. "The Rival Poet"
See Acheson, Arthur;
Disher, M. Wilson; Doug-
las, Lord Alfred; Durrell,
Lawrence; Eagle, R. L.;
Gray, Henry David; Moore,
H.; Murry, J. M.; Need-
ham, F.; Newdigate, B.
H.; Ord, H.; Strachey, C.

128
1252. Robbins, R. H. A.
"A Seventeenth-Century
Manuscript of S's Sonnet 128,"
N & Q, 14 (1967), 137-138.

1253. Rodin, M.
"The Friend in S's Son-
nets," ES, 56 (1922), 390-407.

1254. Roe, J. E.
"The Grave's Tiring
Room," Baconiana, 16 (1908),
p. 114-121; p. 155-165.

1255. .
"F. Bacon in the Son-
nets," Baconiana, 17 (1909),
36-40.

130
1256. Rogers, E. G.
"Sonnet 130: Watson to
Linche to S," SQ, 11 (1960),
232-233.

1257. Rolfe, W. J.
"Two New Studies of the
Sonnets," Critic, 39 (1901),
26-31.

1258. Rolle, Dietrich
"S's Sonnet Technique,"
SNL, 12 (1962), 22. [Albert
S. Gerard, "The Stone as Lily:
A Discussion of S's Sonnet 94,"
SJ, 96 (1960), 155-160.]

1259. .
"The Sonnets: A Long
Pastoral," SNL, 17 (1967), 42.
[Originally in "S's Sonnets and
Pastoral Poetry," SJ, 103
(1967), 81-96.]

1260. Romeo & Juliet
See McClumpha, C. F.

1261. .
See Perrine, L.

1262. Ronsard, Pierre
See Sturtz, S. V.

1263. Rostenberg, Leona
"Thomas Thorpe, Pub-
lisher of 'Shakespeare's Sonnets,' " Papers of the Bibliographical Society of America,
54 (1960), 16-37; SNL, 12
(1962), 34.

1264. .
See Allen, Ned B.

1265. Rowse, Alfred Leslie
See Marder, Louis.

1266. _____.
"A. L. Rowse Solves S's
Sonnets (Interview)," Publishers'
Weekly, 184 (1963), 31.

1267. _____.
"Historian Answers Ques-
tions about S," Times (London),
1 (1963), 13; 2 (1963), 13; 3
(1963), 13; 4 (1963), 13-14 [Sept.
17-20, 1963].

1268. _____.
"Shadow and Substance in
S," TLS, January 16, 1964. p.
47. ["A. L. Rowse and Reviewer,"
Ibid., January 30, 1964. p. 87;
February 13, 1964. p. 127.]

1269. _____.
"William S," Newsweek,
63 (1964), 65.

1270. _____.
"William S," Time, 83
(1964), 83.

1271. Rubow, P. V.
"S's Sonnets," Orbis, 4
(1947), 2-44.

1272. _____.
"S's Sonnets," Orbis Litterarum, 4 (1946), 2-43.

130
1273. Ruthven, K. K.
"The Composite Mistresse,"
AUMLA, 26 (1966), 198-214.

1274. Rutter, Joseph
See Smith, Hallett.

1275. St. Clair, F. Y.
"The Sonnets: Personal
Revelation or Technical Exercise?"
North Dakota Quarterly, 32 (1964),
7-13.

1276. St. Lys, O. (tr.)

"Two Sonnets by S,"
London Mercury, 10 (1924), 15.

27
1277. Salle, J. C.
"S's Sonnet 27 and Keats'
Bright Star!," N & Q, 14
(1967), 24.

36, 96
1278. Sampson, J.
"The Repetition of a
Couplet in Sonnets 36 and 96,"
TLS. October 2, 1919. p.
532.

1279. Sanderlin, George
"The Repute of S's Son-
nets in the Early Nineteenth
Century," MLN, 54 (1939),
462-466.

1280. Sanders, Norman
"Critical Studies," SS,
18 (1965), 156-177. [JC, M
of V, and The Sonnets.]

1281. Schaar, Claes
"Conventional and Uncon-
ventional in the Descriptions of
Scenery in S's Sonnets," ES,
45 (1964), 142-149.

89
1282. _____.
"An Italian Analogue of
S's Sonnet 89," ES, 43 (1962),
253-255. [Cf. B. Tasso's
Libra degli Amori, 111, ii, 1-
13.]

1283. _____.
"Qui me alit me extinguit
(Sonnet 73)," ES, 49 (1968),
362-367.

50, 51
1284. _____.
"S's Sonnets 50-51 and
Tebaldes's Sonnet 107," ES, 38
(1957), 208-209.

1285. Schoen-René, Otto E.

"S's Sonnets in Germany,
1787-1939," Harvard University...
Summaries of Theses, (1942),
284-287.

1286. Schmidtchen, P.W.
"S's Sug'red Sonnets,"
Hobbies, 74 (1969), 104-105.

1287. Schoff, F.G.
"S's 'Fair is Foul,' " N
& Q, 199 (1954), 241-242.

1288. Schroeter, James
"S's Not To-Be-Pitied
Lover," College English, 23 (1962),
250-255. [Discussion in 23 (1962),
672-675.]

1289. Schultz, John H.
"A Glossary of S's Hawking
Language," University of Texas
Studies in English, (1938), 174-
205.

1290. Schwartz, D.
"Gold Morning Sweet
Prince," New Republic, 140 (1959),
15.

1291. Scotland, Catherine, W.
See Lewis, Michael.

1292. Scott, David
"S, Essex, and the Dark
Lady: Solutions to the Problems,"
Dalhousie Review, 49 (1969), 165-
182.

1293. Scott-Espiner, Janet G.
See Scott, Janet G. (1294
1294a)

1294. Scott, Janet G.
"The Names of the Heroines
of Elizabethan Sonnet-Sequences,"
RES, 2 (1926), 159-162.

1294a.   .
"Sonnets Elizabethian by
Hughes Vaganay," Revue de Littérature Comparée, 25 (1935),
107-109.

73

1295. Seib, Kenneth
"S's 'Well': A Note on
Sonnet 73," SNL, 17 (1967), 55.

1296. Seng, Peter J.

See Main, C.F.

1297. Seymour, H.
"The Concealed Author
of the Sonnets," Baconiani, 37
(1929), 106-115.

144

1298. Seymour-Smith, Martin
"Shakespearean Indeli-
cacies (Letter)," New Statesman, October 18, 1963.

1299.   .
"S's Sonnets," TLS,
February 20, 1964, p. 153.

1300. Shackford, Martha Hall
"Rose in S's Sonnets,"
MLN, 33 (1918), 122.

1301. "S and the Earl of Pembroke," Blackwood's Magazine,
169 (1901), 668-683.

1302. "S 's Patron," TLS.
February 9, 1922. p. 85.

1303. "S's Sonnets," Bookman's Journal, 2 (1920), 381-
382.

1304. "S's Sonnets," SR, 134
(July 8, 1922), 60.

1305. "S's Sonnets," SR, 135
(January 13, 1923), 50.

1306. "S's Sonnets," SR, 136
(July 21, 1923), 81; (August 11,
1933), 165.

1307. "S's Sonnets," TLS.
July 22, 1909, p. 265-266.

1308. "S's Sonnets," TSL.
December 11, 1924. p. 845;
December 25, 1924. p. 885.

1309. "S's Sonnets, Alden, and
Pooler," TLS, April 18, 1918.
p. 182.

1310. "S Unlocks His Heart," TLS, December 14, 1922. p. 838.

1311. "S and His Love," Academy, 81 (1911), 678.

1312. "S's Sonnets," Parents' Review. March, 1929. p. 163-175.

1313. S Newsletter "A. L. Rowse Addresses MLA in Chicago on Sonnets," SNL, 13 (1963), 47.

1314. . "A. L. Rowse Continues to Make Headlines," SNL, 14 (1964), 1.

1-6
1315. . "Interpretationships among the Sonnets," (Review of Periodicals), "Famous Elements in S's Sonnets: Sonnets 1-6," EIC, 2 (1952), 76-84; SNL, 3 (1953), 31.

1316. . "Love Conventions and Sonnet Form," EIC, 2 (1951), 119-137; SNL, 3 (1953), 31 (Review of Periodicals, "Sex and the Sonnets" by G. M. Matthews).

1317. . "Oxford Historian Claims Solution of Sonnet Mystery," SNL, 13 (1963), 31.

1318. . "The Sonnet Mystery--1," SNL, 13 (1963), 37.

1319. S Survey, 15 ed. by Allardyce Nicoll. Cambridge: Cambridge University Press, 1962.

1320. Shaw, G. B. See Brown, Ivor.

1321. .

"The Dark Lady of the Sonnets," English Review. 7 (1911), 258-269.

1322. Sherzer, Jane "American Editions of S: 1753-1866," PMLA, 22 (1907), 633-696.

1323. Shield, H. A. "Links with S (6)," N & Q, 195 (1950), 205-206.

9
1324. . "Links with S (9)," N & Q, 197 (1952), 156-157.

1325. Shikoda, Mitsuo "Matter and Manner in S's Sonneteering," Essays and Studies in English Language and Literature (Sendai, Japan), 45-46 (1964), 47-70.

1326. Shipwith, G. H. "S and His Patrons," TLS. July 6, 1916. p. 321; July 20, p. 346; July 27, p. 357-358; August 24, p. 405-406.

1327. Sidebotham, H. (tr.) "Shall I Compare Thee to a Summer's Day?," London Mercury and Bookman, 35 (1937), 454.

1328. Siegel, Paul See Matthews, G. M.

1329. Siegel, Paul N. "The Petrarchan Sonneteers and Neo-Platonic Love," Studies in Philology, 42 (1945), 164-182.

1330. . "Sex and the Sonnet," EIC, 2 (1952), 465-468.

1331. Silverstein, Norman "S's Sonnets in Perspective," Ball State Teachers College Forum, 5 (1964), 67-71.

1332. Singh, S.
"The Theme of Immortality in S's Sonnets," Osmania Journal of English Studies, 4 (1964), 125-140.

1333. Skinner, B. F.
"The Alliteration in S's Sonnets: A Study in Literary Behavior," Psychological Record, 3 (1939), 186-192. [Answered by E. E. Stoll, MLN, 54, (1939), 388-390.]

1334. .
"The Verbal Summator and a Method for the Study of Latent Speech," Journal of Psychology, 2 (1936), 71-107.

1335. Smedley, W. T.
"S's Sonnets," Baconiana, 20 (1912), 9-17.

51
1336. Smith, G. C. M.
"Sonnet 51, Lines 10ff." MLR, 9 (1914), 372-373.

96
1337. .
"Sonnet 96, Line 1," TLS. June 22, 1922. p. 413.

143
1338. Smith, Gordon Ross
"A Note on S's Sonnet 143," American Imago, 14 (1957), 33-36.

1339. Smith, Hallett
" 'No Cloudy Stuffe to Puzzell Intellect': A Testimonial Misapplied to S," SQ, 1 (1950), 18-21. [John Benson's prefatory remarks to 1640 edition of Poems plagiarized from testimonial poem to Joseph Rutter by Thomas May in 1635 volume published by Benson.]

1340. Smith, J. C.
"The Problem of S's Sonnets," MLR, 5 (1910), 273-281.

1341. Somervell, R. U.
"S's Sonnets," TLS, March 5, 1964, p. 199.

1342. "The Sonnet," Academy (London), 69 (1903), 180-181.

1343. "The Sonnets Again," SR, 89 (June 9, 1900), 717-718.

1344. "The Sonnets and Wordsworth," SR, 136 (August 4, 1923), 137; (August 25, 1923), 218.

23-26
1345. "Sonnets 23-26," Baconiana, 6 (1908), 45-48.

116
1346. "Sonnet 116 Analysed," The Poet and the Philosopher, 1 (1913), 10-12.

146
1347. Southam, B. C.
"S's Christian Sonnet? Number 146," SQ, 11 (1960), 67-71.

1348. Southampton, Earl of
See Hinman, C.

1349. .
See Keller, W.

1350. Spencer, T. J. B.
"Confusion and Doubt over the Shakespearean Sonnets: Their Interpretation and Impact Today," Birmingham Post, April 17, 1964, p. xi.

1351. Spitzer, Leo
" 'Runaways Eyes' and 'Children's Eyes' Again," Neuphilologische Mitteilungen, 57 (1956), 257-260.

1352. Stabler, A. P.
"King Hamlet's Ghost in Belleforest?," PMLA, 77 (1962), 18-20.

76
1353. Stainer, C. L.
"A Cipher in Sonnet 76," TLS. April 7, 1932. p. 250.

60
1354. Starnes, D. T.
"S's Sonnet 60: Analogues," N & Q, 194 (1949), 454. [In Ovid and Buchanan's Jephthis.]

146
1355. Stauffer, D. A.
"Critical Principles and Sonnet 146," American Scholar, 12 (1942), 52-62.

1356. Steadman, John M.
"Like Two Spirits: S and Ficino," SQ, 10 (1959), 244-246.

130
1357. _____.
"S's Sonnet 130 and Aretino's Ragionamente," N & Q, 13 (1966), 134-135.

1358. Stirling, Brents
"More S Sonnet Groups," Essays on S, 531 (1962), 115-135.

1359. _____.
"A S Sonnet Group," PMLA, 75 (1960), 340-349.

109-126
1360. _____.
"Sonnets 109-126," The Centennial Review of Arts and Science (Michigan State), 8 (1964), 109-120.

127-154
1361. _____.
"Sonnets 127-154," S 1564-1964, 10 (1964), 134-153.

1362. Stoll, E. E.

"Poetic Alliteration," MLN, 55 (1940), 388-390.

1363. _____.
See Skinner, B. F.

107
1364. Stone, Walter B.
"S and the Sad Augurs," JEGP, 52 (1953), 457-479. [Takes issue with Leslie Hotson over the dating of Sonnet 107.]

1365. Stopes, C. C.
"Mr. W. H." Athenaeum, August 4, 1900. p. 154.

1366. _____.
"S's Patron," Bookman's Journal, 6 (1922), 64.

85
1367. Strachey, C. et al.
"Sonnet 85 & Mary Fitton," TLS. January 5, 1922. p. 13; January 12, p. 29.

1368. _____.
"The Rival Poet & the Youth," TLS. November 16, 1933. p. 795.

1369. Strachey, J. St. L.
"On the Sonnets," Spectator, February 28, 1925. p. 326-327.

1370. Stronach, G.
"Bacon in the Sonnets," Baconiana, 13 (1905), 58-61.

116
1371. Stroup, Thomas B.
"Biron and the 116th Sonnet," PQ, 10 (1931), 308-310.

81
1372. Sturtz, S. V.
"Ronsard & Sonnet 81," Observer (London), June 19, 1927. p. 5.

1373. Sykes, C.
"Trouble with the Bard,"
Nation, 198 (1964), 101.

1374. Sypher, Wylie
"S as Casuist," Sewanee
Review, 58 (1950), 262-280.

1375. Tannenbaum, Samuel A.
"The 'Copy' for S's Son-
nets," PQ, 10 (1931), 393-395.

1376. .
"The Heart of S's Mystery,"
Dial, 56 (1914), 494-496.

20
1377. .
"Sonnet 20, Interpreted,"
S Association Bulletin, 13 (1938),
188.

1378. Tate, Allen
"The Unilateral Imagina-
tion: Or, I, Too, Dislike It,"
Southern Review, New Series 1
(1965), 530-542.

1379. Taylor, Dick, Jr.
"The Earl of Pembroke and
the Youth of S's Sonnets: An Essay in Rehabilitation," Studies in
Philology, 56 (1959), 26-54.

1380. .
"The Third Earl of Pem-
broke As a Patron of Poetry,"
Tulane Studies in English, 5 (1955),
41-67.

1381. The Tempest
See Cranefield, P. F. and
Federn, W.

1382. Texts (1609)
See Bartlett, H. C.; Carter,
Albert.

1383. Texts (1640)
See Alden, Raymond M.

1384. Texts (1710, 1714)
See Alden, Raymond M.

129
1385. Thompson, Karl F.
"S's Sonnet 129," Ex-
plicator, 7 (1949), 27.

98
1386. Thomson, Patricia
"The Date Clue in S's
Sonnet 98," Neophilologus, 50
(1967), 262-269.

106
1387. Thonon, Robert
" 'Still' or 'Skill,' A
Note on S's Sonnet 106," SJ,
97 (1961), 203-207.

1388. Thorpe, Thomas
See Fort, James A.;
Rostenberg, Leona.

1389. Thurston, Herbert
"The 'Mr. W. H.' of S's
Sonnets," Month, 156 (1930),
425-437.

1390. Titherley, Arthur Walsh
" 'Speake of my Lame-
nesse,' " Shakespearean Authorship Review, 5 (1961), 7-9.

1391. Titus Andronicus
See Kirov, Todor T.

1392. Toliver, Harold E.
"S and the Abyss of
Time," JEGP, 64 (1965), 234-
254.

1393. Tonog Lanua, Francisco
G.
"S's Sonnets and Hamlet's
Soliloquies," Far Eastern Uni-
versity Faculty Journal (Manila),
7 (1964), 221-225.

1394. Troilus and Cressida
See Muir, Kenneth.

1395. Turner, L. M.
"Mr. W. H.," TLS,
June 3, 1965. p. 460.

1396. "Unique Illuminated Copy of S's Songs and Sonnets by Sangorski," TLS, December 23, 1926. p. 952.

1397. Viswanathan, K.
"Falstaff and the Sonnets," Triveni (Madras), 20 (1949), 569-573.

1398. Ward, B. R.
"Mr. W. H. and Our Ever-Living Poet," National Review, 80 (1922), 81-93.

1399. _____.
"The Mystery of Mr. W. H.," TLS. May 24, 1923. p. 356.

1400. _____.
"S's Sonnets," Poetry and the Play, 13 (1929-1930), 19-30.

1401. Warren, Clyde T.
See Clarkson, Paul S.

1402. Warren, Roger
"Why Does It End Well? Helena, Bertram, and The Sonnets," SS, 22 (1969), 79-92.

1403. Watson, Wilfred
"Tarquin the Master-Mistress, and the Dark Lady: The Role of the Poet in S's Sonnets," Humanities Association Bulletin (Canada), 15 (1964), 7-16.

1404. Wells, Henry Willis
"A New Preface to S's Sonnets," S Association Bulletin, 12 (1937), 118-129.

1405. _____.
"A New Preface to S's Sonnets," S Association Bulletin, 12 (1937), 118-129. [See Lord Alfred Douglas, "S and Will Hughes," Ibid., May 21, p. 53, 353.... Ibid., May 28, p. 370.]

1406. Wheeler, Charles B. and

Bateson, F. W.
"Bare Ruined Choirs," EIC, 4 (1954), 224-226.

1407. Whitcomb, I. P.
"The Lark in Legend & Song," Poet Lore, 15 (1904), 81-94.

73
1408. White, Robert L.
"Sonnet 73 Again: A Rebuttal and New Reading," College Language Association Journal (Morgan State College, Baltimore), 6 (1962), 125-132.

44
1409. Whorlow, H.
"An Emendation of Sonnet 44, Line 9," TLS. January 16, 1919. p. 34.

1410. Wilder, C. F.
"Sonnet-Hunting," Methodist Review, 91 (1909), 372-385.

1411. Wilkie, K. E.
"O Brave New World," Scholastic, 50 (1947), 17-18.

1412. Wilkins, Ernest H.
"The 'Enuey' in Petrarch and S (Sonnet 66)," MP, 13 (1915), 495-496.

1413. _____.
"The Invention of the Sonnets: The Enuey in Petrarch and in S," MP, 13 (1915), 463+.

104
1414. Wilkinson, L. P.
"S and Horace," TLS, May 6, 1955, p. 237. [Influence of Horace's Epode 11 on S's Sonnet 104.]

1415. Williams, Franklin B., Jr.
"An Initiation Into Initials," Studies in Bibliography,

9 (1957), 163-178.

1416. Wilson, Katharine M.
"S's Sonnets," Calcutta Review, 37 (1930), 179-197; 38 (1931), 46-70.

1417. Wilson, Sir Thomas
(Arte of Rhetorique)
See Peterson, D. L.

1418. Winters, Yvor
"The 16th Century Lyric in England," Poetry, 53 (1939), 258-272, 320-335; 54 (1939), 35-51.

1419. Woodward, P.
"S Sonnets," Baconiana, 20 (1912), 17-23.

1420. Wright, L. B.
"The Male-Friendship Cult in Heywood's Plays," MLN, 42 (1927), 510-514.

1421. Wriothesley, Henry
See Southampton, Earl of.

1422. Wyatt, Thomas
See Muir, Kenneth.

1423. Yates, Frances A.
"The Emblematic Conceit in Giordano Bruno's De Gli Eroici Furori and in the Elizabethan Sonnet Sequences," Journal of the Warburg and Courtlauld Institute, 6 (1944), 101-121.

1424. Yolland, Arthur
"1938-1963: The Cult of S in Hungary," Hungarian Quarterly, 5 (1939), 285-296.

1425. The Youth
See Chambers, Sir Edmund K.; Empson, William; Lynch, A.; Newdigate, B. H.; Nickalls, B.; Rodin, M.; Stopes, C. C.; Strachey, C.; Taylor, Dick, Jr.

1426. Zeydel, Edwin H.
"Fourteenth Sonnet, with

Tieck's Rendering," PMLA, 51 (1936), 234-237.

(2) Book Reviews
(Selective List)

1427. Adams, Hazard
"A Window to Criticism by Murray Krieger," Criticism, 7 (1965), 190-193.

1428. Akrigg, G. P. V.
"The Sonnets ed. by J. Dover Wilson," MP, 65 (1967), 159-161.

1429. Alden, Raymond M.
"Acheson's Mistress Davenant & Chambrun's The Sonnets of William S," JEGP, 14 (1915), 449-459.

1430. Arnold, A.
"A Window to Criticism by Murray Krieger," Personalist, 46 (1965), 401-403.

1430a. Axelrad, A. J.
"The Sense of S's Sonnets ed. by Edward Hubler," Revue de Litterature Comparée, 28 (1955), 496-497.

1431. Bacon, Wallace A.
"The Mutual Flame by G. Wilson Knight," Quarterly Journal of Speech, 42 (1955), 201-202.

1432. Barroll, Leeds
"S's Sonnets by John Dover Wilson," College English, 26 (1964), 61.

1433. Berman, Ronald
"Interpretations in S's Sonnets by Hilton Landry," Kenyon Review, 26 (1964), 564-567.

1434.   .
"S's Sonnets by John Dover Wilson," Kenyon Review, 26 (1964), 564-567.

1435. Blackstone, B.
"K. Muir's The Voyage

to Illyria," Criterion, 17 (1938), (1958), 950.

1436. Bonnerot, L.
"An Explanatory Introduction to Thorpe's Edition... by C. L. DeChambrun," Etudes Anglaises, 5 (1951), 75-76.

1437. Boston, Richard
"Mr. W. H. by Leslie Hotson," TLS, June 17, 1965. p. 519.

1438. Brien, A.
"Afterthought" [Hotson's Identity of Mr. W. H.], Spectator, 212 (Ap 17, 1964), 529.

1439. Brown, Ivor
"S's Sonnets by John Dover Wilson," Observer, Dec. 1, 1963. p. 25.

1440. .
"An Explanatory Introduction to Thorpe's Edition... by C. L. DeChambrun," Observer, April 22, 1951. p. 7.

1441. Bullough, Geoffrey
"The Sense of S's Sonnets by Edward Hubler," MLN, 69 (1953), 514-516.

1442. .
"Themes and Variations in S's Sonnets by J. B. Leishman," RES, 14 (1963), 194-195.

1443. Chamaillard, P.
"The Sense of S's Sonnets by Edward Hubler," Etudes Anglaises, 5 (1950), 243-244.

1444. Connolly, Cyril
"S's Sonnets by John Dover Wilson," Sunday Times, December 1, 1963, p. 36.

1445. Corke, Hilary
"The Portrait of Mr. W. H. by Oscar Wilde," Listener, 60

1446. Cox, R. G.
"Themes and Variations in S's Sonnets by J. B. Leishman," Listener, 65 (1961), 1059.

1447. Craig, John
"S's Sonnets by John Dover Wilson," Spectator. April 24, 1964. p. 555.

1448. Deckner, E.
"J. A. Fort's Two Dated Sonnets of S," Beiblatt, 36 (1925), 367-372.

1449. .
"A. Brandl's S's Sonnets," Beiblatt, 37 (1927), 271-286.

1450. Eliot, T. S.
"J. M. Robertson on The Sonnets," Nation & Athenaeum, 40 (1927), 664-665.

1451. Empson, William
"S's Sonnets by John Dover Wilson," New Statesman, 67 (1964), 216-217.

1452. Forster, M.
"A. Acheson's Mistress Davenant," SJ, 50 (1914), 201-205.

1453. Friedrich, Gerhard
"The Riddle of S's Sonnets by R. P. Blackmur," Books Abroad, 37 (1963), 198.

1454. Gardner, Helen
"Mr. W. H. by Leslie Hotson," Listener, 71 (1964), 887-888.

1455. .
"Mr. W. H. by Leslie Hotson," TLS, September 10, 1964. p. 841.

1456. Grebanier, Bernard
"S's Sonnets ed. by John
Dover Wilson," Saturday Review,
47 (January 11, 1964), 56-57.

1457. Grundy, Joan
"The Riddle of S's Sonnets
by Edward Hubler, et al.," RES,
15 (1964), 73-75.

1458. Harris, F.
"Shaw's The Dark Lady of
the Sonnets," Academy, 79 (1910),
543-544.

1459. Harrison, G. B.
"The Sense of S's Sonnets
by Edward Hubler," Saturday Review, 35 (June, 1952), 28.

1460. .
"S's Sonnets by John Dover
Wilson," New York Herald Tribune
Book Review, April 26, 1964. p.
4, 8.

1461. .
"A Window to Criticism by
Murray Krieger," New York Herald Tribune Book Review, April
26, 1964. p. 4, 8.

1462. Hart, Thomas R.
"A Window to Criticism by
Murray Krieger," Books Abroad,
39 (1965), 211-212.

1463. Hasler, Jörg
"The Riddle of S's Sonnets
ed. by Edward Hubler," English
Studies, 48 (1967), 238-240.

1464. Hayashi, Tetsumaro
"Hilton Landry, Interpreta-
tions in S's Sonnets,"
SNL, 14 (1964), 5.

1465. Henman, C.
"S's Sonnets: Their Rela-
tion to His Life by Barbara Mac-
Kenzie," MLN, 63 (1948), 213-
214.

1466. Henze, R.
"S's Sonnets ed. by
Barbara Herrnstein," College
English, 27 (1966), 339.

1467. Heuer, Hermann
"S's Sonnets by John
Dover Wilson," SJ, 100 (1964),
76.

1468. Hubler, Edward
"S's Sonnets by John
Dover Wilson," New York Times
Book Review, January, 1964,
p. 5, 37.

1469. .
"S's Secret by Rudolf
Melander Holzapfel," SNL, 12
(1962), 21.

1470. .
"S's Sonnets Dated,"
SQ, 1 (1950), 78-83 (A review
of S's Sonnets Dated and Other
Essays by Leslie Hotson, New
York: Oxford University Press,
1949).

1471. Hyde, H. Montgomery
"The Portrait of Mr.
W. H. by Oscar Wilde," TSL,
December 5, 1958. p. 705.

1472. Jiriczek, O.
"S. Butler's S's Son-
nets," Beiblatt, 13 (1902), 100-
104.

1473. Johnson, B. S.
"The Riddle of S's Son-
nets ed. by Edward Hubler,
et al.," Spectator. September
28, 1962. p. 444.

1474. Kaufmann, U. Milo
"A Window to Criticism
by Murray Krieger," JEGP,
65 (1966), 592-595.

1475. Keller, W.
"C. C. Stopes' Life of
Henry Wriothesley," SJ, 58

(1922), 128-130.

1476. Kingsmile, H.
"Mr. W.H., A Review of True History of S's Sonnets by A. Douglas," English Review, 56 (1933), 57-80.

1476a. Knights, Lionel C.
"The Mutual Flame by G. Wilson Knight," RES, 8 (1957), 302-304.

1477. Landry, Hilton
"A Window to Criticism by Murray Krieger," S Studies, 1 (1964), 328-332.

1478. _____.
"The Sonnets," SNL, 14 (1964), 41. Review by T. Hayashi.

1479. Lawrence, W. J.
"S. Butler's S's Sonnets Reconsidered." Irish Statesman, 9 (1927), 137-138.

1480. _____.
"Thomson's Book on the Sonnets," Spectator, May 6, 1938. p. 818.

1481. Lerner, Laurence
"Interpretations in S's Sonnets by Hilton Landry." Listener, 71 (1964), 686.

1482. _____.
"A Window to Criticism by Murray Krieger," MLR, 60 (1965), 430-432.

1483. Lever, J. W.
"The Riddle of S's Sonnets ed. by Edward Hubler, et al.," MLR, 58 (1963), 406-407.

1484. Levin, Harry
"A Window to Criticism by Murray Krieger," Yale Review, 54 (1965), 261-265.

1485. Lüdeke, H.
"The Sense of S's Sonnets by Edward Hubler," English Studies, 38 (1958), 79-82.

1486. McClumpha, C. F.

"P. Godwin's New Study of The Sonnets," MLN, 16 (1901), 106-111.

1487. McManaway, James G.
"An Explanatory Introduction to Thorpe's Edition of S's Sonnets, 1609, with Text Transcription by C. L. De Chambrun," SQ, 2 (1951), 366.

1488. Marshall, W.
"D. Bray's Original Order of S's Sonnets," Beiblatt, 39 (1928), 99-102.

1489. Mincoff, M.
"S's Sonnets by John Dover Wilson," English Studies, 45 (1964), 401-403.

1490. Nearing, Homer, Jr.
"Interpretations in S's Sonnets by Hilton Landry." SQ, 15 (1964), 234-235.

1491. Nicoll, A.
"J. Robertson's The Problems of S's Sonnets." MLR, 22 (1927), 330-333.

1492. Nowottny, Winifred
"Elizabethan Sonnet Themes & The Dating of S's Sonnets by Claes Schaar," RES, 15 (1964), 423-429.

1493. Palmer, H. E.
"A. Douglas on 'Mr. W. H.,'" Everyman, 9 (1933), 331.

1494. Palmer, D. J.
"The Riddle of S's Sonnets ed. by Edward Hubler, et al.," Critical Quarterly, 4 (1962), 379-380.

1495. Paret, M.
"F. Harris's S & His Love," Vassar Miscellany Monthly, 1 (1916), 491-493.

1496. Poirier, Michael
"A Casebook on S's Sonnets
eds. by Gerald Willen and Victor
B. Reed," Etudes Anglaises, 19
(1966), 296.

1497.   .
"S's Sonnets by J. Dover
Wilson," Etudes Anglaises, 18
(1965), 70-71.

1498.   .
"Themes and Variations in
S's Sonnets by J.B. Leishman,"
Etudes Anglaises, 15 (1962), 75-
76.

1499.   .
"A Window to Criticism by
Murray Krieger," Etudes Anglaises,
19 (1966), 296-297.

1500. Praz, Mario
"S's Sonnets: Their Rela-
tion to His Life by Barbara Mac-
Kenzie," ES, 29 (1948), 53-58.

1501. Prince, F. T.
"Elizabethan Sonnet Themes
and the Dating of S's Sonnets by
Claes Schaar," Studia Neophilologia, 35 (1963), 307-310.

1502. Ricks, Christopher
"S's Sonnets by John Dover
Wilson," Listener, 70 (1963), 938.

1503. Salyer, Sandford
"The Sense of S's Sonnets
by Edward Hubler," Books Abroad,
26 (1953), 82.

1504. S Newsletter
"The Dark Lady," A Review of
Dark Ladies by Ivor Brown."
SNL, 7 (1957), 21.

1505.   .
"Hotson's Sonnet Theories
Astound Scholars," SNL, 14
(1964), 61.

1506.   .

"Knight's Mutual
Flame," Kenyon Review, 18
(1956), 659-663; SNL, 7 (1957),
23. [A Review of G. Wilson
Knight's The Mutual Flame.]

1507. Strathmann, Ernest A.
"The Sense of S's Son-
nets by Edward Hubler," JEGP,
52 (1953), 577-581.

1508. Smith, Hallett
"Interpretations in S's
Sonnets by Hilton Landry," S
Studies, 1 (1965), 332-334.

1509. T. L. S.
"The Sense of S's Son-
nets by Edward Hubler," TLS,
March 6, 1953. p. 151.

1510.   .
"The Sonnets Illustrated
by Steven Spurrier," TLS, December 29, 1950. p. 830.

1511. Walton, J. K.
"John Dover Wilson's
The Sonnets," SS, 20 (1968),
170-172.

1512. Whitaker, Virgil K.
"On the Literary Genet-
ics of S's Poems & Sonnets by
T. W. Baldwin," SQ, 2 (1951),
137-139.

1513. Williams, Philip
"A Review of The Sense
of S's Sonnets by Edward Hubler," South Atlantic Quarterly,
52 (1953), 490.

1514. Wimsatt, W. K.
"A Window to Criticism
by Murray Krieger," MP, 64
(1966), 71-74.

(3) Book Reviews
("See References")

1515. Acheson, Arthur
See Alden, Raymond M.

1516. _____.
See Foster, M.

1517. Baldwin, T. W.
See Whitaker, Virgil K.

1518. Blackmur, R. P.
See Friedrich, Gerhard.

1519. Brandle, A.
See Deckner, E.

1520. Bray, D.
See Marshall, W.

1521. Brown, Ivor
See S Newsletter.

1522. Butler, S.
See Jiriczek, O.

1523. _____.
See Lawrence, W. J.

1524. De Chambrun, Clara Longworth
See Pineton, Clara Long-
worth (Countess de Cham-
brun). (See 1564 in ref-
erence below)

1525. Douglas, Lord Alfred
See Kingsmile, H.

1526. _____.
See Palmer, H. E.

1527. Fort, J. A.
See Deckner, E.

1528. Godwin, P.
See McClumpha, C. F.

1529. Harris, F.
See Paret, M.

1530. Herrnstein, Barbara
See Henze, R.

1531. Holzapfel, R. M.
See Hubler, Edward.

1532. Hotson, Leslie
See Boston, Richard.

1533. _____.
See Brien, A.

1534. _____.
See Gardner, Helen;
Hubler, Edward.

1535. _____.
See SNL.

1536. Hubler, Edward
See Axalrad, A. J.
[in 1430a]

1537. _____.
See Bullough, Geoffrey.

1538. _____.
See Chamaillard, P.

1539. _____.
See Grundy, Joan;
Harrison, G. B.;
Hasler, Jörg; John-
son, B. S.; Lever,
J. W.

1540. _____.
See Lüdeke, H.;
Palmer, D. J.

1541. _____.
See Salyer, S.;
Strathmann, E. A.

1542. _____.
See TLS.

1543. _____.
See Williams, Philip.

1544. Knight, G. Wilson
See Bacon, Wallace A.

1545. _____.
See Knights, Lionel C.

1546. _____.
See S Newsletter.

1547. Krieger, Murray
See Adams, Hazard.

1548. _____.

See Arnold, A.

1549.
     .
See Harrison, G. B.
Hart, Thomas R.
Kaufmann, U. M.

1550.
     .
See Landry, Hilton;
Lerner, Laurence;
Levin, Harry.

1551.
     .
See Poirier, M.

1552.
     .
See Wimsatt, W. K.

1553. Landry, Hilton
See Berman, Ronald;
Hayashi, Tetsumaro.

1554.
     .
See Lerner, L.

1555.
     .
See Nearing, Homer, Jr.;
Smith, Hallett.

1556. Leishman, J. B.
See Bullough, Geoffrey.

1557.
     .
See Cox, R. G.

1558.
     .
See Poirier, Michael.

1559. MacKenzie, Barbara
See Henman, C.; Pruz,
Mario.

1560. Muir, K.
See Blackstone, B.

1561. Pineton, Clara Longworth
(Countess De Chambrun)
See Alden, Raymond M.;
Bonnerot, L.

1562. Reed, Victor B.
See Willen, Gerard item
1571 below.

1563. Robertson, J. M.
See Eliot, T. S.

1564.
     .
See Nicoll, A.

1565. Schaar, Claes
See Nowottny, W.;
Prince, F. T.

1566. Shaw, G. B.
See Harris, F.

1567. Spurrier, Steven
See TLS.

1568. Stopes, C. C.
See Keller, W.

1569. Wilde, Oscar
See Corke, Hilary;
Hyde, H. M.

1570. Thomson, Walter (ed.)
See Lawrence, W. J.

1571. Willen, Gerard and Reed,
Victor B.
See Poirier, M.

1572. Wilson, John Dover
See Akrigg, G. P. V.

1573.
     .
See Barroll, Leeds.

1574.
     .
See Berman, Ronald.

1575.
     .
See Brown, Ivor.

1576.
     .
See Connolly, Cyril.

1577.
     .
See Craig, John.

1578.
     .
See Empson, William.

1579.
     .
See Grebanier, Bernard

Harrison, G.B.; Heuer, Hermann; Hubler, Edward.

1580. ____ .

See Mincoff, M.; Poirier, M.; Ricks, C.; Walton, J.K.

D. Individual Sonnet Criticism (In Numerical Order)

1
1581. Booth, Stephen
An Essay on S's Sonnets. New Haven: Yale University Press, 1969. p. 42-43, passim.

1
1582. Nowottny, Winifred M.
"Formal Elements in S's Sonnets (1-6)," in Discussions of S's Sonnets. ed. by B. Herrnstein. Boston: D.C. Heath and Co., 1964. p. 152-159.

1-6
1583. ____ .
"Formal Elements in S's Sonnets 1-6," EIC, 2 (1952), 76-84.

1-6
1584. S Newsletter
"Interpretationships among the Sonnets," (Review of Periodicals) "Formal Elements in S's Sonnets 1-6," EIC, 2 (1952), 76-84; SNL, 3 (1953), 31.

1-17
1585. Blackmur, R.P.
"Poetics for Infatuation," Venture, 3 (1963), 38-59.

1-27
1586. Pirkhofer, Anton M.
" 'A Pretty Pleasing Pricket'--On the Use of Alliteration in S's Sonnets," SQ, 14 (1963), 3-14.

1-154
1587. Holzapfel, Rudolf Melander

S's Secret: A New and Correct Interpretation of S's Sonnets. Dublin: Melander S Society, 1961.

2
1588. Nowottny, Winifred M.T.
"Formal Elements in S's Sonnets (1-6)," in Discussions of S's Sonnets, ed. B. Herrnstein. Boston: D.C. Heath, 1964. p. 152-158.

2
1589. Mahood, M.M.
"The Fatal Cleopatra: S and the Pun," EIC, 1 (1951), 193-207.

3
1590. Nowottny, Winifred M.T.
"Formal Elements in S's Sonnets (1-6)," in Discussions of S's Sonnets ed. B. Herrnstein. p. 152-159.

4
1591. ____ .
"Formal Elements in S's Sonnets (1-6)," in Discussions of S's Sonnets ed. B. Herrnstein. p. 152-158.

5
1592. Elman, Paul
"S's Gentle Hours," SQ, 4 (1953), 301-309.

5
1593. Nowottny, Winifred M.T.
"Formal Elements in S's Sonnets (1-6)," in Discussions of S's Sonnets, ed. Barbara Herrnstein. p. 152-158.

6
1594. ____ .
"Formal Elements in S's Sonnets (1-6)," in Discussions in S's Sonnets, ed. B. Herrnstein. p. 152-158.

6
1595. Shield, H.A.

"Links with S (Sonnet 6),"
N & Q, 195 (1950), 205-206.

8
1596. Banks, Theodore H.
"S's Sonnet 8," MLN, 63
(1948), 541-542.

8
1597. Booth, Stephen
An Essay on S's Sonnets.
New Haven: Yale University
Press, 1969. p. 53-45, passim.

8
1598. Hemingway, S. B.
"Sonnet 8 and Mr. William
Hughes, Musician," MLN, 25
(1910), 210.

8, 128
1599. Naylor, Edward W.
"Sonnets 128 and 8," The
Poets and Music, London: Dutton,
1928. p. 91-92; 109-110.

9
1600. Shield, H. A.
"Links with S (Sonnet 9),"
N & Q, 197 (1952), 156-157.

12
1601. Berry, J. Wilkes
"S's Sonnet 12," Explica-
tor, 27 (1968), Item 13.

12
1602. Booth, Stephen
An Essay on S's Sonnets.
New Haven: Yale University
Press, 1969. p. 64-66, 69-84,
passim.

12, 30
1603. Herbert, T. Walter
"Sound and Sense in Two
S Sonnets (12 & 30)," Tennessee
Studies in Literature, 3 (1958),
43-52.

12, 99
1604. Anderton, Basil
"Barton's Translation of

Sonnets 99 and 12," Sketches
from a Library Window. Cambridge: W. Heffer, 1922. p.
50, 70.

15
1605. Booth, Stephen
An Essay on S's Sonnets.
New Haven: Yale University
Press, 1969. p. 174-186, 209-
214.

15
1606. Kirk, Richard Ray, and
McCutcheon, Roger P.
An Introduction to the
Study of Poetry. New York:
American Book Co., 1934. p.
39-41.

16
1607. Empson, William
Seven Types of Ambiguity.
Cleveland: World Publishing Co.,
1955. p. 70-74 [1947 ed. 54-
57].

18
1608. Blackmur, R. P.
"Poetics for Infatuation,"
Venture, 3 (1963), 38-59.

18
1609. Smith, Hallett
Elizabethan Poetry.
Cambridge: Harvard University
Press, 1966. p. 178.

18, 20
1610. Mahony, P.
"Aptness & Two Shake-
spearean Sonnets," Etudes
Anglaises et Americaines, 2
(1964), 67-78 [Formerly
Travaux du Centre d'Etudes
Anglaises et Americaines].

18, 33
1611. Law, Robert A.
"Two Notes on Shake-
spearean Parallels," University
of Texas Studies in English, 9
(1929), 82-85.

20
1612. Chambers, Sir Edmund
"The Youth of S's Sonnets;
Significance of Hews in Sonnet
20," RES, 21 (1945), 331.

20
1613. Reichert, John F.
"Sonnet 20 and Erasmus'
'Epistle to Perswade a Young Gentleman to Marriage,' " SQ, 16
(1965), 238-240.

20
1614. Tannenbaum, Samuel A.
"Sonnet 20." S Association
Bulletin, 13 (1938), 188.

20,18
1615. "Aptness & Two S Sonnets," Etudes Anglaises et Americaines, 2 (1964), 67-78.

21
1616. Booth, Stephen
An Essay on S's Sonnets.
New Haven: Yale University
Press, 1969. p. 192-193, passim.

23
1617. .
An Essay on S's Sonnets.
p. 38-39, passim.

23-26
1618. "Sonnets 23-26," Baconiana,
16 (1908), 45-48.

24
1619. Orange, Linwood E.
"S's Sonnet 24." Southern
Quarterly, 4 (1966), 409-410.

27
1620. Salle, J. C.
"S's Sonnet 27 and Keats'
'Bright Star!' " N & Q, 14
(1967), 24.

29
1621. Booth, Stephen
An Essay on S's Sonnets.
New Haven: Yale University

Press, 1969. p. 48-49,
passim.

29
1622. Broun, Malcolm
"The Sweet Crystalline
Cry," Western Review, 16
(1952), 264-265.

29
1623. Frankenberg, Lloyd (ed.)
Invitation to Poetry; a
Round of Poems from John
Skelton to Dylan Thomas. Garden City, N.Y.: Doubleday,
1956. p. 239.

29
1624. Nearing, Homer, Jr.
"S as a Nondramatic
Poet; Sonnet 29," SQ, 13
(1962), 15-20.

29
1625. No entry.

30
1626. Aiken, Ralph
"Note on S's Sonnet 30,"
SQ, 14 (1963), 93-94.

30
1627. Dean, Leonard
English Masterpieces,
ed. by Maynard Mack (7 vols.)
Renaissance Poetry. Englewood
Cliffs, N.J.: Prentice-Hall,
1961. III, 9.

30
1628. Hendricks, W.O.
"Sonnet 30," Language,
42 (1966), 3.

30
1629. Knights, Lionel C.
Explorations: Essays in
Criticism, Mainly in the Literature of the 17th Century.

New York: G. W. Stewart, 1947.
p. 74-75.

30
1630. .
"S's Sonnets," Scrutiny,
3 (1934), 153.

30
1631. Kock, E. A.
"On Sonnet 30, Lines 1-4,"
Anglia, 31 (1908), 134.

30
1632. Krenzer, James R.
Elements of Poetry. New
York: Macmillan, 1955. p. 67-
70.

30
1633. Main, C. F. and Seng, Peter J.
Poems, Wadsworth Hand-
book and Anthology. Belmont,
California: Wadsworth, 1965 (1961).
p. 246-247.

30
1634. Pepper, Stephen C.
The Basis of Criticism in
the Arts. Cambridge: Harvard
University Press, 1945. p. 115-
127. Reprinted in part Poetry as
Experience. ed. by Norman C.
Stageberg and Wallace L. Ander-
son. New York: American Book
Co., 1952. p. 461. Abridged in
The Case for Poetry. ed. by
Frederick L. Gwynn et al. Engle-
wood Cliffs, N. J.: Prentice-Hall,
1965. p. 307-309.

30
1635. Zahniser, Howard
"Lake Solitude Sermon,"
Nature, (n. v.), (1958), 452-453.

30, 12
1636. Herbert, T. Walter
"Sound and Sense in Two
Sonnets 12 and 30," Tennessee
Studies in Literature, 3 (1958),
43-52.

31
1637. Piper, W. H.
"S's 31st Sonnet," TLS,
April 13, 1951. p. 229.

31
1638. SNL
Piper, H. W. "Sonnet
31," (Review of Periodicals;
S's 31st Sonnet," TLS, April
13, 1951. p. 229), SNL, I
(1951), 12.

32
1639. Booth, Stephen
An Essay on S's Sonnets.
New Haven: Yale Univ. Press,
1969, p. 38-39, passim.

33
1640. .
An Essay on S's Sonnets.
p. 3-12, 39-41, 88-90.

33
1641. Dean, Leonard
English Masterpiece;
(7 vols.) ed. Maynard Mark.
Renaissance Poetry. Englewood
Cliffs, N. J.: Prentice-Hall,
1961. III, 10.

33
1642. Ransom, John Crowe
The World's Body. New
York: Scribner s, 1938. p.
279-282.

33, 18
1643. Law, Robert A.
"Two Notes in Shake-
spearean Parallels," Studies in
English, 9 (1929), 82-85.

33-35, 40-42, 57, 58
1644. Landry, Hilton
"The Civil War: Sonnets
33-35, 40-42, and 57-58," in
his Interpretations in S's Sonnets. Berkeley: University of
California Press, 1964. p. 56-
80.

33,124
1645. Mahood, M. M.
"Love's Confined Doom,"
SS, 15 (1962), 50-61.

34
1646. Booth, Stephen
An Essay on S's Sonnets.
New Haven: Yale University
Press, 1969. p. 3-12, passim.

34
1647. Kallsen, T. J.
"S's Sonnet 34," Explicator,
27 (1969), 3.

35
1648. Booth, Stephen
An Essay on S's Sonnets.
New Haven: Yale University
Press, 1969. p. 3-12, 58-59,
passim.

34
1649. Knights, Lionel C.
Explorations. New York:
G. W. Stewart, 1947. p. 64-66.

35
1650. _____.
"S's Sonnets," Scrutiny, 3
(Sept., 1934) 142-143. Reprinted
in Understanding Poetry ed. by
Cleanth Brooks and Robert Penn
Warren. New York: Holt, Rinehart and Winston, 1960. p. 292-
293.

36
1651. Booth, Stephen
An Essay on S's Sonnets.
New Haven: Yale University
Press, 1969. p. 8-12, 111-113,
passim.

36, 96
1652. Sampson, J.
"The Repetition of a Couplet
in Sonnets 36 and 96," TLS. October 2, 1919. p. 532.

37
1653. Booth, Stephen

An Essay on S's Son-
nets. New Haven: Yale University Press, 1969. p. 9-14,
112-113.

39
1654. _____.
An Essay on S's Son-
nets. p. 113-114, 197-198,
passim.

40-42, 33-35, 57, 58
1655. Landry, Hilton
"The Civil War: Son-
nets 33-35, 40-42, and 57-58,"
in his Interpretations in S's
Sonnets. Berkeley: University
of California Press, 1964. p.
56-80.

44
1656. Booth, Stephen
An Essay on S's Son-
nets. New Haven: Yale University Press, 1969. p. 47-48,
passim.

44
1657. Whorlow, H.
"An Emendation of Son-
net 44, Line 9," TLS. January 16, 1919. p. 34.

46
1658. Clarkson, Paul S. and
Warren, C. T.
"Pleading & Practice in
S's Sonnet 46," MLN, 62
(1947), 102-110.

47
1659. Booth, Stephen
An Essay on S's Son-
nets. New Haven: Yale University Press, 1969. p. 53-
54, 189-190, passim.

48
1660. _____.
An Essay on S's Son-
nets. p. 42-43, passim.

50, 51
1661. Schaar, Claes

"S's Sonnets 50-51 and
Tabaldo's Sonnet 107," ES, 38
(1957), 208-209.

51
1662. Davenport, A.
"S's Sonnet 51 Again,"
N & Q, 198 (1953), 15-16.

51
1663. Smith, G. C. M.
"Sonnet 51, Lines 10ff." MLR,
9 (1914), 372-373.

53
1664. Booth, Stephen
An Essay on S's Sonnets.
New Haven: Yale University
Press, 1969. p. 96-110, passim.

53, 54, 69, 70
1665. Landry, Hilton
"The Canker in the Rose:
Sonnets 69 and 70, 53 and 54,"
in his Interpretations in S's Sonnets. Berkeley: University of
California Press, 1964. p. 28-
55.

55
1666. Eccles, C. M.
"S and Jacques Amyot:
Sonnet 55 and Corialanus," N & Q,
12 (1965), 100-102.

55
1667. Smith, Hallett
Elizabethan Poetry. Cam-
bridge: Harvard University Press,
1966. p. 178-181.

55
1668. Whalley, George
Poetic Process: An Essay
in Poetics. Cleveland: World
Publishing Co., 1967. (M 246).
p. 48-49, 209-210.

57-58, 33-35, 40-42
1669. Landry, Hilton
"The Civil War: Sonnets
33-35, 40-42, and 57-58," in his

Interpretations in S's Sonnets.
Berkeley: University of California Press, 1964. p. 56-80.
"A Slave to Slavery: S's Sonnets 57 and 58," in his Interpretations in S's Sonnets. Berkeley: University of California
Press, 1963. Also in A Casebook on S's Sonnets ed. G.
Willen and V. B. Reed, p. 282-
288.

59-61
1670. Suddard, Sarah J. M.
"Sonnets 59, 60, and
61," Keats, Shelley, and S
Studies. New York: Broadway
Press, 1912. p. 177-181.

60
1671. Booth, Stephen
An Essay on S's Son-
nets. New Haven: Yale University Press, 1969. p. 130-
143, passim.

60
1672. Lamson, Roy, et al.
(eds.)
The Critical Reader.
New York: Norton, 1962. p.
56-59.

60
1673. Ransom, John Crowe
"S's Sonnets," Southern
Review, 3 (1938), 548-549.

60
1674. ___.
The World's Body. New
York: Scribner's, 1938. p.
296-297.

60
1675. Starnes, D. T.
"S's Sonnet 60: Ana-
logues," N & Q, 194 (1949),
454.

63
1676. Booth, Stephen
An Essay on S's Sonnets.

98

New Haven: Yale University
Press, 1969. p. 37-38, passim.

64
1677. Caldwell, James R.
"State of Mind: States of
Consciousness," EIC, 4 (1954),
168-179.

64
1678. Hussey, R.
"S and Gower," N & Q,
180 (1941), 386.

64
1679. Levin, Richard
"S's Sonnet 64," Explicator,
24 (1965), 39.

64
1680. Van Doren, Mark
Introduction to Poetry.
New York: Dryden Press, 1951.
p. 117-120.

65
1681. Millett, Fred B.
Reading Poetry, N.Y.:
Harper, 1950. p. 60-61.

65
1682. Reeves, James
The Critical Sense. Lon-
don: Heinemann, 1956. p. 105-
107.

65
1683. Wassal, G.
"Since Brass Nor Stone
(Sonnet 65)," A S Song Cycle.
Cincinnati: [n.p.], 1904. p. 34-
37.

66
1684. Allen, Ned B.
See Levin, Richard. "S's
Sonnet 66," Explicator, 22
(1964), 36; SNL, 14 (1964),
76.

66
1685. Davies, H. Neville
"S's Sonnet 66 Echoed in

All for Love," N & Q, 15
(1968), 262-263.

66
1686. Levin, Richard
"S's Sonnet 66," Ex-
plicator, 22 (1964), 36.

66
1687. Lundquist, Carole
"Sonnet 66," Kerygma,
4 (1964), 22-23.

66
1688. Main, C. F. and Seng,
Peter J.
Poems, Wadsworth Hand-
book and Anthology. Belmont,
California: Wadsworth, 1961
(1965). p. 259-330.

1689. No entry

66, 121, 129
1690. Landry, Hilton
"This Vile World: Son-
nets 66, 121, and 129," in
his Interpretations in S's Sonnets. Berkeley: University of
California Press, 1964. p. 81-
104.

67
1691. Kellner, Loon
"Sonnet 67, Line 7,
Emended," Restoring S.
New York: Knopf, 1925. p.
57.

68
1692. Holzer, G.
"The Grave's Tiring-
room and Sonnet 68," Baconiana,
15 (1907), 201-209.

69, 70, 53, 54
1693. Landry, Hilton
"The Canker in the
Rose: Sonnets 69 and 70; 53
and 54," in his Interpretations
in S's Sonnets. Berkeley: Uni-

versity of California Press, 1964.
p. 28-55.

71
1694. Booth, Stephen
An Essay on S's Sonnets.
New Haven: Yale University
Press, 1964. p. 43-46, passim.

71
1695. Davis, Jack M. and Grant,
J. E.
"A Critical Dialogue in S's
Sonnet 71," Texas Studies in Literature and Language, I (1959),
214-232.

71
1696. Van Doren, Mark
Introduction to Poetry.
New York: Dryden Press, 1951.
p. 117-120.

71-74
1697. Moore, Carlisle
"S's Sonnets 71-74," Ex-
plicator, 7 (October 1949), Item
2; Also in A Casebook on S's
Sonnets. ed. Gerald Willen and
Victor B. Reed. New York:
Thomas Y. Crowell, 1964. p.
271-272.

73
1698. Berkelman, Robert
"The Drama in S's Son-
nets," College English, 10 (1948),
139.

73
1699. Bishop, Henry Rowley
"That Time of Year (Son-
net 73)," Two Gentlemen of Verona. London: Goulding, D'Al-
maine, Potter, 1821 (1921). p.
11-13.

73
1700. Booth, Stephen
An Essay on S's Sonnets.
New Haven: Yale University
Press, 1969. p. 116-130.

73
1701. Keogh, J. G.
"S's Sonnet 73," Ex-
plicator, 28 (1969), 6.

73
1702. Krenzer, James R.
Elements of Poetry.
New York: Macmillan, 1955.
p. 150-151.

73
1703. Lumiansky, R. M.
"S's Sonnet 73," Ex-
plicator, 6 (1948), Item 55;
Also in A Casebook on S's Sonnets ed. G. Willen & V. B.
Reed. p. 269.

73
1704. Moore, Carlisle
"Sonnet 73," Explicator,
8 (1949), 2.

73
1705. Nolan, Edward F.
"S's Sonnet 73," Ex-
plicator, 7 (1948), 13.

73
1706. .
"S's Sonnet 73," Ex-
plicator, 7 (1948), Item 13;
Also in A Casebook on S's Sonnets ed. G. Willen & V. B.
Reed. p. 270.

73
1707. Ransom, John Crowe
The World's Body. New
York: Scribner's, 1938. p.
297-298.

73
1708. Rosenthal, M. Louis,
and Smith, A. J. M.
Exploring Poetry. New
York: Macmillan, 1955. p.
91-94.

73
1709. Schaar, C.
"Qui me alit me extinguit

(Sonnet 73)," ES, 49 (1968), 362-367.

73
1710. Schroeter, James
"S's 'Not To-Be-Pitied Lover' (Sonnet 73)," College English, 23 (1962), 250-255.

73
1711. Seib, Kenneth
"S's 'Well': A Note on Sonnet 73," SNL, 17 (1967), 55.

73
1712. Smith, Hallett
Elizabethan Poetry. Cambridge: Harvard Univ. Press, 1966. p. 182-185.

73
1713. Thomas, Wright, and Brown, S.G. (eds.)
Reading Poems: An Introduction to Critical Study. New York: Oxford University Press, 1941. p. 744-748.

73
1714. White, Robert L.
"Sonnet 73 Again," College Language Association Journal, 6 (1962), 125-132.

73
1715. Winifred, Lynskey
"A Critic in Action: Mr. Ransom," College English, 5 (1944), 244-245.

74
1716. Chambrun, Longworth
"The Rival Poet," TLS, February 2, 1951. p. 69.

76
1717. Stainer, C. L.
"A Cipher in Sonnet 76," TLS. April 7, 1932. p. 250.

77
1718. Booth, Stephen
An Essay On S's Sonnets.

p. 198-199, passim.

77
1719. Winters, Yvor
"The 16th Century Lyric in England," Poetry, 54 (1939), 49-51.

77,105,140
1720. Loane, G.G.
"Sonnets 77, 105, and 140," TLS. March 19, 1925. p. 200.

78
1721. Booth, Stephen
An Essay on S's Sonnets. p. 195-196, passim.

79
1722. .
An Essay on S's Sonnets. p. 56-57, passim.

80
1723. Schaar, C.
"Italian Analogue of S's Sonnet 80," ES, 43 (1962), 253-255.

81
1724. Empson, William
Seven Types of Ambiguity. Cleveland: World Publishing, 1955. p. 69-70. (1947 ed., 53-54).

81
1725. Sturtz, S. V.
"Ronsard & Sonnet 81," Observer. June 19, 1927. p. 5.

83
1726. Empson, William
Seven Types of Ambiguity. Cleveland: World Publishing, 1955. p. 168-175. (1947 ed., 133-139).

85
1727. Booth, Stephen
An Essay on S's Sonnets. p. 145-148, passim.

85
1728. Creighton, Charles
"A New Reading in Sonnet
85," TLS. January 23, 1919.
p. 46.

85
1729. Richmond, O. et al.
"A Reading in Sonnet 85,"
TLS. Dec. 26, 1918, p. 657;
Jan. 2, 1919, p. 10; Jan. 9, p.
21; Jan. 16, p. 34; Jan. 23, p.
46.

85
1730. Strachey, C. et al.
"Sonnet 85 and Mary Fit-
ton," TLS. January 5, 1922. p.
13; January 12, p. 29.

85, 86
1731. Bradbook, M. C.
"A Reading of Sonnets 85
and 86," Filoloski Pregled, 1 and
2 (1964), 155-157.

86
1732. Booth, Stephen
An Essay on S's Sonnets.
p. 200-201, passim.

86
1733. Frankenberg, Lloyd (ed.)
Invitation to Poetry. Garden City, N.Y.: Doubleday,
1956. p. 94-95.

87
1734. Daniels, Earl R. K.
The Art of Reading Poetry.
New York: Farrar & Rinehart,
1941. p. 212.

89
1735. Booth, Stephen
An Essay on S's Sonnets.
p. 91-94, passim.

89
1736. Schaar, Claes
"An Italian Analogue of S's
Sonnet 89," ES, 43 (1962), 253-
255.

90
1737. Jorgensen, V.
"Of Love and Hate; S's
Sonnet 90," English Journal,
53 (1964), 459-461.

90-91
1738. Wassal, G.
"Then Hate Me If Thou
Wilt (Sonnet 90)," A S Song
Cycle. Cincinnati: [n.p.],
1904. p. 12-15.

94
1739. Booth, Stephen
An Essay on S's Sonnets.
New Haven: Yale University
Press, 1969. p. 152-168.

94
1740. Empson, William
"They That Have Power
(Sonnet 94)," in Some Versions
of Pastoral. London: Chatto
& Windus, 1935; New York:
New Directions, 1950.

94
1741. Gerard, Albert S.
"The Stone As Lily: A
Discussion of S's Sonnet 94,"
SJ, 96 (1960), 155-160; SNL,
12 (May 1962), 22.

94
1742. Knights, Lionel C.
Explorations. New York:
G. W. Stewart, 1947. p. 69-70.

94
1743. .
"S's Sonnets," Scrutiny,
3 (1934), 147-149.

94
1744. Landry, Hilton
"The Unmoved Movers:
Sonnet 94 and The Contexts of
Interpretation," in his Interpre-
tations in S's Sonnets. Berk-
eley: University of California
Press, 1964. p. 7-27.

94
1745. Rolle, Dietrich
"S's Sonnet Technique,"
SNL, 12 (1962), 22.

94
1746. Smith, Hallett
Elizabethan Poetry. Cambridge: Harvard University Press, 1966. p. 188-191.

96
1747. A Memorial of the Quater-Centenary Year of William S., 1564-1964, April 23. Callow End, Eng: Stanbrook Abbey Press, 1964.

96
1748. Smith, G. C. M.
"Sonnet 96, Line 1," TLS. June 22, 1912. p. 413.

96, 36
1749. Sampson, J.
"The Repetition of a Couplet in Sonnets 36 and 96," TLS. October 2, 1919. p. 532.

97
1750. Evans, E. C.
"S's Sonnet 97," RES, 14 (1963), 379. [Reply: R. Levin, RES, 15 (1964), 408-409.]

97
1751. Krenzer, James R.
Elements of Poetry. New York: Macmillan, 1955. p. 10-11.

97
1752. Levin, Richard
"Sonnet 97," RES, 15 (1964), 408-409. [Reply to Art. by E. C. Evans, Ibid., 14 (1963), 370-380.]

98
1753. Thomson, Patricia
"The Date Clue in S's Sonnet 98," Neophilologus, 50 (1967), 262-269.

99
1754. MacKenzie, A. C.

"The Forward Violet,"
Monthly Musical Record, 46 (1916), 113-116.

99, 12
1755. Anderton, Basil
"Barton's Translation of Sonnets 99 and 12," Sketches from a Library Window. Cambridge: W. Heffer, 1922. p. 50 and 70.

104
1756. Wilkinson, L. P.
"S and Horace," TLS. May 6, 1955. p. 237.

104, 107
1757. Fort, James A.
The Two Dated Sonnets of S (Sonnets 104 and 107). London: Oxford University Press, 1924.

105, 77, 140
1758. Loane, G. G.
"Sonnets 77, 105, and 140," TLS. March 19, 1925. p. 200.

106
1759. Allen, Ned B. and Brussels, Robert T.
" 'Still' or 'Skill,' A Note on S's Sonnet 106," SJ, 97 (1961), 203-207; SNL, 13 (1963), 10.

106
1760. Brussels, Robert T.
" 'Still' or 'Skill,' A Note on S's Sonnet 106," SJ, 97 (1961), 203-207. [SNL, 13 (1963), 10.]

106
1761. May, Louis F., Jr.
"The Figure in Sonnet 106," SQ, 11 (1960), 93-94.

106
1762. Thonon, Robert
" 'Still or Skill,' A Note on S's Sonnet 106," SJ, 97

(1961), 203-207.

107
1763. Bateson, F.W.
"Elementary, My Dear
Hotson," EIC, 1 (1951), 81-88.

107
1764. Fort, James A.
"The Date of S's 107th
Sonnet," Library, 4th Series, 9
(1929), 381-384.

107
1765. Harrison, G.B.
"On Sonnet 107," TLS.
November 29, 1928. p. 938.

107
1766. Mattingly, G.
"Date of S's Sonnet 107,"
PMLA, 48 (1933), 705-721.

107
1767. Michael, L.
"S's Sonnet 107 [in Light
of L. Hotson's Argument]," JEGP,
54 (1955), 301-305.

107
1768. Murry, John Middleton
"Concerning Sonnet 107,"
New Adelphi, 2 (1929), 251-254.

107
1769.   .
John Clare and Other
Studies. London: Neville, 1950.
p. 246-252.

107
1770. Ransom, John Crowe
The World's Body. New
York: Scribner's, 1938. p. 298-
299.

107
1771. Stone, Walter B.
"S and the Sad Augurs,"
JEGP, 52 (1953), 457-479. [Takes
issue with Leslie Hotson over the
dating of Sonnet 107.]

107,104
1772. Fort, James A.
The Two Dated Sonnets
of S (Nos. 104 and 107). London: Oxford University Press,
1924.

107,123
1773. Harbage, Alfred
"Dating S's Sonnets 107
and 123," SQ, 1 (1950), 57-63.

107,123,124
1774. Hotson, Leslie
"When S Wrote the Son-
nets," Atlantic, 184 (1949),
61-67.

108,123,124
1775. Nosworthy, J.M.
"All Too Short a Date:
Internal Evidence in S's Sonnets," EIC, 2 (1952), 311-324.

109
1776. Barrell, Charles Wisner
"The Wayward Water-
Bearer Who Wrote S's Sonnet
109," S Fellowship Quarterly,
6 (1945), 37-39.

109
1777. Parry, Sir Charles H.H.
"Sonnet 109," English
Lyrics. London: [n.p.], 1907.
p. 15-18.

109-126
1778. Stirling, Brents
"Sonnets 109-126," The
Centennial Review of Arts and
Science (Michigan State), 8
(1964), 109-120.

110
1779. Larbaud, V.
" 'Motley' in Sonnet
110," TLS. June 24, 1926.
p. 432.

110
1780. Radley, Virginia L. and
Redding, David C.

"S: Sonnet 110, a New
Look," SQ, 12 (1961), 462-463.

111
1781. Edwards, H.L.R.
"Emending Sonnet 111,
Line 12," TLS. October 25,
1934. p. 735.

111
1782. Kenyon, J.S.
"An Emendation in Sonnet
111, Line 12," TLS. October 18,
1934. p. 715.

111
1783.   .
"S, Sonnet 111," MLN, 60
(1945), 357-358.

113
1784. Louthan, Doniphan
"Sonnet 113," TLS, July
6, 1951. p. 421.   ·

113
1785. S Newsletter
"Sonnet 113," (Review of
Periodicals: TLS, by Doniphan
Louthan, July 1951. p. 421),
SNL, 1 (Oct. 1951), 22.

114
1786. Booth, Stephen
An Essay on S's Sonnets.
p. 191-192, passim.

116
1787.   .
An Essay on S's Sonnets.
p. 194-195, passim.

116
1788. Burckhardt, Sigurd
"The Poet as Fool and
Priest," JELH, 23 (1956), 289-
298.

116
1789. Clark, W.R.
"Poems for Study: Sonnet
116," Clearing House, 34 (1960),
316.

116
1790. Doebler, J.
"A Submerged Emblem
in Sonnet 116," SQ, 15 (1964),
109-110.

116
1791. Evans, W.M.
"Lawes' Version of S's
Sonnet 116; with Text and Music Facsimile," PMLA, 51
(1938), 120-122.

116
1792. Frankenberg, Lloyd (ed.)
Invitation to Poetry.
Garden City, N.Y.: Doubleday,
1956. p. 398-399.

116
1793. Landry, Hilton
"The Marriage of True
Minds: Truth and Error in
Sonnet 116," SS, 3 (1968), 98-
110.

116
1794. MacLeish, Archibald
Poetry and Experience.
Baltimore: Penguin Books,
1960 (1964). p. 38-41, Passim.

116
1795.   .
"The Proper Pose of
Poetry," SR, (1955), 11-12,
47-49.

116
1796. Smith, Hallett
Elizabethan Poetry.
Cambridge: Harvard University Press, 1966. p. 172-176.

116
1797. "Sonnet 116 Analysed,"
The Poet & the Philosopher,
1 (1913), 10-12.

116
1798. Stroup, Thomas B.
"Bion and The 116th Son-
net," PQ, 10 (1931), 308-310.

118
1799. Booth, Stephen
An Essay on S's Sonnets.
p. 206-207, Passim.

120
1800. Frankenberg, Lloyd (ed.)
Invitation to Poetry. Garden City, N. Y.: Doubleday, 1956. p. 285.

121
1801. Knights, L. C.
"S's Sonnets," Scrutiny, 3 (1930), 155-156.

121, 66, 129
1802. Landry, Hilton
"This Vile World: Sonnets 66, 121 and 129," in his Interpretations in S's Sonnets. p. 81-104.

123
1803. Knights, Lionel C.
Explorations. New York: G. W. Stewart, 1947. p. 79-80.

123
1804.   .
"S's Sonnets," Scrutiny, 3 (1934), 158-160.

123
1805. Murry, John Middleton
"The Meaning of Sonnet 123," Wanderer, 1 (1934), 64.

123, 107
1806. Harbage, Alfred
"Dating S's Sonnets 107 and 123," SQ, 1 (1950), 57-63.

123, 107, 124
1807. Hotson, Leslie
"When S Wrote the Sonnets," Atlantic, 184 (1949), 61-67.

123-125
1808. Landry, Hilton
"Constancy to an Ideal Object: Sonnets 123, 124, and 125," in his Interpretations in S's Sonnets. p. 105-128.

123, 107, 108, 124
1809. Nosworthy, J. M.
"All Too Short a Date: Internal Evidence in S's Sonnets," EIC, 2 (1952), 311-324.

124
1810. Bercovitch, Sacvan
"S's Sonnet 124," Explicator, 27 (1968), 22.

124
1811. Booth, Stephen
An Essay on S's Sonnets.
p. 207-208, Passim.

124
1812. Mizener, Arthur
"The Structure of Figurative Language in S's Sonnets," Southern Review, 5 (1940), 734-747.

124, 107, 123
1813. Hotson, Leslie
"When S Wrote the Sonnets," Atlantic, 184 (1949), 61-67.

124, 33
1814. Mahood, M. M.
"Love's Confined Doom (Sonnets 33 and 124)," SS, 15 (1962), 50-61.

124, 108, 123
1815. Nosworthy, J. M.
"All Too Short a Date: Internal Evidence in S's Sonnets," EIC, 2 (1952), 311-324.

126
1816. Fox, Charles Overbury
"S's Sonnet 126, Line 1 and 2," N & Q, 197 (1952), 134-135.

126, 127
1817. Blackmur, R. P.
"Poetics for Infatuation," Venture, 3 (1963), 38-59.

106

127-154
1818. Stirling, Brents
"Sonnets 127-154," S 1564-
1964, 10 (1964), 134-153.

128
1819. Brushy, James
"S's 'Saucy Jacks, ' "
ELN, 1 (1963), 11-13.

128
1820. McNeal, Thomas H.
"Every Man Out of His
Humour and S's Sonnets (128),"
N & Q, 197 (1952), 376.

128, 8
1821. Naylor, Edward W.
"Sonnets 128 and 8," The
Poets and Music. London: Dutton, 1928. p. 91-92, and 109-
110.

128
1822. Purdum, R.
"S's Sonnet 128," JEGP,
63 (1964), 235-239.

128
1823. Robbins, R. H. A.
"17th Century Manuscript
of S's Sonnet 128," N & Q, 14
(1967), 137-138.

129
1824. Booth, Stephen
An Essay on S's Sonnets.
p. 148-151, passim.

129
1825. Fox, Charles A. O.
"Thomas Lodge and S,"
N & Q, 3 (1956), 190.

129
1826. Graves, Robert, and Rid
ing, Laura
"A Study in Original Punctuation and Spelling," in Discussions of S's Sonnets ed. Barbara
Herrnstein. Boston: D. C. Heath,
1964. p. 116-124.

129
1827. Johnson, C. W. M.

"S's Sonnet 129," Ex-
plicator, 7 (1949), 41.

129
1828. .
"S's Sonnet 129," Ex-
plicator, 7 (1949), Item 41;
Also in A Casebook on S's Sonnets ed. G. Willen and V. B.
Reed. p. 274-275.

129
1829. Levin, R.
"Sonnet 129 as a Dramatic
Poem," SQ, 16 (1965), 175-181.

129
1830. Peterson, Douglas L.
"A Probable Source for
S's Sonnet 129," SQ, 5 (1954),
381-384.

129
1831. Riding, Laura, and
Graves, Robert
A Survey of Modernist
Poetry. Folcroft, Pa.: Fol-
croft, 1927. p. 63-75, 78-80.

129
1832. Smith, Hallett
Elizabethan Poetry.
Cambridge: Harvard University
Press, 1966. p. 187-188.

129
1833. Thomas, Karl F.
"S's Sonnet 129," Ex-
plicator, 7 (1949), 27.

129
1834. Thompson, Karl F.
"S's Sonnet 129," Explicator, 7 (Feb. 1949), Item 27; Also
in A Casebook on S's Sonnets ed.
G. Willen and V. B. Reed. New
York: T. Y. Crowell, 1964. p. 273-
274.

129, 66, 121
1835. Landry, Hilton
"This Vile World: Son-
nets 66, 121, and 129," in his
Interpretations in S's Sonnets.

p. 81-104.

130
1836. Booth, Stephen
An Essay on S's Sonnets.
p. 144-145, passim.

130
1837. John, Lisle Cecil
The Elizabethan Sonnet
Sequences. New York: Russell
& Russell, 1964. p. 143, 150,
159.

130
1838. Lever, J. W.
"S's French Fruits (Sonnet
130)," SS, 6 (1953), 83-84.

130
1839. McNeal, Thomas H.
"Studies in the Greene-S
Relationships," S Application Bulletin, 15 (1940), 210-218.

130
1840. Rogers, E. G.
"Sonnet 130: Watson to
Linche to S," SQ, 11 (1960), 232-
233.

130
1841. Richmond, H. M.
"Traditions and Lyric: An
Historical Approach to Value,"
Comparative Lit. Studies, 1 (1964),
119-132.

130
1842. Rogers, E. G.
"Sonnet 130: Watson to
Linche to S," SQ, 11 (1960), 232-
233.

130
1843. Ruthven, K. K.
"The Composite Mistress,"
AUMLA, 16 (1966), 198-214.

130
1844. Steadman, J. M.
"S's Sonnet 130 and Aretino's
Ragionamente," N & Q, 13 (1966),

134-135.

138
1845. Hux, Samuel
"S's Sonnet 138," Ex-
plication, 25 (1969), 45.

138,144
1846. Adams, Joseph Quincy
"Sonnets 138 and 144
Collated," in his edition The
Passionate Pilgrim. New York:
Scribner's, 1939. p. xlvi-
xlvii.

138,144
1847. Lee, Sir Sidney
"Sonnets 138 and 144,"
in his edition of The Passionate
Pilgrim. Oxford: [n. p.], 1905.
p. 22-24.

140, 77, 105
1848. Loane, G. G.
"Sonnets 77, 105, and
140," TLS. March 19, 1925.
p. 200.

141
1849. Booth, Stephen
An Essay on S's Sonnets.
p. 57-58, passim.

142
1850. Herbert, T. Walter
"S's Sonnet 142," Ex-
plicator, 13 (1955), 38.

143
1851. Hamer, D.
"S: Sonnet 143," N & Q,
16 (1969), 129-130.

143
1852. Smith, Gordon Ross
"A Note on S's Sonnet
143," American Imago, 14
(1957), 33-36; Also in A Casebook on S's Sonnets ed. G.
Willen and V. B. Reed. p. 276-
278.

144
1853. Leith, A.A.
"Sonnet 144," Baconiana,
23 (1915), 85-87.

144
1854. Seymour-Smith, Martin
"Shakespearean Indelicacies
(Letter)," New Statesman, October
18, 1963.

144
1855. Steadman, John M.
"Like Two Spirits: S and
Ficino," SQ, 10 (1959), 244-246.

144,138
1856. Adams, Joseph Quincy
"Sonnets 138 and 144 Collated," in his edition The Passionate Pilgrim. New York:
Scribner's, 1939. p. xlvi-xlvii.

144,138
1857. Lee, Sir Sidney
"Sonnet 138 and 144," in
his facsimile edition of The Passionate Pilgrim. Oxford: [n.p.],
1905. p. 22-24.

145
1858. Booth, Stephen
An Essay on S's Sonnets.
p. 51-53, passim.

145
1859. Fussell, Paul Jr.
"Sonnet 145" in his Poetic
Meter and Poetic Form. New
York: Random House, 1965. p.
130-131.

146
1860. Allen, Ned B.
"S's Sonnet Artistry,"
SNL, 12 (1962), 26. [Albert S.
Gerard, "Ironic Organization in
S's Sonnet 146," ES, 42 (1961),
157-159.]

146
1861. Berkelman, Robert
"The Drama in S's Sonnets," College English, 10 (1948),
139-141.

146
1862. Clarke, Robert F.
"An Emendation of Sonnet 146," SNL, 8 (1958), 11.

146
1863. Fox, Charles A.O.
"S's Sonnet 146," N &
Q, 199 (1954), 83.

146
1864. Gerard, Albert S.
"Ironic Organization in
S's Sonnet 146," English
Studies, 42 (1961), 157-159;
Also in A Casebook on S's Sonnets ed. G. Willen and V.B.
Reed. p. 279-282.

146
1865. _____.
"Ironic Organization in
S's Sonnet 146," English
Studies, 42 (June 1961), 157-
159; SNL, 12 (May 1962), 26.

146
1866. Huttar, C.A.
"The Christian Basis of
S's Sonnet 146," SQ, 19 (1968),
355-365.

146
1867. Krenzer, James R.
Elements of Poetry.
New York: Macmillan, 1955.
p. 91-92.

146
1868. Leisi, Ernest
"A Possible Emendation
of S's Sonnet 146," ES, 47
(1966), 271-285.

146
1869. Maxwell, J.C.
"Rebel Powers: S and
Daniel," N & Q, 14 (1967),
119-127. [Daniel's Cleopatra
(1594).]

146
1870. Parsons, Howard
"S's Sonnet 146," N & Q,
11 (1955), 97.

146
1871. Santayana, George
Interpretations of Poetry
and Religion. New York: Harper
1957. p. 151-152.

146
1872. Southam, B. C.
"S's Christian Sonnet?
No. 146," SQ, 11 (1960), 67-71.

146
1873. Stauffer, Donald A., et al.
"Critical Principles and a
Sonnet," American Scholar, 12
(1942), 52-62. Abridged in The
Case for Poetry. p. 317-319.

147
1874. Smith, Hallett
Elizabethan Poetry. Cam-
bridge: Harvard University Press,
1966. p. 186-187.

147,148
1875. Alter, Jean V.
"Apollinaire and Two S
Sonnets (147-148)," Comparative
Lit., 14 (1962), 377-385.

149
1876. Bray, Denys
"Sonnet 149," TLS, (July
4, 1942), 331.

152
1877. Blackmur, R. P.
"Poetics for Infatuation,"
Venture, 3 (1963), 38-59.

153
1878. Booth, Stephen
An Essay on S's Sonnets.
p. 46-47, passim.

153,154
1879. Hutton, James
"Analogues of S's Sonnets,

153-154," MP, 38 (1941), 399-
403.

154
1880. Booth, Stephen
An Essay on S Sonnets.
p. 49-50, passim.

See References

1881. Allen, Ned B.
See Levin, Richard (Son-
net 66).

1882. Anderson, Wallace L.
(ed.)
See Stephen, Pepper (30).

1883. Brooks, Cleanth (ed.)
See Knights, L. C. (35).

1884. Brown, S. G. (ed.)
See Thomas, Wright
(ed.) (73).

1885. Brussels, R. T.
See Allen, Ned B. (106).

1886. Evans, E. C.
See Levin, Richard (97).

1887. Gerard, A. S.
See Allen, Ned B. (146).

1888. _____.
See Rolle, Dietrich (94).
[in 1745]

1889. Grant, J. E.
See Davis, Jack M. (71).

1890. Graves, Robert
See Riding, Laura (129).

1891. Gwynn, Frederick L. (ed.)
See Pepper, Stephen C. (30).

1892. Herrnstein, Barbara (ed.)
See Graves, Robert (129);
Riding, Laura (129).

1893. _____.
See Nowottny, Winifred

M. (1-6).

1894. Hotson, Leslie
See Michael, L. (Sonnet 107).

1895. _____.
See Stone, Walter B. (107).

1896. Levin, R.
See Evans, E. C. (97).

1897. Mack, Maynard (ed.)
See Dean, Leonard (30, 33).

1898. McCutcheon, Roger P.
See Kirk, Richard R. (15).

1899. Piper, H. W.
See S Newsletter (31).

1900. Redding, David C.
See Radley, Virginia L. (110).

1901. Reed, V. B. (ed.)
See Gerard, Albert S. (146).

1902. _____.
See Johnson, C. W. M. (129).

1903. _____.
See Landry, Hilton (57, 58).

1904. _____.
See Lumiansky, R. M. (73).

1905. _____.
See Moore, Carlisle (71-74).

1906. _____.
See Nolan, Edward F. (73).

1907. _____.
See Smith, Gordon Ross (143).

1908. _____.
See Thompson, Karl F. (129).

1909. Riding, Laura

See Graves, Robert (129).

1910. Seng, Peter J.
See Main, C. F. (30, 66).

1911. Smith, A. J. M.
See Rosenthal, M. L. (73).

1912. Stageberg, Norman C. (ed.)
See Pepper, Stephen C. (30).

1913. Warren, C. T.
See Clarkson, Paul S. (46).

1914. Warren, Robert Penn (ed.)
See Knights, L. C. (35).

1915. Willen, G. (ed.)
See Gerard, Albert S. (146).

1916. _____.
See Johnson, C. W. M. (129).

1917. _____.
See Landry, Hilton (57, 58).

1918. _____.
See Lumiansky, R. M. (73).

1919. _____.
See Moore, Carlisle (71-74).

1920. _____.
See Nolan, Edward F. (73).

1921. _____.
See Smith, Gordon Ross (143).

1922. _____.
See Thompson, Karl F. (129).

E. Biography

1923. Adams, Joseph Q.
A Life of William S. Boston: Houghton Mifflin, 1923.

1924. Akrigg, George Philip Vere
S and the Earl of Southampton. London: Hamilton, 1969.

1925. Alexander, Peter
See Smart, J. S.

1926. .
S's Life and Art. London:
James Nisbet, 1939; New York
University Press, 1961.

1927. Archer, William (tr.)
See Brandes, George M. C.

1928. Baldwin, T. W.
William S's Small Latine
and Lesse Greeke. 2 v. Urbana:
University of Illinois Press, 1944.

1929. Bentley, Gerald E.
S: A Biographical Handbook. New Haven: Yale University Press, 1961.

1930. Brandes, George M. C.
William S: A Critical
Study, tr. by William Archer.
London: Heinemann, 1902.

1931. Brooke, C. F. Tucker (ed.)
S of Stratford. New Haven:
Yale University Press, 1926.

1932. Brown, Ivor
S. Garden City, N. Y.:
Doubleday, 1949.

1933. Campbell, Oscar James
and Quinn, Edward G. (eds.)
The Reader's Encyclopedia
of S. New York: Thomas Y.
Crowell, 1966.

1934. Chambers, Sir Edmund K.
Shakespearean Gleanings.
Oxford: The Clarendon Press,
1944.

1935. .
William S: A Study of
Facts and Problems. 2 vols.
London: Oxford University
Press, 1930.

1936. .
"William S," Encyclopaedia Britannica. Chicago:
Encyclopaedia Britannica, Inc.,
1929.

1937. Chute, Marchette
S of London. New York:
E. P. Dutton, 1949.

1938. Creighton, Charles
S's Story of His Life.
London: G. Richards, 1904.

1939. De Chambrun, Clara
Longworth
See Pineton, Clara Longworth (Countess de
Chambrun).

1940. De Groot, J. H.
The Shakespeares and
"The Old Faith." New York:
King's Crown Press, 1946.

1941. Eccles, Mark
S in Warwickshire.
Madison: University of Wisconsin Press, 1961.

1942. Eliot, T. S.
See Fluchere, Henri.

1943. Fluchere, Henri
S and the Elizabethans,
tr. by Guy Hamilton, with a
Foreword by T. S. Eliot. New
York: Hill & Wang, 1956.

1944. Fripp, Edgar Innes
S, Man and Artist, 2
vols. London: Oxford University Press, 1938.

1945. .
S's Stratford. London:
Oxford University Press, 1928.

1946. Gray, Arthur
A Chapter in the Early
Life of S. Cambridge, England:
University Press, 1926.

1947. Halliday, Frank Ernest
The Life of S. London:
Gerald Duckworth, 1961.

1948. .
A S Companion 1564-1964.
London: Gerald Duckworth, 1964.

1949. .
S: A Pictorial Biography.
New York: Thomas Y. Crowell,
1956; London: Thames & Hudson,
1956.

1950. Hamilton, Guy (tr.)
See Fluchere, Henri.

1951. Holzknecht, Karl J.
The Backgrounds of S's
Plays. New York: American
Book Co., 1950.

1952. Hotson, Leslie
S vs. Shallow. Boston:
Little Brown, 1931.

1953. .
I, William S, Do Appoint.
New York: Oxford University
Press, 1938.

1954. .
Mr. W. H. London: Rupert
Hart-Davis, 1964.

1955. Keen, A., and Lubbock, R.
The Annotator: the Pursuit
of an Elizabethan Reader of Halle's
"Chronicle" Involving some Sur-
mises About the Early Life of
William S. London: Macmillan,
1954.

1956. Lee, Sir Sidney
A Life of William S. Lon-
don: Smith, Elder, 1915; New
York: Macmillan, 1929.

1957. Lubbock, R.
See Keen, A.

1958. McCurdy, H. G.
The Personality of S.
New Haven: Yale University
Press, 1953.

1959. Pineton, Clara Long-
worth (Countess de
Chambrun)
S Actor-Poet. New York:
D. Appleton, 1927.

1960. Pollard, Alfred William,
et al.
S's Hand in the Play of
"Sir Thomas More." Cam-
bridge, England: University
Press, 1923.

1961. Quennell, Peter
S: A Biography. Cleve-
land: World Publishing, 1963.

1962. Quinn, Edward G. (ed.)
See Campbell, Oscar
James (ed.).

1963. Raleigh, Walter
S (English Men of Let-
ters Series). New York: Macmillan, 1907.

1964. Reese, M. M.
S: His World and His
Work. New York: St. Martin's
Press, 1953.

1965. Rolfe, William James
A Life of William S.
Boston: D. Estes, 1904.

1966. Rowse, Alfred Leslie
William S, A Biography.
New York: Harper & Rowe,
1964.

1967. Sisson, Charles Jasper
The Mythical Sorrows
of S. Oxford: Annual British
Academy Lecture, 1934.

1968. Smart, J. S.
    S: Truth and Tradition.
New ed. with Preface by Peter
Alexander. Oxford: Clarendon
Press, 1966.

1969. Snider, Denton J.
    A Biography of William S.
St. Louis: William Harvey Miner,
1922.

1970. Spencer, Hazelton
    The Art and Life of Wil-
liam S. New York: Harcourt,
Brace, 1940.

1971. Stopes, Mrs. Charlotte
    (Carmichael)
    S's Family. London: E.
Stock, 1901; New York: J. Pott,
1901.

1972. Van Doren, Mark
    S. New York: Doubleday,
1953.

1973. Wallace, C. W.
    S and His London Associ-
ates. Lincoln: University of
Nebraska Press, 1905.

1974. Wilson, John Dover
    The Essential S. Cam-
bridge, England: University Press,
1932.

Chapter Three

BACKGROUND SOURCES

A. Life in Shakespeare's
England

1975. Adams, Joseph Quincy
A Life of William S. Boston: Houghton Mifflin, 1923.

1976. Bentley, Gerald E.
S: A Biographical Handbook. New Haven: Yale University Press, 1901.

1977. Black, J.B.
The Reign of Elizabeth, 1558-1603. London: Oxford University Press, 1936.

1978. Bush, Douglas
S and the Natural Condition. Cambridge, Mass.: Harvard University Press, 1956; London: Oxford University Press, 1956.

1979. Buxton, John
Elizabethan Taste. London: Macmillan, 1963.

1980. Byrne, M. St. Clare
Elizabethan Life in Town and Country. London: Methuen, 1950; New York: Barnes and Noble, 1925 (1961).

1981. Camden, Carroll
The Elizabethan Woman. New York: Elsevier Press, 1953.

1982. Campbell, Mildred
The English Yeoman under Elizabeth and the Early Stuarts. New Haven: Yale University Press, 1942.

1983. Chambers, Sir Edmund K.
William S: A Study of Facts and Problems. 2 vols. London: Oxford University Press, 1930.

1984. Chute, Marchette
S of London. New York: E.P. Dutton, 1949 (1956).

1985. Clemen, Wolfgang H.
The Development of S's Imagery. Cambridge, Mass.: Harvard University Press, 1951.

1986. Craig, Hardin
The Enchanted Glass: The Elizabethan Mind in Literature. New York: Oxford University Press, 1936.

1987. _____.
An Interpretation of S. Columbia, Missouri: Lucas Brothers, 1948.

1988. Cruickshank, C.G.
Elizabeth's Army. Oxford: Clarendon Press, 1946.

1989. Curtis, M.H.
Oxford and Cambridge in Transition, 1558-1642. Oxford: Clarendon Press, 1959.

1990. Dean, Leonard F. (ed.)
S: Modern Essays in Criticism. New York: Oxford University Press, 1957.

1991. Eliot, T.S.
Essays on Elizabethan Drama. New York: Harcourt,

Brace, 1956.

1992. Ferguson, A. B.
The Articulate Citizen and
the English Renaissance. Durham,
N. C.: Duke University Press,
1965.

1993. Fripp, Edgar I.
S's Stratford. New York:
Oxford University Press, 1928.

1994. Froude, J. A.
English Seamen in the
Sixteenth Century. London: Har-
rap, 1925.

1995. Goddard, Harold C.
The Meaning of S. 2 v.
Chicago: University of Chicago
Press, 1950.

1996. Granville-Barker, Harley,
and Harrison, G. B. (eds.)
A Companion to S Studies.
Garden City, N. Y.: Doubleday,
1960.

1997. _____.
Prefaces to S. 2 vols.
Princeton, N. J.: Princeton Uni-
versity Press, 1946.

1998. Harbage, Alfred
As They Like It. New
York: Macmillan, 1947.

1999. Harrison, G. B. (ed.)
See Granville-Barker,
Harley.

2000. _____.
The Elizabethan Journals,
1591-1603. Ann Arbor: University of Michigan Press, 1929
(1955).

2001. _____.
A Jacobean Journal...
1603-1616. London: Macmillan,
1941.

2002. _____.

A Second Jacobean
Journal...1607-1610. Ann
Arbor: University of Michigan
Press, 1958.

2003. Jenkins, Elizabeth
Elizabeth the Great.
New York: Coward-McCann,
1959.

2004. Judges, A. V. (ed.)
The Elizabethan Under-
world. New York: E. P. Dutton, 1930.

2005. Kelso, Ruth
The Doctrine of the Eng-
lish Gentleman in the Sixteenth
Century. Urbana: University
of Illinois Press, 1929.

2006. Lee, Sir Sidney and
Onions, C. T. (eds.)
S's England: An Ac-
count of the Life and Manners
of his Age. 2 v. Oxford:
Clarendon Press, 1916.

2007. Lewis, Clive Staple
English Literature in the
16th Century Excluding Drama.
Oxford: Clarendon Press, 1954.

2008. Leys, M. D. R.
See Mitchell, R. J.

2009. McClure, N. E. (ed.)
The Letters of John
Chamberlain. New York:
American Philosophical Society,
1939.

2010. Meyer, A. O.
England and the Catholic
Church under Queen Elizabeth.
London: Kegan Paul, 1916;
New York: Barnes and Noble,
1967.

2011. Miller, E. H.
The Professional Writer
in Elizabethan England. Cambridge, Mass.: Harvard Uni-

versity Press, 1959.

2012. Mitchell, R. J., and Leys, M. D. R.
A History of London Life. London: Longmans, Green, 1958.

2013. Moulton, Richard Green
S as Dramatic Artist. Oxford: Clarendon Press, 1929.

2014. Nicoll, Allardyce (ed.)
The Elizabethans. London: Cambridge University Press, 1957.

2015. .
S in His Own Age (S Survey 17). Cambridge: University Press, 1964.

2016. Onions, C. T. (ed.)
See Lee, Sir Sidney.

2017. Powell, C. L.
English Domestic Relations, 1487-1653. New York: Columbia University Press, 1917.

2018. Quennell, Peter
S: A Biography. Cleveland: World Publishing Co., 1963.

2019. Raleigh, Sir Walter, et al. (eds.)
S's England: An Account of the Life and Manners of His Age. 2 vols. Oxford: Oxford University Press, 1917 (1919).

2020. Ridler, Anne Bradby (ed.)
S Criticism, 1935-1960. New York: Oxford University Press, 1963.

2021. Rowse, Alfred Leslie
William S: A Biography. New York: Harper & Rowe, 1964.

2022. Sanders, Gerald De Witt
A S Primer. New York: Rinehart, 1950.

2023. S's England: An Account of the Life and Manners of His Age. 2 vols. Oxford: Clarendon Press, 1916.

2024. Smith, D. Nichol (ed.)
S Criticism. New York: Oxford University Press, 1916.

2025. Spencer, Hazelton
The Art and Life of William S. New York: Harcourt, Brace, 1940.

2026. Spencer, Theodore
S and the Nature of Man. New York: Macmillan, 1942.

2027. Steeholm, Cara and Hardy
James I of England. New York: Covici, 1938.

2028. Stevens, John
Music and Poetry in the Early Tudor Court. Lincoln: University of Nebraska Press, 1961.

2029. Stow, John
A Survey of London. London: Oxford University Press, 1908. New York: Dutton, 1956.

2030. Stowe, A. R. M.
English Grammar Schools in the Reign of Queen Elizabeth. New York: Columbia University Press, 1908.

2031. Stroll, Elmer Edgar
S and Other Masters. Cambridge, Mass.: Harvard University Press, 1940; London: Oxford University Press, 1940.

2032. Tillyard, E. M. W.
The Elizabethan World Picture. New York: Macmillan, 1944; London: Chatto & Windus, 1943.

117

2033. Traversi, D. A.
An Approach to S. Rev.
ed. New York: Doubleday, 1956.

2034. Trevelyan, G. M.
History of England. Vol.
II: The Tudors and the Stuart
Era. London: Longmans, Green,
1945 (1952).

2035. Unwin, G.
The Gilds and Companies
of London. London: Methuen,
1908.

2036. Van Doren, Mark
S. New York: Henry Holt,
1939; New York: Doubleday,
1953.

2037. Whitaker, Virgil K.
S's Use of Learning. San
Marino, Calif.: Huntington Li-
brary, 1953.

2038. Wilson, F. P.
The Plague in S's London.
Oxford: Clarendon Press, 1927.

2039. Wilson, John Dover (ed.)
Life in S's England. Cam-
bridge: University Press, 1911.

2040. _____ (ed.)
Life in S's England. 2nd
ed. New York: Macmillan, 1913.

2041. Wright, L. B.
Middle-Class Culture in
Elizabethan England. Chapel
Hill: University of North Caroli-
na Press, 1935.

2042. _____.
S for Everyman. New
York: Washington Square Press,
1964.

2043. Zilboorg, Gregory
The Medical Man and the
Witch during the Renaissance.
Baltimore: Johns Hopkins Univer-
sity Press, 1935.

B. English Renaissance

2044. Allen, J. A.
A History of Political
Thought in the Sixteenth Cen-
tury. London: Methuen, 1928.

2045. Allen, J. W.
English Political Thought,
1603-60. London: Methuen,
1938.

2046. Alston, L. (tr.) (ed.)
See Smith, Sir Thomas.

2047. Baker, Herschel
The Image of Man: A
Study of the Idea of Human
Dignity in Classical Antiquity,
the Middle Ages and the Ren-
aissance. Cambridge, Mass.:
Harvard University Press, 1947.

2048. _____.
The Wars of Truth:
Studies in the Decay of Christian Humanism in the Earlier
Seventeenth Century. Cam-
bridge, Mass.: Harvard University Press, 1952.

2049. Baumer, F. L.
The Early Tudor Theory
of Kingship. New Haven: Yale
University Press, 1940.

2050. Bindoff, S. T.
Tudor England. Balti-
more: Penguin Books, 1950.

2051. Black, J. B.
The Reign of Elizabeth,
1558-1603. Oxford: Clarendon
Press, 1936.

2052. Briggs, K. M.
The Anatomy of Puck:
An Examination of Fairy Beliefs Among S's Contemporaries
and Successors. London: Routledge and Kegan Paul, 1959.

2053. _____.

Pale Hecate's Team: An
Examination of the Beliefs on
Witchcraft and Magic Among S's
Contemporaries and His Immediate
Successors. London: Routledge
and Kegan Paul, 1962.

2054. Buckley, G. T.
Atheism in the English
Renaissance. Chicago: Univer-
sity of Chicago Press, 1932.

2055. Bush, Douglas
The Renaissance and Eng-
lish Humanism. Toronto: University of Toronto Press, 1939.

2056. ____.
Prefaces to Renaissance
Literature. Cambridge, Mass.:
Harvard University Press, 1966.

2057. Butterfield, Herbert
The Origins of Modern
Science. Rev. ed. New York:
Macmillan, 1959.

2058. Caspari, Fritz
Humanism and the Social
Order in Tudor England. Chicago:
University of Chicago Press, 1954.

2059. Cassirer, Ernst
The Platonic Renaissance
in England. Austin: University
of Texas Press, 1953.

2060. Cheyney, E. P.
A History of England from
the Defeat of the Armada to the
Death of Elizabeth. 2v. London:
Longmans, Green, 1914-26.

2061. Craig, Hardin
The Enchanted Glass: The
Elizabethan Mind in Literature.
New York: Oxford University
Press, 1936.

2062. Danby, J. F.
S's Doctrine of Nature.
London: Faber and Faber, 1949.

2063. Einstein, Lewis

The Italian Renaissance
in England. New York: Co-
lumbia University Press, 1907.

2064. ____.
Tudor Ideals. New York:
Harcourt, Brace, 1921.

2065. Elton, G. R.
The Tudor Revolution in
Government. Cambridge: Uni-
versity Press, 1953.

2066. ____.
England Under the Tudors.
London: Methuen, 1955.

2067. Figgis, J. N.
The Divine Right of
Kings. Cambridge: University
Press, 1922.

2068. Garret, C. H.
The Marian Exiles: A
Study in the Origins of Eliza-
bethan Puritanism. Cambridge:
University Press, 1938.

2069. Haller, William
The Rise of Puritanism,
1570-1642. New York: Co-
lumbia University Press, 1938.

2070. Haydn, Hiram
The Counter-Renaissance.
New York: Charles Scribner,
1950.

2071. Helton, Tinsley (ed.)
The Renaissance: A
Reconsideration of the Theories
and Interpretations of the Age.
Madison: University of Wis-
consin Press, 1961.

2072. Hoopes, Robert
Right Reason in the Eng-
lish Renaissance. Cambridge,
Mass.: Harvard University
Press, 1962.

2073. Hughes, Philip
The Reformation in Eng-
land. 3 vols. London: Hollis

and Carter, 1950-4.

2074. Huizinga, J.
The Waning of the Middle
Ages. Baltimore: Penguin
Books, 1955.

2075. Kittredge, George Lyman
Witchcraft in Old and New
England. Cambridge, Mass.:
Harvard University Press, 1928.

2076. Knappen, M. M.
Tudor Puritanism. Chi-
cago: University of Chicago
Press, 1939.

2077. Knights, Lionel Charles
Drama and Society in the
Age of Jonson. London: Chatto
and Windus, 1937.

2078. Kocher, P. H.
Science and Religion in
Elizabethan England. San Marino:
Huntington Library, 1953.

2079. Latham, M. W.
The Elizabethan Fairies.
New York: Columbia University
Press, 1930.

2080. Lewis, Clive Staple
The Discarded Image: An
Introduction to Medieval and Ren-
aissance Literature. Cambridge:
University Press, 1964.

2081. Lovejoy, A. O.
The Great Chain of Being.
Cambridge, Mass.: Harvard Uni-
versity Press, 1936.

2082. Mazzeo, J. A.
Renaissance and Revolution:
Backgrounds to Seventeenth-Cen-
tury Literature. New York:
Pantheon Books, 1965.

2083. Morris, C.
Political Thought in Eng-
land: Tyndale to Hooker. London: Oxford University Press,
1953.

2084. Murray, R. H.
The Political Conse-
quences of the Reformation:
Studies in Sixteenth Century
Political Thought. London:
Ernest Benn, 1926.

2085. Neale, J. E.
Queen Elizabeth I: A Biography.
London: Jonathan Cape, 1934.

2086. .
The Elizabethan House
of Commons. New Haven:
Yale University Press, 1949.

2087. .
Elizabeth I and Her
Parliaments. 2v. London:
Jonathan Cape, 1953-7.

2088. Pearson, A. F. S.
Church and State: Po-
litical Aspects of 16th Century
Puritanism. Cambridge: University Press, 1928.

2089. Penrose, Boies
Travel and Discovery in
the Renaissance, 1420-1620.
Cambridge, Mass.: Harvard
University Press, 1955.

2090. Pollen, J. H.
The English Catholics in
the Reign of Elizabeth. London: Longmans, Green, 1920.

2091. Powicke, F. M.
The Reformation in Eng-
land. London: Oxford University Press, 1941.

2092. Raab, Felix
The English Face of
Machiavelli. London: Routledge
and Kegan Paul, 1964.

2093. Read, C. J.
Mr. Secretary Walsing-
ham and the Policy of Queen
Elizabeth. 3v. Oxford:
Clarendon Press, 1925.

2094. _____.
The Tudors: Personalities and Politics in Sixteenth Century England. New York: Henry Holt, 1936.

2095. _____.
Mr. Secretary Cecil and Queen Elizabeth. New York: Alfred Knopf, 1955.

2096. Rice, E. F., Jr.
The Renaissance Idea of Wisdom. Cambridge, Mass.: Harvard University Press, 1958.

2097. Rowse, Alfred Leslie
The England of Elizabeth: The Structure of Society. London: Macmillan, 1951.

2098. Sellery, G. C.
The Renaissance: Its Nature and Origins. Madison: University of Wisconsin Press, 1950.

2099. Smith, Sir Thomas
De Republica Anglorum. Eng. tr. ed., L. Alston. Cambridge: University Press, 1906.

2100. Spencer, Theodore
S and the Nature of Man. New York: Macmillan, 1942.

2101. Tawney, R. H.
Religion and the Rise of Capitalism. New York: Harcourt, Brace, 1926.

2102. Tayler, E. W.
Nature and Art in Renaissance Literature. New York: Columbia University Press, 1964.

2103. Taylor, Henry Osborn
Thought and Expression in the Sixteenth Century. 2v. New York: Macmillan, 1920.

2104. Tillyard, E. M. W.
The Elizabethan World Picture. London: Chatto and Windus, 1943.

2105. Watson, Curtis Brown
S and the Renaissance Concept of Honor. Princeton: Princeton University Press, 1960.

2106. Wilson, F. P.
Elizabethan and Jacobean. Oxford: Clarendon Press, 1945.

2107. Zeeveld, W. G.
Foundations of Tudor Policy. Cambridge, Mass.: Harvard University Press, 1948.

C. Pre-Shakespearean Drama

2108. Adams, H. H.
English Domestic or Homiletic Tragedy 1575-1642. New York: Columbia University Press, 1943.

2109. Baker, Howard
Induction to Tragedy. Baton Rouge: Louisiana State University Press, 1939.

2110. Baskervill, C. R.
The Elizabethan Jig and Related Song Drama. Chicago: University of Chicago Press, 1929.

2111. Bevington, D. M.
From Mankind to Marlowe: Growth of Structure in the Popular Drama of Tudor England. Cambridge, Mass.: Harvard University Press, 1962.

2112. Boas, F. S.
University Drama in the Tudor Age. Oxford: The Clarendon Press, 1914.

2113. _____.
An Introduction to Tudor Drama. Oxford: The Clarendon Press, 1933.

2114. Bowers, Fredson
Elizabethan Revenge Tragedy: 1587-1642. Princeton: Princeton University Press, 1940.

2115. Bradbrook, M. C.
Themes and Conventions of Elizabethan Tragedy. Cambridge: University Press, 1935.

2116. ___ .
The Growth and Structure of Elizabethan Comedy. London: Chatto and Windus, 1955.

2117. Brooke, C. F. Tucker
The Tudor Drama. Boston: Houghton Mifflin, 1911.

2118. Campbell, Lily B.
Divine Poetry and Drama in Sixteenth Century England. Cambridge: University Press, 1959.

2119. Chambers, Sir Edmund K.
The Medieval Stage. 2v. Oxford: Clarendon Press, 1903.

2120. ___ .
The Elizabethan Stage. 4v. Oxford: Clarendon Press, 1923.

2121. ___ .
The English Folk-Play. Oxford: Clarendon Press, 1933.

2122. Charlton, H. B.
The Senecan Tradition in Renaissance Tragedy. Manchester: University of Manchester Press, 1946.

2123. Clemen, Wolfgang
English Tragedy Before S: The Development of Dramatic Speech. Tr. by T. S. Dorsch. London: Methuen, 1961.

2124. Craig, Hardin
English Religious Drama of the Middle Ages. Oxford:

Clarendon Press, 1955.

2125. Cunliffe, J. W.
The Influence of Seneca on Elizabethan Tragedy. London: Macmillan, 1893.

2126. ___ (ed.)
Early English Classical Tragedies. Oxford: Clarendon Press, 1912.

2127. Dixon, W. M.
Tragedy. London: Edward Arnold, 1924.

2128. Doran, Madeleine
Endeavors of Art: A Study of Form in Elizabethan Drama. Madison: University of Wisconsin Press, 1954.

2129. Dorsch, T. S. (tr.)
See Clemen, Wolfgang.

2130. Farnham, Willard
The Medieval Heritage of Elizabethan Tragedy. Berkeley: University of California Press, 1936.

2131. Foakes, R. A. and Richert, R. T. (eds.)
Henslowe's Diary. Cambridge: University Press, 1961.

2132. Gardiner, H. C.
Mysteries End: The Last Days of the Medieval Stage. New Haven: Yale University Press, 1946.

2133. Green, A. Wigfall
The Inns of Court and Early English Drama. New Haven: Yale University Press, 1931.

2134. Greg, W. W.
A Bibliography of the English Printed Drama to the Restoration. 4v. London: The Bibliographical Society,

1939-59.

2135. _____.
Pastoral Poetry and Pas-
toral Drama. London: A.H.
Bullen, 1906; New York: Russell
and Russell, 1959.

2136. Harbage, Alfred
Annals of English Drama,
975-1700. Rev. by S. Schoen-
baum. London: Methuen, 1964.

2137. Hardison, O.G., Jr.
Christian Rite and Chris-
tian Drama in the Middle Ages:
Essays in the Origin and Early
History of Modern Drama. Bal-
timore: Johns Hopkins University
Press, 1965.

2138. Hogrefe, Pearl
The Sir Thomas More
Circle: A Program of Ideas and
Their Impact on Secular Drama.
Urbana: University of Illinois
Press, 1959.

2139. Kolve, V.A.
The Play Called Corpus
Christi. Palo Alto: Stanford
University Press, 1966.

2140. Lea, K.M.
Italian Popular Comedy.
2v. Oxford: Clarendon Press,
1934.

2141. Lucas, F.L.
Seneca and Elizabethan
Tragedy. Cambridge: University
Press, 1922.

2142. Mackenzie, W.R.
The English Moralities from
the Point of View of Allegory.
Boston: Houghton Mifflin, 1914.

2143. Margeson, J.M.R.
The Origins of English
Tragedy. Oxford: Clarendon
Press, 1968.

2144. Motter, T.H.V.
The School Drama in
England. London: Longmans,
Green, 1929.

2145. Owst, G.R.
Literature and Pulpit in
Medieval England. Rev. ed.
New York: Barnes and Noble,
1961.

2146. Pettet, E.C.
S and the Romance Tra-
dition. London: Staples Press,
1949.

2147. Prosser, Eleanor
Drama and Religion in
the English Mystery Plays: A
Re-evaluation. Palo Alto:
Stanford University Press, 1961.

2148. Reed, A.W.
Early Tudor Drama.
London: Methuen, 1926.

2149. Ribner, Irving
The English History
Play in the Age of S. Rev.
ed. London: Methuen, 1965.

2150. Rickert, R.T. (ed.)
See Foakes, R.A.

2151. Rossiter, A.P.
English Drama from
Early Times to the Elizabethans:
Its Background, Origins, and
Developments. London: Hutch-
inson's University Library,
1950.

2152. Salter, F.M.
Medieval Drama in
Chester. Toronto: University
of Toronto Press, 1955.

2153. Spivack, Bernard
S and the Allegory of
Evil. New York: Columbia
University Press, 1958.

2154. Talbert, E.W.

123

Elizabethan Drama and S's
Early Plays. Chapel Hill: University of North Carolina Press, 1963.

2155. Thompson, E. N. S.
The English Moral Play.
New Haven: Connecticut Academy of Arts and Letters, 1910.

2156. Thorndike, A. H.
English Comedy. New York: Macmillan, 1929.

2157. Tiddy, R. J. E.
The Mummer's Play. Oxford: Clarendon Press, 1923.

2158. Welsford, Enid
The Court Masque. Cambridge: University Press, 1927.

2159. Young, Karl
The Drama of the Medieval Church. 2v. Oxford: The Clarendon Press, 1933.

D. Shakespeare In The Theatre

2160. Adams, John Cranford
The Globe Playhouse: Its Design and Equipment. Cambridge, Mass.: Harvard University Press, 1942; New York: Barnes & Nobles, 1961.

2161. Adams, Joseph Quincy
Shakespearean Playhouses: A History of English Theatres from the Beginnings to the Restoration. Boston: Houghton Mifflin, 1917.

2162. Armstrong, W. A.
"Actors and Theatres,"
SS, 17. Cambridge: University Press, 1964. p. 191-204.

2163. _____ .
"The Art of Shakespearean Production in the Twentieth Century," Essays and Studies, 15 (1962), 74-87.

2164. Baldwin, T. W.
The Organization and Personnel of the Shakespearean Company. Princeton: Princeton University Press, 1927 (1929).

2165. _____ .
Organization and Personnel of the Shakespearean Company. Princeton University Press, 1927.

2166. Beckerman, Bernard
S at the Globe, 1559-1609. New York: Macmillan, 1962.

2167. Bentley, Gerald Eades
The Jacobean and Caroline Stage. 5 vols. Oxford: Clarendon Press, 1941-56.

2168. _____ .
"S and the Blackfriars Theatre," SS, 1 (1948), 38-50.

2169. _____ .
S and His Theatre. Lincoln: University of Nebraska Press, 1964.

2170. Bradbrook, M. C.
The Rise of the Common Player: A Study of Actor and Society in S's England. London: Chatto and Windus, 1964.

2171. Bradley, Andrew Cecil
Shakespearean Tragedy. London: Macmillan, 1929 (1955).

2172. Branam, George Curtis
Eighteenth-Century Adaptations of S's Tragedies. Berkeley: University of California Press, 1956.

2173. Brown, John Russell
"On the Acting of S's Plays," Quarterly Journal of Speech, 39 (1953), 474-85.

124

2174. _____.
S's Plays in Performance.
New York: St. Martin's Press,
1967.

2175. Campbell, Lily Bess
Scenes and Machines in the
English Stage during the Renais-
sance. Cambridge: University
Press, 1923.

2176. Chambers, Sir Edmund K.
The Elizabethan Stage. 4
vols. New York: Oxford University Press, 1924.

2177. _____.
William S: A Study of
Facts and Problems. Oxford:
1930.

2178. Cowling, G. H.
Music on the Shakespearian
Stage. Cambridge: The Univer-
sity Press, 1913.

2179. Craik, T. W.
The Tudor Interlude.
Leicester: University of Leicester
Press, 1958.

2180. Dean, Winton
"S in the Opera House,"
SS, 18. Cambridge: University
Press, 1965. p. 75-93.

2181. De Banke, Cecile
Shakespearean Stage Produc-
tion, Then and Now. A Manual
For the Scholar Player. New
York: McGraw-Hill, 1953.

2182. Deelman, Christian
The Great S Jubilee. New
York: Viking Press, 1964.

2183. Downer, Alan S.
The Eminent Tragedian,
William Charles Macready. Cambridge, Mass.: Harvard University Press, 1966.

2184. Dunn, Esther Cloudman
S in America. New
York: Macmillan, 1939.

2185. England, M. W.
Garrick's Jubilee.
Columbus: Ohio State Univer-
sity Press, 1964.

2186. Farnham, Willard
The Medieval Heritage
of Elizabethan Tragedy. Berkeley: University of California
Press, 1936.

2187. Foakes, R. A.
"The Player's Passion:
Some Notes on Elizabethan
Psychology and Acting," Essays
and Studies Collected for the
English Association, 7 (1954),
62-77.

2188. Gildersleeve, V. C.
Government Regulation
of the Elizabethan Drama.
New York: Columbia University Press, 1908.

2189. Glick, Claris
"William Poel: His
Theories and Influence," SQ,
15 (1964), 15-25.

2190. Greg, W. W.
Dramatic Documents
from the Elizabethan Playhouses. 2 vols. Oxford University Press, 1931.

2191. _____ (ed.)
Henslowe's Diary and
Henslowe's Papers. London:
Bullen, 1904-1908.

2192. Harbage, Alfred
S's Audience. New
York: Columbia University
Press, 1941.

2193. _____.
A Theatre for S. To-
ronto: University of Toronto
Press, 1955.

2194. _____ .
"Elizabethan Acting,"
PMLA, 54 (1939), 685-708.

2195. _____ .
S's Audience. New York:
Columbia University Press, 1941.

2196. Harrison, G. B.
Elizabethan Plays and
Players. Ann Arbor: University
of Michigan Press, 1940 (1956).

2197. Henslowe's Diary (2 vols.)
and Henslowe's Papers (1 vol.)
ed. by W. W. Greg. London:
Bullen, 1904-1908.

2198. Henslowe, Philip
See Henslowe's Diary.
Greg, W. W. (ed.)

2199. Hillebrand, H. N.
The Child Actors. Urbana:
University of Illinois Press, 1926.

2200. Hodges, C. Walter
The Globe Restored: A
Study of the Elizabethan Theatre.
New York: Coward-McCann, 1954.

2201. _____ .
The Globe Restored. Lon-
don: Ernest Benn, 1953; New
York: Coward-McCann, 1954.

2202. Hogan, Charles Beecher
S in the Theatre, 1701-
1800. 2v. Oxford: Clarendon
Press, 1952-57.

2203. Hosley, Richard
"An Approach to the Eliz-
abethan Stage," Renaissance
Drama, 6 (1963), 71-8.

2204. _____ .
"The Origins of the Shakespearian Playhouse," SQ, 15
(1964), 29-39.

2205. _____ .
"The Origins of the So-

called Elizabethan Multiple
Stage," Theatre and Drama Review, 12 (1968), 28-50.

2207. Hotson, Leslie
S's Wooden O. London:
Rupert Hart-Davis, 1959.

2208. Joseph, B. L.
Acting S. New York:
Theatre Arts Books, 1960.

2209. _____ .
Elizabethan Acting.
Rev. ed. Oxford: Clarendon
Press, 1964.

2210. _____ .
The Tragic Actor. Lon-
don: Routledge and Kegan Paul,
1959.

2211. Kernodle, G. R.
From Art to Theatre:
Form and Convention in the
Renaissance. Chicago: Univer-
sity of Chicago Press, 1944.

2212. Kitchin, Laurence
Drama in the Sixties:
Form and Interpretation. Lon-
don: Faber and Faber, 1966.

2213. _____ .
"S on the Screen," SS,
18 (1965), 70-74.

2214. Knight, George Wilson
Shakespearian Production,
with Especial Reference to the
Tragedies. London: Methuen,
1964.

2215. Lawrence, W. J.
The Elizabethan Play-
house and Other Studies. Stratford-upon-Avon: S Head Press,
1912; New York: Russell &
Russell, 1963.

2216. _____ .
Pre-Restoration Stage
Studies. Cambridge, Mass.:

Harvard University Press, 1927.

2217. _____ .
The Physical Conditions of
the Elizabethan Public Playhouse.
Cambridge, Mass.: Harvard University Press, 1927.

2218. _____ .
Speeding Up S. London:
Argonaut Press, 1937.

2219. _____ .
Those Nut-Cracking Elizabethans. London: Argonaut
Press, 1935.

2220. Linthicum, M. C.
Costume in the Drama of
S and His Contemporaries. Oxford: Clarendon Press, 1936.

2221. Manheim, Ralph (tr.)
See Nagler, A. M.

2222. Marder, Louis
His Exits and His Entrances:
The Story of S's Reputation. Philadelphia: Lippincott, 1963.

2223. Murray, J. T.
English Dramatic Companies, 1558-1642. Boston: Houghton Mifflin, 1910.

2224. Nagler, A. M.
S's Stage. New Haven:
Yale University Press, 1958.

2225. _____ .
S's Stage. tr. by Ralph
Manheim. New Haven: Yale
University Press, 1958.

2226. Naylor, Edward W.
S and Music. New York:
Dutton, 1896 (1931).

2227. Nicoll, Allardyce
Masques, Mimes and Miracles. London: Harrap, 1931.

2228. _____ .

Stuart Masques and the
Renaissance Stage. London:
Harrap, 1937.

2229. _____ .
"Studies in the Elizabethan Stage Since 1900," SS, 1
(1948), 1-17.

2230. _____ .
The World of Harlequin.
Cambridge: University Press,
1963.

2231. Noble, Richmond
S's Use of Song. Oxford University Press, 1923.

2232. Nungezer, Edwin
A Dictionary of Actors
and Other Persons Associated
with the Public Representation
of Plays in England Before
1642. New Haven: Yale University Press, 1929.

2233. Odell, George C. D.
S from Betterton to
Irving. 2 vols. New York:
Scribner's, 1920 (1931); New
York: Dover, 1966.

2234. Poel, William
S in the Theatre. London: Sidgwick and Jackson,
1913.

2235. Reynolds, G. F.
The Staging of Elizabethan Plays at the Red Bull
Theater, 1605-1625. New York:
MLA, 1940.

2236. Rosenberg, Marvin
"Elizabethan Actors:
Men or Marionettes," PMLA,
69 (1954), 915-27.

2237. Saunders, J. W.
"Staging at the Globe,
1599-1613," SQ, 11 (1960),
401-25.

2238. Seltzer, Daniel
"The Staging of the Last
Plays," The Later S (Stratford-
on-Avon Studies No. 8). London:
Edward Arnold, 1966. p. 127-66.

2239. Sharpe, R. B.
The Real War of the The-
atres. Boston: Heath, 1935.

2240. Shattuck, C. H.
The S Promptbooks.
Urbana: University of Illinois
Press, 1965.

2241. Shirley, F. A.
S's Use of Off-Stage
Sounds. Lincoln: University of
Nebraska Press, 1963.

2242. Smith, Irwin
S's Blackfriars Playhouse.
New York: New York University
Press, 1965.

2243. .
S's Globe Playhouse: A
Modern Reconstruction in Text and
Scale Drawings. New York:
Charles Scribner's, 1957.

2244. Southern, Richard
The Medieval Theatre in
the Round. London: Faber and
Faber, 1957.

2245. .
The Open Stage. New
York: Theatre Arts Books, 1959.

2246. Speaight, William
William Poel and the Eliz-
abethan Revival. Cambridge:
The University Press, 1954.

2247. Spencer, Hazelton
S Improved: The Restora-
tion Versions in Quarto and on the
Stage. Cambridge, Mass.: Harvard University Press, 1927.

2248. Sprague, Arthur Colby
The Doubling of Parts in

S's Plays. London: Society
for Theatre Research, 1966.

2249. .
S and the Actors: The
Stage Business in His Plays
(1660-1905). Cambridge, Mass.:
Harvard University Press, 1944.

2250. .
Shakespearian Players
and Performances. Cambridge,
Mass.: Harvard University
Press, 1953.

2251. Steele, Mary S.
Plays and Masques at
Court During the Reigns of
Elizabeth, James, and Charles.
New Haven: Yale University
Press, 1926.

2252. Stockholm, J. M.
Garrick's Folly. Lon-
don: Methuen, 1964.

2253. Thaler, Alwin
S to Sheridan: A Book
About the Theatre of Yesterday
and Today. Cambridge, Mass.:
Harvard University Press,
1922.

2254. Thompson, E. N. S.
The Controversy Between
the Puritans and the Stage.
New Haven: Yale University
Press, 1903.

2255. Thorndike, A. H.
S's Theatre. New York:
Macmillan, 1916.

2256. Trewin, J. C.
S on the English Stage,
1900-1964. London: Barrie
and Rockliff, 1964.

2257. Venezky, Alice S.
Pageantry on the Shake-
spearean Stage. New York:
Twayne Publishers, 1951.

2258. Wallace, C.W.
The Children of the Chapel
at Blackfriars, 1597-1603. Lincoln: University of Nebraska
Press, 1908.

2259. Watkins, Ronald
On Producing S. London:
M. Joseph, 1950. New York:
Norton, 1950.

2260. Watson, Ernest Bradlee
Sheridan to Robertson: A
Study of the 19th Century London
Stage. Cambridge, Mass.: Harvard University Press, 1926.

2261. Webster, Margaret
S Today. London: J.M.
Dent, 1957.

2262. .
S without Tears. New
York: McGraw Hill, 1942.
Cleveland: World Pub. Co., 1955
(1957).

2263. Welsford, Enid
The Court Masque; A Study
in the Relationship Between Poetry
& the Rebels. Cambridge: University Press, 1927.

2264. Wickham, Glynne
Early English Stages, 1300
to 1660. 2v. New York: Columbia University Press, 1959-60.

2265. Wilson, Harold S.
On the Design of Shakespearian Tragedy. Toronto: University of Toronto Press, 1957.

2266. Withington, Robert
English Pageantry: An
Historical Outline. 2v. Cambridge, Mass.: Harvard University Press, 1918-20.

2267. Yates, Frances A.
The Art of Memory. London: Routledge and Kegan Paul,
1966.

E. Shakespeare's Drama

(1) Comedies

2268. Barber, Cesar Lombardi
S's Festive Comedy.
Princeton: Princeton University Press, 1959.

2269. Bonazza, Blaze O.
S's Early Comedies: A
Structural Analysis. The Hague,
Netherlands: Mouton, 1966.

2270. Bradbrook, Muriel C.
The Growth and Structure
of Elizabethan Comedy. Berkeley: University of California
Press, 1956.

2271. Brown, John Russell
S and His Comedies.
London: Methuen, 1957.

2272. Chambers, Sir Edmund
K.
S: A Survey. London:
Sidgwick & Jackson, 1925
(1935; 1958).

2273. Charlton, Henry Buckley
Shakespearean Comedy:
The Consummation. London:
John Rylands Library, 1937
[Reprinted from the Bulletin of
the John Rylands Library]. 4th
ed., 1949.

2274. Evans, Bertrand
S's Comedies. Oxford:
Clarendon Press, 1960.

2275. Frye, Northrop
A Natural Perspective:
the Development of Shakespearean Comedy and Romance. New
York: Columbia University
Press, 1965.

2276. Gordon, George
Shakespearian Comedy
and Other Studies. London:
Oxford University Press, 1944.

2277. Granville-Barker, Harley
Prefaces to S. 5 vols.
London: Sidgwick & Jackson,
1927-1948; 1958.

2278. Harbage, Alfred
William S: A Reader's
Guide. New York: Farrar,
Straus, 1963.

2279. Hunter, G. K.
William S: The Late
Comedies. London: Longmans,
Green, 1962 [MND, Much Ado,
AYLI, TN].

2280. Hunter, Robert G.
S and the Comedy of For-
giveness. New York: Columbia
University Press, 1965.

2281. Lawrence, W. W.
S's Problem Comedies.
New York: Macmillan, 1931.

2282. Meader, William G.
Courtship in S. New York:
King's Crown Press, Columbia
University, 1954.

2283. Muir, Kenneth
S's Sources: Comedies
and Tragedies. London: Methuen,
1957.

2284. Palmer, John
Political & Comic Charac-
ters of S. London: Macmillan,
1964.

2285. Parrott, Thomas M.
Shakespearean Comedy.
New York: Oxford University
Press, 1949.

2286. Pettet, Ernest C.
S and the Romance Tradi-
tion. London & New York: Staples Press, 1949.

2287. Phialas, Peter G.
S's Romantic Comedies:
The Development of Their Form

and Meaning. Chapel Hill:
University of North Carolina
Press, 1966.

2288. Reese, M. M.
The Cease of Majesty;
A Study of S's History Plays.
London: E. Arnold, 1961.

2289. Sen Gupta, S. C.
Shakespearian Comedy.
Calcutta: Oxford University
Press, 1950.

2290. Stoll, Elmer Edgar
S's Young Lovers. Lon-
don: Oxford University Press,
1937.

2291. Tillyard, E. M. W.
The Nature of Comedy
and S. London: Oxford University Press, 1958.

2292. .
S's Early Comedies.
London: Chatto and Windus,
1966.

2293. Traversi, Derek
William S: The Early
Comedies. London: Longmans,
Green, 1960.

2294. Wilson, John Dover
S's Happy Comedies.
Evanston, Illinois: Northwest-
ern University Press, 1962.

(2) Histories

2295. Campbell, Lily Bess
S's "Histories"; Mirrors
of Elizabethan Policy. San
Marino, California: Huntington
Library, 1947.

2296. Jenkins, Harold
"S's History Plays:
1900-1951," S Survey, 6 (1953),
1-15.

2297. Jorgensen, Paul A.

S's Military World. Berkeley: University of California Press, 1956.

2298. Knights, Lionel Charles
William S, the Histories: Richard III, King John, Richard II, Henry V. London: Longmans, Green, 1962.

2299. Leech, Clifford
William S, The Chronicles. London: Longmans, Green, 1962.

2300. Marriott, Sir John A. R.
English History in S. London: Chapman & Hall, 1918.

2301. Maxwell, J. C.
"S's Roman Plays, 1900-1956," S Survey, 10 (1957), 1-11.

2302. Palmer, John
Political Characters of S. London: Macmillan, 1945 (1961).

2303. Reese, Max Meredith
The Cease of Majesty: A Study of S's History Plays. London: Arnold, 1961; New York: St. Martin's Press, 1962.

2304. Ribner, Irving
The English History Play in the Age of S. Princeton: Princeton University Press, 1947.

2305. Schelling, Felix E.
The English Chronicle Play; A Study in the Popular Historical Literature Environing S. New York: Macmillan, 1902.

2306. Sen Gupta, Subodh Chandra
S's Historical Plays. London: University Press, 1964.

2307. Sprague, Arthur Colby
S's Histories: Plays for the Stage. London: Society for Theatre Research, 1964.

2308. Talbert, Ernest W.

The Problem of Order: Elizabethan Political Commonplaces and An Example of S's Art. Chapel Hill: University of North Carolina Press, 1962.

2309. Tillyard, Eustace M. W.
S's History Plays. London: Chatto & Windus, 1948.

2310. Traversi, Derek Antona
S from Richard II to Henry V. Stanford, California: Stanford University Press, 1957.

2311. Wilson, Frank P.
Marlowe and the Early S. Oxford: Clarendon Press, 1953.

(3) Problem Plays

2312. Campbell, Oscar James
Comicall Satyre and S's Troilus and Cressida. San Marino: Huntington Library, 1938.

2313. Lawrence, William W.
S's Problem Comedies. New York: Macmillan, 1931.

2314. Ornstein, Robert (ed.)
Discussions of S's Problem Comedies. Boston: Heath, 1961.

2315. Schanzer, Ernest
The Problem Plays of S; a Study of Julius Caesar, Measure for Measure, Antony and Cleopatra. New York: Schocken, 1963.

2316. Tillyard, Eustace M. W.
S's Problem Plays. Toronto: University of Toronto Press, 1949; London: Chatto & Windus, 1950.

2317. Toole, William B.
S's Three Problem Plays; Studies in Form and

131

Meaning. The Hague, Netherlands: Mouton, 1966.

2318. Ure, Peter
William S: The Problem
Plays. London: Longmans,
Green, 1961.

(4) Tragedies

2319. Bowers, Fredson T.
Elizabethan Revenge Trag-
edy, 1587-1642. Princeton, N.J.:
Princeton University Press, 1940.

2320. Bradley, Andrew C.
Shakespearean Tragedy;
Lectures on Hamlet, Othello,
King Lear, Macbeth. London:
Macmillan, 1904.

2321. Bush, Geoffrey
S and the Natural Condi-
tion. Cambridge: Harvard University Press, 1956.

2322. Campbell, Lily Bess
S's Tragic Heroes: Slaves
of Passion. Cambridge: University Press, 1930.

2323. Charlton, Henry Buckley
Shakespearian Tragedy.
Cambridge: University Press,
1948.

2324.   .
S's Tragic Frontier: The
World of His Final Tragedies.
Berkeley: U. of California Press,
1950.

2325. Farnham, Willard
The Medieval Heritage of
Elizabethan Tragedy. Berkeley:
University of California Press,
1936.

2326.   .
S's Tragic Frontier; The
World of His Final Tragedies.
Berkeley: University of Califor-
nia Press, 1950.

2327. Frye, Northrop
Fools of Time: Studies
in Shakespearian Tragedy. Toronto: University of Toronto
Press, 1967.

2328. Harbage, Alfred (ed.)
S: The Tragedies; a
Collection of Critical Essays.
Englewood Cliffs, N.J.:
Prentice-Hall, 1964.

2329. Hawkes, Terence
S and the Reason; a
Study of the Tragedies and the
Problem Plays. London:
Routledge & Paul, 1964.

2330. Holloway, John
The Story of the Night:
Studies in S's Major Tragedies.
London: Routledge & Paul,
1961.

2331. Knight, George Wilson
The Wheel of Fire; In-
terpretations of Shakespearian
Tragedy, with Three New Essays. London: Methuen, 1954
(1957).

2332. Lawlor, John
The Tragic Sense in S.
New York: Harcourt, Brace,
1960.

2333. Leech, Clifford (ed.)
S: The Tragedies; a
Collection of Critical Essays.
Toronto: University of Toronto
Press, 1965.

2334.   .
S's Tragedies and Other
Studies in Seventeenth Century
Drama. London: Chatto and
Windus, 1950.

2335. McFarland, Thomas
Tragic Meanings in S.
New York: Random House,
1966.

2336. Muir, Kenneth
S and the Tragic Pattern
in British Academy Proceedings.
London: British Academy, 1958.

2337. ____.
William S: The Great
Tragedies. London: Longmans,
Green, 1961.

2338. Proser, Matthew N.
The Heroic Image in Five
Shakespearean Tragedies. Prince-
ton, N.J.: Princeton University
Press, 1965.

2339. Rosen, William
S and the Craft of Tragedy.
Cambridge: Harvard University
Press, 1960.

2340. Sisson, Charles J.
S's Tragic Justice. Scar-
borough, Ontario: W.J. Gage,
1961; London: Methuen, 1964.

2341. Spencer, Terence John B.
William S, the Roman
Plays. London: Longmans, Green,
1963.

2342. Stirling, Brents
Unity in Shakespearian
Tragedy; the Interplay of Theme
and Character. New York: Columbia University Press, 1956.

2343. Traversi, Derek Antona
S: the Roman Plays.
London: Hollis & Carter, 1963.

2344. Weisinger, Herbert
Tragedy and the Paradox
of the Fortunate Fall. Lansing:
Michigan State College Press,
1953.

2345. Whitaker, Virgil K.
The Mirror up to Nature;
the Technique of S's Tragedies.
San Marino, California: Huntington Library, 1965.

2346. Wilson, Harold S.
On the Design of Shake-
spearian Tragedy. Toronto:
University of Toronto Press,
1957.

(5) Tragicomic Romances

2347. Edwards, Philip
S Survey, II (1958).
"A survey of the 20th century
criticism of the last plays."

2348. Frye, Northrop
A Natural Perspective:
The Development of Shakespear-
ean Comedy and Romance.
New York: Columbia Univer-
sity Press, 1965.

2349. Hunter, Robert G.
S and the Comedy of
Forgiveness. New York: Co-
lumbia University Press, 1965.

2350. Kermode, John Frank
William S: The Final
Plays. London: Longmans,
Green, 1963.

2351. Knight, George Wilson
The Crown of Life; Es-
says in Interpretation of S's
Final Plays. London: Oxford
University Press, 1947.

2352. Muir, Kenneth
Last Periods of S,
Racine and Ibsen. Detroit:
Wayne State University Press,
1961.

2353. Pettet, Ernest C.
S and the Romance Tra-
dition. London: Staples Press,
1949.

2354. Tillyard, Eustace M.W.
S's Last Plays. Lon-
don: Chatto and Windus, 1938.

2355. Traversi, Derek Antona
S: The Last Phase.

London: Hollis & Carter, 1954.

F. Language and Style

2356. Alexander, Peter
S's Punctuation. (British
Academy Lecture) London: Ox-
ford University Press, 1945.

2357. Bradbrook, M. C.
S and Elizabethan Poetry.
London: Chatto & Windus, 1951.

2358. Carter, Albert H.
"The Punctuation of S's
Sonnets of 1609." Joseph Quincy
Adams Memorial Studies. Edited
by Giles E. Dawson and Edwin E.
Willoughby. Washington: Folger
S Library, 1948. p. 409-428.

2359. .
"The Punctuation of S's
Sonnets of 1609," J. Q. Adams
Memorial Studies, (1948), p.
409-428.

2360. .
"The Punctuation of S's
Sonnets of 1609." Joseph Quincy
Adams Memorial Studies, ed. by
J. G. McManaway et al. Washing-
ton, D. C.: Folger S Library,
1948. p. 409-428.

2361. Dawson, Giles E. (ed.)
See Carter, Albert H.

2362. Dobson, E. J.
English Pronunciation, 1700.
1500-1700. 2v. Oxford: Clarendon Press, 1957.

2363. Empson, William
Seven Types of Ambiguity.
London: Chatto & Windus, 1950.

2364. .
Some Versions of Pastoral.
London: Chatto & Windus, 1935-50.

2365. Fries, Charles C.
"Shakespearian Punctuation,"

Studies in S, Milton, and
Donne. New York: Macmillan,
1925. p. 67-86.

2366. Gordon, George
S's English (Society for
Pure English Tract No. 29).
Oxford: Clarendon Press,
1928.

2367. Joseph, Sister Miriam
S's Use of the Arts of
Language (Studies in English
and Comparative Literature,
165). New York: Columbia
University Press, 1947.

2368. Kökeritz, Helge
S's Pronunciation. New
Haven: Yale University Press,
1953.

2369. McManaway, J. G. (ed.)
See Carter, Albert H.

2370. Mahood, M. M.
S's Wordplay. London:
Methuen, 1957.

2371. Mayhew, A. L. (ed.)
See Skeat, W. W.

2372. Ness, F. W.
The Use of Rhyme in
S's Plays. New Haven: Yale
University Press, 1941.

2373. Onions, C. T.
A S Glossary. London:
Oxford University Press, 1911.

2374. Partridge, Eric
S's Bawdy. New York:
E. P. Dutton, 1955.

2375. Rendall, Gerald Henry
Shake-spear: Handwrit-
ing and Spelling. London: C.
Palmer, 1931.

2376. Rylands, George Humphrey W.
Words and Poetry. Lon-

134

don: L. & V. Woolf, 1928.

2377. Simpson, Percy
Shakespearian Punctuation.
Oxford: Clarendon Press, 1911.

2378. Skeat, W. W.
A Glossary of Tudor and
Stuart Words. ed. with additions
by A. L. Mayhew. Oxford: Clarendon Press, 1914.

2379. Tannenbaum, S. A.
The Handwriting of the
Renaissance. New York: Columbia University Press, 1930.

2380. Vietor, Wilhelm
S's Pronunciation. New
York: Lemacke & Buechner,
1906.

2381. Willcock, Gladys D.
"S and Rhetoric," Essays
and Studies of the English Association (29), 2 v. Oxford: Clarendon Press, 1943.

2382. Willoughby, Edwin E. (ed.)
See Carter, Albert H.

2383. Wright, T.
Dictionary of Obsolete and
Provincial English. 2v. London:
Bell, 1904.

G. Textual Problems

2384. Alexander, Peter
S's Henry VI and Richard
III. Cambridge: University
Press, 1929.

2385. Baldwin, T. W.
On Act and Scene Division
in the S First Folio. Carbondale:
Southern Illinois University Press,
1065.

2386. Bennett, H. S.
English Books and Readers,
1558 to 1603, Being a Study in
the History of the Book Trade in

the Reign of Elizabeth I. Cambridge: University Press,
1965.

2387. Bowers, Fredson
On Editing S and the
Elizabethan Dramatists. Philadelphia: University of Pennsylvania Library, 1955.

2388. _____.
Textual Study and Literary Criticism. Cambridge:
University Press, 1959.

2389. _____.
Bibliography and Textual
Criticism. Oxford: Clarendon
Press, 1964.

2390. _____.
On Editing S. Charlottesville: University of Virginia Press, 1966.

2391. Duthie, G. I.
Elizabethan Shorthand
and the First Quarto of "King
Lear." Oxford: Clarendon
Press, 1949.

2392. Ford, Herbert L.
S 1700-1740; A Collation of the Editions and Separate
Plays. Oxford: Oxford University Press, 1935.

2393. Greg, Walter Wilson
"The Rationale of Copy-
Text," Studies in Bibliography,
3 (1950), 19-36.

2394. _____.
The Editorial Problem
in S: A Survey of the Foundations of the Text. 3rd ed.
Oxford: Clarendon Press, 1954.

2395. _____.
The S First Folio: Its
Bibliographical and Textual
History. Oxford: Clarendon
Press, 1955.

135

2396. _____ .
Some Aspects and Problems of London Publishing Between 1550 and 1650. Oxford: Clarendon Press, 1956.

2397. Hart, Alfred
Stolen and Surreptitious Copies: A Comparative Study of S's Bad Quartos. Oxford: Clarendon Press, 1942.

2398. Hinman, Charlton
The Printing and Proof-Reading of the First Folio of S. 2v. Oxford: Clarendon Press, 1963.

2399. _____ .
"S's Text--Then, Now and Tomorrow," SS, 18 (1965), 23-33.

2400. Honigmann, E. A. J.
The Stability of S's Text. London: Edward Arnold, 1965.

2401. Jewkes, W. T.
Act Division in Elizabethan and Jacobean Plays, 1583-1616. Hamden, Conn.: Shoestring Press, 1958.

2402. Kirchbaum, Leo
S and the Stationers. Columbus: Ohio State University Press, 1955.

2403. Kökeritz, Helge, and Prouty, Charles Tyler (eds.)
The First Folio of S's Plays, in a Facsimile Edition. New Haven: Yale University Press, 1955.

2404. Lounsbury, Thomas R.
The Text of S. New York: Scribner's, 1906.

2405. MacCallum, Sir Mungo W.
S's Roman Plays and Their Background. London: Macmillan, 1910.

2406. McKerrow, Ronald B.
A Dictionary of Printers and Booksellers in England... 1557-1640. London: Bibliographical Society, 1910.

2407. _____ .
An Introduction to Bibliography for Literary Students. Oxford: Clarendon Press, 1927.

2408. _____ .
Printers and Publishers' Devices in England and Scotland 1485-1640. London: Bibliographical Society, 1913.

2409. _____ .
Prolegomena for the Oxford S. Oxford: Clarendon Press, 1939.

2410. Nosworthy, J. M.
S's Occasional Plays: Their Origin and Transmission. New York: Barnes and Noble, 1965.

2411. Partridge, A. C.
Orthography in S and Elizabethan Drama. Lincoln: University of Nebraska Press, 1964.

2412. Pollard, Alfred William
S's Fight with the Pirates and the Problem of Transmission of the Text. London: Cambridge University Press, 1920-37.

2413. _____ .
S's Fight with the Pirates and the Problems of Transmission of His Text. Cambridge: University Press, 1920.

2414. _____ .
S Folios and Quartos: A Study in the Bibliography of S's Plays, 1594-1685. Lon-

don: Methuen, 1909.

2415. Prouty, Charles Tyler (ed.)
See Kökeritz, Helge.

2416. Shroeder, J. W.
The Great Folio of 1623:
S's Plays in the Printing House.
Hamden, Conn.: Shoestring
Press, 1956.

2417. Sisson, Charles Jasper
New Readings in S. Cam-
bridge: University Press, 1956;
London: Dawsons of Pall Mall,
1961.

2418. Walker, Alice
Textual Problems in the
First Folio. Cambridge: Uni-
versity Press, 1953.

2419.   .
"Edward Capell and His
Edition of S." Proceedings of
the British Academy, 46 (1962),
131-45.

2420. Willoughby, Edwin E.
The Printing of the First
Folio of S. Oxford: Clarendon
Press, 1932.

2421. Wilson, John Dover
"The New Way with S's
Texts: An Introduction for Lay
Readers. I. The Foundations,"
SS, 7 (1954), 48-56.

2422.   .
"The New Way with S's
Texts: II. Recent Work on the
Text of Romeo and Juliet," SS,
8 (1955), 81-99.

II. Reference Books

2423. Alden, Raymond Macdonald
A S Handbook. New York:
F. S. Crofts, 1925.

2424. Allen, John (tr.)
See Calvin, John.

2425. Apperson, G. L.
English Proverbs and
Proverbial Phrases. London:
J. M. Dent; New York: E. P.
Dutton, 1929.

2426. Aquinas, St. Thomas
Basic Writings ed.
Anton G. Pegis, 2v. New
York: Random House, 1945.

2427. Aristotle
The Works Translated
into English, ed. W. D. Ross,
12 vols. Oxford: Clarendon
Press, 1908-1952.

2428. Armi, A. M. (tr.)
See Mommsen, T. E.

2429. Bartlett, John
A New and Complete
Concordance or Verbal Index
to Words, Phrases, & Pas-
sages in the Dramatic Works
of S. London: Macmillan,
1937.

2430. Bullough, Geoffrey
Narrative and Dramatic
Sources of S. 4 vols. (5 &
6 in preparation). New York:
Columbia University Press;
London: Routledge & Kegan
Paul, 1957.

2431. Calvin, John
Institutes of the Chris-
tian Religion, tr. John Allen,
7th American ed., 2 vols.
Philadelphia: Presbyterian
Board of Christian Education,
1936.

2432. Campbell, Oscar James
and Quinn, Edward G.
(eds.)
The Reader's Encyclo-
pedia of S. New York: Thomas Y. Crowell, 1966. p.
1013-1014.

2433. Chambers, Sir Edmund K.

137

See Munro, John.

2434.   .
William S, A Study of
Facts and Problems, 2 vols. Ox-
ford: Clarendon Press, 1930.

2435. Cornford, Francis M. (tr.)
See Plato.

2436. Daniel, Samuel
Poems and A Defence of
Ryme, ed. A. C. Sprague. Cambridge, Mass.: Harvard University Press, 1930.

2437. Dean, Leonard (tr.)
See Erasmus, Desiderius.

2438. De Selincourt, E. (ed.)
See Spenser, Edmund.

2439. Detmold, C. E. (tr.)
See Machiavelli, Niccolo.

2440. Donne, John
The Songs and Sonnets, ed.
Theodore Redpath. London:
Methuen, 1956.

2441. Donow, Herbert S.
A Concordance to the Son-
net Sequences of Daniel, Drayton,
S, Sidney, and Spenser. Carbon-
dale: Southern Illinois University
Press, 1969.

2442. Erasmus, Desiderius
The Praise of Folly, trans.
Leonard Dean. Chicago: Packard,
1946.

2443. Fellowes, E. H. (ed.)
English Madrigal Verse,
1588-1632. Oxford: Clarendon
Press, 1929.

2444. Feuillerat, Albert (ed.)
See Sidney, Sir Philip.

2445. Furness, Helen K.
Concordance to S's Poems.
New York: AMS Press, 1875
(1970).

2446. Granville-Barker, Harley, and Harrison, G.
B. (eds.)
A Companion to S
Studies. New York: Macmillan, 1934; Cambridge: University Press, 1934.

2447. Greg, W. W.
The S First Folio. New
York and London: Oxford Uni-
versity Press, 1955.

2448. Halliday, Frank Ernest
A S Companion, 1550-
1950. London: Gerald Duckworth, 1952. p. 607-610.

2449. Hardison, O. B., Jr. (ed.)
See Warnke, Frank J.
(ed.).

2450. Harrison, G. B.
See Granville-Barker, H.

2451.   .
The Elizabethan Journals.
2v. London: Rutledge, 1938-55.

2452. Kökeritz, Helge
S's Names. New Haven:
Yale University Press, 1959;
London: Oxford University
Press, 1960.

2453.   .
S's Pronunciation. New
Haven: Yale University Press;
London: Oxford University
Press, 1953.

2454. Linthicum, Marie C.
Costume in the Drama
of S and His Contemporaries.
New York & London: Oxford
University Press, 1936.

2455. Luce, Morton
A Handbook to the Works
of S. London: G. Bell, 1906.

2456. Machiavelli, Niccolo
The Prince and The Dis-
courses, tr. Luigi Ricci and

138

C. E. Detmold. New York: Modern Library, 1940.

2457. Martin, L. C. (ed.)
See Marlowe, Christopher.

2458. Mayhew, A. L. (ed.)
See Skeat, W. W.

2459. Miller, Frank (tr.)
See Ovid.

2460. Miller, Walter (tr.)
See Cicero.

2461. Mommsen, T. E.
"Introduction," Petrarch:
Sonnets and Songs, tr. A. M.
Armi. New York: Pantheon
Books, 1946.

2462. Muir, Kenneth
S's Sources. London:
Methuen, 1957.

2463. _____ and O'Loughlin, Sean
The Voyage to Illyria; a
New Study of S. London: Methuen,
1937.

2464. Munro, John
The S Allusion-Book, 2
vols. London and New York,
1909. [The same, reissued with
an introduction by Sir E. K.
Chambers, 2 vols., Oxford, 1932.]

2465. Neilson, William Allan,
and Thorndike, A. H.
The Facts about S. New
York: Macmillan, 1913.

2466. Norton, Thomas (tr.)
See Calvin, John.

2467. O'Loughlin, Sean
See Muir, Kenneth.

2468. Onions, C. T. (ed.)
A Oxford S Glossary. London: Oxford University Press,
1953. Oxford: Clarendon Press,
1919.

2469. Ovid
Metamorphoses, tr.
Frank Miller (Loeb Library),
2 vols. London: William
Heinemann, 1916, 1926.

2470. Parrott, Thomas Marc
William S A Handbook.
New York: Scribner's, 1934.

2471. Partridge, Eric
S's Bawdy. New York:
E. P. Dutton, 1948; London:
Routledge & Kegan Paul, 1955.

2472. Pegis, Anton G. (ed.)
See Aquinas, St. Thomas

2473. Plato
The Republic, tr. Francis M. Cornford. London: Oxford University Press, 1941.

2474. Pollard, Alfred William
S's Fight with the Pirates and the Problem of Transmission of the Text. London:
Cambridge University Press,
1920-37.

2475. _____ and Redgrave,
G. R.
A Short-Title Catalogue
of Books...1475-1640. London:
Bibliographical Society, 1926
(1946).

2476. Quinn, Edward G. (ed.)
See Campbell, Oscar
James (ed.)

2477. Redgrave, G. R.
See Pollard, A. W.

2478. Redpath, Theodore (ed.)
See Donne, John.

2479. Ricci, Luigi (tr.)
See Machiavelli, Niccolo.

2480. Rollins, Hyder E. (ed.)
England's Helicon, 2
vols. Cambridge, Mass.: Har-

vard University Press, 1935.

2481. Ross, W. D. (ed.)
See Aristotle.

2482. Rowse, Alfred Leslie
The England of Elizabeth.
London: Macmillan, 1950.

2483. Sarrazin, G. (tr.) (ed.)
See Schmidt, Alexander.

2484. Schmidt, Alexander
S-Lexicon (1874-5). 3rd
ed. with supplement, tr. and ed.
by G. Sarrazin. Berlin: Georg
Reimer, 1902.

2485. Shilleto, A. R. (ed.)
See Burton, Robert.

2486. Simpson, Percy
Shakespearian Punctuation.
Oxford: Clarendon Press, 1910.

2487. Sisson, Charles Jasper
New Readings in S. 2v.
London: Cambridge University
Press, 1956.

2488. Skeat, W. W.
A Glossary of Tudor and
Stuart Words. ed. with additions
by A. L. Mayhew. Oxford: Clarendon Press, 1914.

2489. Smith, Gordon Ross
A Classified S Bibliography
1936-1958. University Park:
Pennsylvania State University
Press, 1963.

2490. Smith, J. C. (ed.)
See Spenser, Edmund.

2491. Smith, William George
The Oxford Dictionary of
English Proverbs. Oxford: Clar-
endon Press, 1935.

2492. Spenser, Edmund
The Poetical Works, ed.
J. C. Smith and E. De Selincourt.

London: Oxford University
Press, 1912.

2493. Sprague, Arthur Colby (ed.)
See Daniel, Samuel.

2494. Squire, John C.
Life and Letters. Lon-
don: Hodder & Stoughton, 1920.

2495. Taylor, A. E.
Plato: The Man and
His Work. New York: Meridian
Books, 1956.

2496. Thompson, A. H. (ed.)
See Suckling, Sir John.

2497. Thorndike, A. H.
See Neilson, W. A.

2498. Tilley, Morris Palmer
Elizabethan Proverb Lore
in Lyly's Euphues and in Pet-
tie's Petite Pallace with Parallels from S. London & New
York: Macmillan, 1926.

2499. _____.
A Dictionary of the Prov-
erbs in England in the Sixteenth
and Seventeenth Centuries. Ann
Arbor: University of Michigan
Press, 1950.

2500. Vietor, Wilhelm
S's Pronunciation. New
York: Lemacke & Buechner, 1906.

2501. Warnke, Frank J. and
Hardison, O. B., Jr. (eds.)
Encyclopedia of Poetry
and Poetics. Princeton, N. J.:
Princeton University Press,
1965. p. 781-784.

2502. Wright, T.
Dictionary of Obsolete
and Provincial English. 2v.
London: Bell, 1904.

2503. Wyld, H. C.
A Short History of Eng-
lish. London: Murray, 1914.

Appendix A

A LIST OF REFERENCE GUIDES CONSULTED

Abstracts of English Studies.

Annual Bibliography of English Language and Literature (Modern
Humanities Research Association, England).

Bateson, F. W. (ed.). See CBEL.

British Humanities Index.

British Museum General Catalogue of Printed Books.

The Cambridge Bibliography of English Literature (CBEL). ed.
by F. W. Bateson. 4 vols. London: Cambridge University
Press, 1940; 1947; Supplement, 1957.

Campbell, Oscar James and Quinn, Edward G. (eds.). The Reader's Encyclopedia of Shakespeare. New York: Thomas Y.
Crowell Co., 1966. P. 803-809.

Cumulative Book Index.

Ebisch, W., and Schucking, Levin L. A Shakespeare Bibliography. Oxford: Clarendon Press, 1931. ("Sonnets," p.
263-269).

Ebisch, W., and Schucking, L. L. Supplement for the Years
1930-1935 to A Shakespeare Bibliography. London: Oxford
University Press, 1936; (New York: Benjamin Blom, 1964).
("Sonnets, p. 93-94")

Education Index.

Essay and General Literature Index.

International Index to Periodicals (now called Social Sciences and
Humanities Index).

Jaggard, William. Shakespeare Bibliography: A Dictionary of
Every Known Issue of the Writings of Our National Poet and
of Recorded Opinion Thereon in the English Language. Stratford-on-Avon: Shakespeare Press, 1911. "Sonnets," p.
452-456.

Journal of English and Germanic Philology (JEGP).

Library of Congress Catalog of Printed Books.

Modern Humanities Association. See Annual Bibliography of English Language and Literature. Cambridge, England; MHA, 1921-date.

Paperbound Books in Print.

PMLA (Annual Bibliography).

Poetry Exposition by Joseph M. Kuntz. Chicago: Swallow Press, 1962 (Sonnets, p. 220-226).

Quinn, Edward G. (ed.). See Campbell, Oscar J. (ed.).

Reader's Guide to Periodical Literature.

Schucking, L. L. See Ebisch, W.

Shakespeare Association Bulletin (Annual Bibliography).

Shakespeare Newsletter (Bibliography).

Shakespeare Quarterly (Annual Bibliography).

Shakespeare Survey.

Studies in Philology (Annual Bibliography).

Subject Guide to Books in Print.

Tannenbaum, Samuel A. Shakespeare's Sonnets (A Concise Bibliography). New York: S. A. Tannenbaum, 1940. (Elizabethan Bibliographies, No. 10) (88 p.).

The Year's Work in English Studies (London, England)

Smith, Gordon Ross. A Classified Shakespeare Bibliography, 1936-1958. University Park, Pa.: Pennsylvania State University Press, 1963 ("Sonnets," p. 764-772).

Appendix B

A LIST OF ANNUALS, NEWSPAPERS, AND PERIODICALS INDEXED

(For further information consult the following:
1. Ulrich's International Periodicals Directory,
2. the Standard Periodical Directory, 3. Ayer's
Directory of Newspapers and Periodicals.)

Academy.

American Imago.

American Journal of Philology.

American Scholar.

Anglia (Germany).

Anglica (Japan).

Archiv für das Studium....
(Archiv) (W. Germany).

Arion (University of Texas).

Athenaeum (England).

Atlantic Monthly.

Atlas.

AUMLA (Journal of the
Australasian Universities)

Baconiana.

Baker Street Journal.

Ball State Teachers College Forum (Later Ball State University
Forum).

Beiblatt.

Bibliotheca Sacra (a Theological
Quarterly) (Texas).

Birmingham Post (England).

Blackwood's Magazine (Scotland).

Bookman (England).

Bookman's Journal.

Book Monthly.

Books Abroad.

Bucknell Review.

Bulletin of the New York Public
Library.

Calcutta Review (India).

Cambridge Review (England).

Carnegie Series in English.

Catholic World.

The Centennial Review of Arts
and Science (Michigan State
University).

Christian Science Monitor.

Clearing House (a Journal for
Modern Junior and Senior High
School Faculties).

College English.

143

Colorado Quarterly.

Comparative Literature (University of Oregon).

Comparative Literature Studies (University of Illinois).

Contemporary Review (England).

Cornhill Magazine.

Criterion.

Critic.

Critical Quarterly (London).

Criticism.

Culture (Canada).

Daily Telegraph (London).

Dalhousie Review. (Canada)

Dial.

Discourse (Concordia College, Minn.).

Elizabethan Poetry.

Englische Studien (Germany).

English (Magazine of the English Association).

English Institute Essays (Annual, Columbia University).

English Journal (NCTE).

English Language Notes (University of Colorado) (ELN).

English Record.

English Review (England).

English Studies (ES) (Netherlands).

Essays and Studies.

Essays and Studies Collected for the English Association.

Essays and Studies by Members of the English Association.

Essays and Studies in English Language and Literature (Sendai, Japan).

Essays in Criticism (EIC) (England).

Essays of Studies by Members of the English Association (England).

Essays on Shakespeare.

Etudes Anglaises et Americaines (Etudes Anglaises) (France).

Etudes Classiques (Belgium).

Everyman.

Explicator.

Far Eastern University Faculty Journal (Manila).

Fifties (Madison, Minn.).

Filoloski Pregled (Belgrade).

Gaya College Journal.

Golden Book (New York).

Good Housekeeping.

Harper's Magazine.

Harvard University--Summaries of Theses.

Hispania (U.S.).

Hobbies.

Holborn Review.

Hudson Review.

Humanities Association Bulletin (Canada).

Hungarian Quarterly (New York).

Huntington Library Quarterly.

International Journal of Psycho-Analysis (London).

Irish Statesman.

John Rylands Library Bulletin (England).

Journal of English and Germanic Philology (JEGP).

Journal of English Literary History (JELH).

Journal of Nervous and Mental Diseases.

Journal of Psychology.

Journal of the Warbury and Courtauld Institute (JWCI).

Kenyon Review.

Kerygma.

Language.

Library (England).

Listener (England).

Literary Half Yearly (England).

Literary Review.

Literature (New York).

Living Age (Boston).

London Mercury (England).

London Mercury and Bookman (England).

Manchester Guardian Weekly (England).

Massachusetts Review (University of Mass.).

Methodist Review.

Midwest Folklore.

Mitteldeutsche for Shungen (Germany).

Modern Language Notes (MLN).

Modern Language Quarterly (MLQ) (University of Washington).

Modern Language Review (MLR) (England).

Modern Philology (MP).

Month (England).

Monthly Musical Record.

Nation.

Nation and Athenaeum.

National Review.

Nature (England).

Neophilologus (Netherlands).

Neuphilologische Mitteilungen.

New Adelphi (London).

New Republic.

New Shakespeareana.

New Statesman (England).

Newsweek.

New York Herald Tribune Book Review.

New York Times Book Review.

19th Century (Philadelphia).

North American Review (University of Northern Iowa).

North Dakota Quarterly.

Notes and Queries (N & Q) (England).

Observer (London).

Orbis (University of Pennsylvania).

Orbis Litterarum (Copenhagen).

Osmania Journal of English Studies (India).

Outlook (London, England).

Papers of the Bibliographical Society of America.

Parents' Review.

The Personalist.

Philological Quarterly (PQ).

PMLA (Publications of the Modern Language Association of America).

The Poet and the Philosopher.

Poet Lore.

Poetry (Chicago).

Poetry and the Play (England).

Poetry Review (England).

Proceedings of the American Philosophical Society.

Proceedings of the British Academy.

Psychological Record (Denisen University, Ohio).

Publishers' Weekly.

Punch (England).

Quarterly Journal of Speech.

Quarterly Review (Washington, D. C.).

Queen's Quarterly (Canada).

Quest.

Reedy's Mirror.

Renaissance Drama.

Research Studies (Washington State University).

Review of English Studies (RES) (England).

Review of Reviews (England).

Revue de Littérature Comparée (France).

Revue des Langues Vivantes (Brussels).

Satire Newsletter.

Saturday Review (SR).

Saturday Review of Literature (New York).

Scholastic.

Scrutiny (England).

Sewanee Review.

Shakespeare.

Shakespeare Association Bulletin (England).

Shakespeare Authorship Review (Shakespeare Authorship Society, London, England).

Shakespeare Fellowship Quarterly.

Shakespeare Jahrbuch (SJ) (Germany). Jahrbuch der Deutscben Shakespeare-Gesellnbaft (Germany) [SJ(O) = SJ Ost; SJ(W) = SJ West]

Shakespeare Newsletter (SNL).

Shakespeare 1564-1964.

Shakespeare Problems (New York University).

Shakespeare Quarterly (SQ).

Shakespeare Research and Opportunities.

Shakespeare Stage (Shakespeare Stage Society, London, England).

Shakespeare Studies (Japan).

Shakespeare Studies (University of Cincinnati).

Shakespeare Scudies (Vanderbilt University).

Shakespeare Survey (SS) (England).

South Atlantic Bulletin.

Southern Quarterly (University of Southern Mississippi).

Southern Review.

Spectator (England).

Studia Neophilologia (Sweden).

Studies in Bibliography.

Studies in English.

Studies in English Literature (Tokyo, Japan).

Studies in English Literature 1500-1900 (Rice University).

Studies in Philology.

Studies in the Renaissance.

Sunday Times Magazine (London, England).

Teachers College Journal.

Tennessee Studies in Literature.

Texas Studies in Literature and Language.

Theatre Arts.

Theatre and Drama Review.

Time.

Time and Tide (England).

Times (London).

Times (London) Literary Supplement (TLS) (England).

Tokyo Imperial University Studies in English Literature (Japan). See Studies in English Literature.

Triveni (Madras, India).

Tulane Studies in English.

Twentieth Century (Australia).

University Magazine.

University of California Chronicle.

University of Mississippi Studies in English.

University of Texas Studies in English.

University of Virginia Magazine.

Vassar Miscellany Monthly.

Venture.

Wanderer.

Yale Review.

Year's Work in English Studies.

Author Index

(numbers are to entries in main sequence)

Abend, Murray 756
Acheson, Arthur 155-157, 757-
760, 874a, 1251, 1515, 1516
Adams, H.H. 1427, 1547, 2108
Adams, John Crawford 2160
Adams, Joseph Quincy 273, 274,
761, 983, 1846, 1856, 1923,
1975, 2160, 2161
Aiken, Ralph 762, 1626
Ainger, A. 763, 804a
Ainslie, Douglas (tr.) 275
Akrigg, George P. Vere 764,
1428, 1572, 1924
Alden, Raymond M. (ed.) 1, 10,
158, 276-279, 502, 765-770,
874a, 1383, 1384, 1429, 1515,
1561, 2423
Alexander, Peter 771, 1925,
1926, 2356, 2384
Allen, Don Cameron (ed.) 280
Allen, John (tr.) 2424
Allen, J.A. 2044
Allen, J.W. 2045
Allen, Ned B. 773-775, 834,
951, 1228, 1264, 1684, 1759,
1860, 1881, 1885, 1887
Allen, Percy 159, 265, 281, 282,
776, 777, 1148a
Alpers, Paul J. (ed.) 283, 284
Alston, Z. (tr.) (ed.) 2046
Alter, Jean V. 778, 1875
Anders, H.R.D. 285
Anderson, Wallace L. 1882
Anderton, Basil 286, 1604, 1755
Angell, Pauline K. 779, 780,
788, 874a
Anspacher, Louis 160
Appearson, G.L. 2425
Aquinas, St. Thomas 2426, 2472
Archer, C. 782
Archer, William (tr.) 783, 1927
Aretino 784
Aring, Charles D. 785

Aristotle 2427, 2481
Armi, A.M. (tr.) 2428
Armstrong, Edward A. 287
Armstrong, W.A. 2162, 2163
Arnold, A. 1430, 1548
Atkinson, Charles F. (tr.) 288
Auden, W.H. 12, 33, 289,
290, 348, 349, 389, 786
Auslander, Joseph (ed.) 13
Axelrad, A.J. 1430a, 1536

Babb, Lawrence 291
Babcock, R.W. 292
Bacon, Francis 749
Bacon, Wallace A. 1431, 1544
Bagg, R. 787
Bailey, John 293
Baker, Herschel 2047, 2048
Baker, Howard 2109
Baldwin, T.W. 161, 780, 788,
874a, 1517, 1928, 2164,
2165, 2385
Ballou, Robert O. (ed.) 14
Banks, Theodore H. 789, 1596
Bannerjie, S. 294
Barber, Cesar Lombardi 15,
162, 214, 283, 295-297,
522, 678, 790, 2268
Barker, G.A. 791, 1208
Barnard, E.A.B. 298
Barnard, Finch 163
Barnstoff, D. 164
Barrell, Charles W. 792,
1776
Barrol, Leeds 1432, 1573
Bartlett, Henrietta C. 299,
793, 1382
Bartlett, John 2429
Barton, A.T. 16, 69
Barton, Sir Dunbar P. 300,
301
Basdekis, P. 794
Baskervill, C.R. 2110

Bates, E.S. 795
Bates, Paul A. 796, 797, 1204
Bateson, F.W. 302, 303, 798-
801, 915, 1406, 1763
Bathurst, C. 304
Baugh, Albert C. (ed.) 305
Baumer, F.L. 2049
Bayfield, Matthew A. 306
Baym, Max I. 802
Beach, Elizabeth 307
Beatty, Arthur 308, 309
Beaty, John Owen 17
Beck, James Montgomery 300,
310
Beckerman, Bernard 2166
Beckwith, Elizabeth 803, 874b
Beddoes, Thomas Lovell 49
Beeching, Henry C. (ed.) 18,
311, 804
Begley, Walter E. 312
Belloc, H. 313
Benezet, Louis P. 314
Bennett, H.S. 2386
Bennett, Josephine (ed.) 315,
805, 806
Benson, John 316, 807
Bentley, Gerald Eades 317,
1929, 1930, 1976, 2167-2169
Berconitch, Sacvan 808, 1810
Berkelman, Robert G. 809,
1698, 1861
Berman, Ronald 1433, 1434,
1553, 1574
Berry, Francis 318, 810, 930
Berry, J. Wilkes 811, 1601
Berryman, John 812
Best, C. 813
Bevington, D.M. 2111
Beza, Marcer 319
Biggs, Alan J. 814, 843
Bindoff, S.T. 2050
Birchenough, J. 815, 816, 874a,
961
Bishop, Henry Rowley 320, 1699
Black, J.B. 1977, 2051
Black, Matthew W. (ed.) 19,
321
Blackmur, R.P. 165, 322, 474,
817, 1518, 1585, 1608, 1817,
1877
Blackstone, B. 1435, 1560
Blatt, William M. 818
Blind, Mathilda (ed.) 20, 21

Bliven, Bruce 323
Bloom, Edward A. (ed.) 324
Bluestone, Max 325, 475
Boaden, J. 166
Boas, F.S. (ed.) 326, 327,
819, 874b, 2112, 2113
Bock, Vera (illus.) 22
Bodtker, A.T. 328
Bonazza, Blaze O. 2269
Bonnerot, L. 1436, 1561
Booth, Stephen 167, 329, 330,
1581, 1597, 1602, 1605,
1616, 1617, 1621, 1639,
1640, 1646, 1648, 1651,
1653, 1654, 1656, 1659,
1660, 1664, 1671, 1676,
1694, 1700, 1718, 1721,
1722, 1727, 1732, 1736,
1739, 1786, 1787, 1799,
1811, 1824, 1836, 1849,
1858, 1878, 1880
Borghesi, Piertro 331
Boston, Richard 1437, 1532
Bowen, Gwynneth 820
Bower, John W. (ed.) 23
Bowers, Fredson T. 2114,
2319, 2387-2390
Bradbrook, Muriel C. 332,
821, 1731, 2115, 2116,
2170, 2270, 2357
Bradby, Anne (ed.) 333
Bradby, Godfrey Fox 334
Bradley, Andrew Cecil 335,
336, 2171, 2320
Bradley, Holdeen 822
Bradner, Leicester 337
Branan, George Curtis
2172
Brandes, George M.C. 1927
Brandle, A. 1519
Bray, Sir Denys (ed.) 24, 25,
168, 169, 823-825, 1520,
1876
Brett-Smith, H.F.B. 26
Brewer, Wilmon 338
Bridges, H.J. 339
Brien, A. 1438, 1533
Briggs, K.M. 2052, 2053
Broadbent, J.B. 340
Broadus, Edmund Kemper 341
Brooke, Arthur 826
Brooke, C.F.T. (ed.) 27, 28,
170, 305, 342, 1931, 2117

Brooks, Alden 343
Brooks, C. 827, 828, 1883
Brooks, H. F. 829, 963, 1247
Brophy, James 830
Broun, Malcolm 1622
Brown, Charles A. 344
Brown, George H. 345
Brown, Harry 346, 566
Brown, Henry 171, 347, 755
Brown, Ivor 172, 804a, 831-833,
 846, 874a, 1439, 1440, 1521,
 1561, 1575, 1932
Brown, John Russell 2173, 2174,
 2273
Brown, S. G. 1713, 1884
Brushy, James 1819
Brussels, Robert T. 775, 834,
 1760, 1885
Bucke, Richard Maurice 348
Buckley, G. T. 2054
Bullen, A. Henry (ed.) 29-
 32
Bullock, W. L. 835
Bullough, Geoffrey 1441, 1442,
 1537, 1556
Burckhardt, Sigurd 836, 1788
Burto, William (ed.) 33, 289,
 348, 349
Burton, Robert 2485
Bush, Douglas (ed.) 34, 35, 63,
 350, 351, 455, 1978, 2055,
 2056, 2323
Bush, Geoffrey 2321
Butler, Samuel 36, 173, 1522,
 1523
Butterfield, Herbert 2057
Buxton, John 837, 1979
Byars, W. V. 838, 874a
Byrne, M. St. Clare 1980
Byvanck, William G. C. 333, 352

Cabaniss, Allen 839
Caldwell, James R. 840, 1677
Calvin, I. 841
Calvin, John 2424, 2431, 2466
Camden, Carroll 842, 1901
Cameron, G. M. 174
Campbell, Lily Bess 353, 2118,
 2175, 2295, 2322
Campbell, Mildred 1982
Campbell, Oscar J. (ed.) 38-40,
 175, 354, 1933, 2312, 2432,
 2476

Carew T. 843
Cargill, Alexander 355
Cargill, Oscar (ed.) 356
Carpenter, B. F. 844
Carter, Albert H. 845, 1382,
 2358-2361, 2369, 2382
Carter, Thomas 357
Cavendish, G. 846
Caspari, Fritz 2058
Cassirer, Ernst 2059
Cazamian, Louis 358, 530
Chamaillard, P. 1443, 1538
Chambers, Sir Edmund K. 176,
 359, 360, 847-849, 874b,
 1148a, 1425, 1612, 1934-
 1936, 1983, 2119-2121, 2176,
 2177, 2272, 2433, 2434
Chambers, R. W. (ed.) 361
Chambrun, Longworth 1716
Chapman, G. 850-852
Chapman, J. A. 853
Chapman, J. J. 362
Charlton, Henry Buckley 2122,
 2273, 2323, 2324
Chaucer, G. 854
Cheyney, E. P. 2060
Chute, Marchette 363, 1937,
 1984
Cicero 3462
Clark, Cumberland 364, 365
Clark, W. R. 856, 1789
Clarke, Robert F. 857, 1862
Clarkson, Paul S. 366, 725,
 858, 859, 1138, 1658, 1913
Clemen, Wolfgang H. 367,
 1985, 2123
Clutton-Brock, Arthur 368
Cohen, H. L. 860
Coleridge, Samuel T. 369-
 372, 620
Collins, John Churton 373, 374
Collison-Morley, Lacey 375
Colvin, I. 861
Conklin, Groff (ed.) 323, 376
Connolly, Cyril 1444, 1576
Conway, Eustace 377
Cook, I. R. W. 862, 988
Corke, Hilary 1445, 1569
Cormican, L. A. 864
Cornford, Francis (tr.) 2435,
 2473
Courthope, William John 378
Cowling, G. H. 379, 2178

Cox, R.G. 1446, 1557
Craig, Edward Gordon 380
Craig, Hardin (ed.) 381-383,
865, 874a, 1986, 1987, 2061,
2124
Craig, John 1447, 1577
Craig, W.J. (ed.) 43
Craik, T.W. 2179
Cranefield, P.F. 866, 927, 1381
Creighton, Charles 867, 868,
1728, 1938
Cripps, A.R. 869, 890
Croce, Benedetto 275, 384
Crosland, Thomas W.H. 385
Cruickshank, C.G. 1988
Cruttwell, Patrick 386-388, 501,
870
Cunliffe, J.W. 2125, 2126
Curtis, M.H. 1989

D., A. 871
Dam, Bastiaan A.P.V. 389
Danby, J.F. 2062
Daniel, Samuel 872, 2436
Daniels, Earl R.K. 1734
Dannenfeldt, Karl H. 873
Darby, Robert H. 874, 874b
Davenport, A. 875, 876, 1662
David, Richard 390
Davies, H. Neville 877, 894,
1685
Davies, Jack M. 878, 965, 1695,
1889
Davies, Randall 178
Davis, Herbert (ed.) 391
Davis, Latham (ed.) 392
Dawson, Giles E. (ed.) 2361
Day, Martin S. 393
Day Lewis, Cecil 393a
Dean, Leonard (ed., tr.) 394,
1614, 1627, 1897, 1990, 2437
Dean, Winton 2180
DeBanke, Cecile 2181
DeBruce, Robert 395
DeChambrun, C.L. see: Pineton,
Clara Longworth
Deckner, G. 1448, 1449, 1519,
1527
Deelman, Christian 2182
DeGroot, J.H. 1940
Dellinger, J. Howard 880
DeMontmorency, J.E.G. 881,
882

Denning, W.H. 883
DeSanctis, Francesco 622
DeSelincourt, E. 46, 2438
Detmold, C.E. (tr.) 2439,
2456
Disher, M. Wilson 884, 1154,
1251
Dixon, W.M. 2127
Dobree, Bonamy (ed.) 398
Dobson, E.J. 2362
Dodd, Alfred 47, 48, 180, 399
Dodge, R.E.N. 400, 401
Doebler, John 886, 1790
Donne, John 2440, 2478
Donner, H.W. (ed.) 49
Donow, Herbert S. 2441
Doran, Madeleine 2128
Dorsch, T.S. (tr.) 2129
Douglas, Lord Alfred 50, 181,
850, 869, 887-890, 1020a,
1251, 1525, 1526
Douglas, Montagne W. 402
Douse, T.L.M. 891
Dowden, Edward (ed.) 51,
804a, 892
Downer, Alan S. 893, 2183
Downing, Charles 403
Dryden, John 894
Dunn, Esther Cloudman 404,
2184
Durrell, Lawrence 895, 1251
Duthie, G.I. 2391

Eagle, Robert L. 874a, 896-
900, 1251
Eagle, Roderick L. 2, 182,
183, 405
Eastman, Arthur M. 406, 407,
461
Eccles, C.M. 863, 901, 1666
Eccles, Mark 902, 1148a,
1941
Echhoff, Lorentz 903
Edward, Philip 2347
Edwards, H.L.R. 906, 1781
Einstein, Lewis 2063, 2064
Eliot, T.S. 408-410, 907,
1450, 1563, 1942, 1991
Elman, Paul 908, 1592
Elonen, Paul 909
Elson, L.C. 411, 412
Elton, C.I. 714
Elton, G.R. 2065, 2066

Elton, Oliver 413
Emerson, John M. 184, 185
Emerson, Oliver Farrar 910
Empson, William 414-417, 799,
　911-915, 1138, 1425, 1451,
　1578, 1607, 1724, 1726, 1740,
　2363, 2364, 3365, 3366
England, M. W. 2185
Enright, D. J. 916, 1138
Erasmus, Desiderius 917, 2437,
　2442
Erskine, John 418
Ervine, St. J. 918
Essex, Robert Devereaux 919
Evans, Bertrand 2274
Evans, E. C. 920, 921, 1076,
　1750, 1886, 1896
Evans, Willa McClung 419, 922,
　1791

Farnham, Willard 2130, 2186,
　2325, 2326
Farr, Henry 926, 1229
Federn, W. 866, 927, 1381.
Feldman, A. Bronson 928
Fellowes, E. H. (ed.) 2443
Ferguson, A. B. 1992
Ferguson, Francis (ed.) 52, 53,
　125
Feuillerat, Albert (ed.) 2444
Ficino, Marsilio 929
Fielder, Leslie 186
Figgis, Darrell 420
Finkenstaldt, Thomas 930
Finney, Claude Lee 421
Flatter, Richard 931, 946
Fletcher, Charles R. L. 422
Flower, Margaret (ed.) 54
Fluchere, Henri 1942, 1943
Foakes, R. A. 932, 2131,
　2187
Forbis, J. F. 423
Ford, Herbert L. 2392
Forrest, Henry T. S. 187
Forster, M. 1452, 1516
Fort, James A. 57, 188, 189,
　874b, 933-939, 1148a, 1193,
　1388, 1527, 1757, 1764, 1772
Fox, Charles A. O. 940-944,
　1091, 1203, 1816, 1825, 1863
Fox, Levi (ed.) 42, 58
Frankenberg, Lloyd (ed.) 59, 72,
　1623, 1733, 1792, 1800

Frazer, Robert 424
Freeman, A. 945, 1247
Freud, Sigmund 946
Friedrich, Gerhard 1453, 1518
Fries, Charles C. 3365
Friggis, J. N. 2067
Fripp, Edgar Innes 425, 426,
　1944, 1945, 1993
Froude, J. A. 1994
Frye, Northrop 190, 427, 2275,
　2327, 2348
Frye, Prosser Hall 428
Furness, Helen K. 2445
Furnivall, F. J. 947
Fussell, Paul Jr. 429, 1859

Gahan, C. J. 948, 1138
Gardiner, H. C. 2132
Gardner, Helen (ed.) 430,
　1454, 1455, 1534
Garnett, Richard M. 191,
　431, 437, 174b, 949
Garret, C. H. 2068
Garwood, H. P. 1073
Gerard, Albert S. 433, 951,
　953, 954, 1741, 1864, 1887,
　1888, 1901, 1915
Gerard, M. Albert 952
Gerritsen, Johan 955
Gilbank, P. E. 956
Gildersleeve, V. C. 2188
Gittings, Robert (ed.) 174,
　192, 197, 244
Gleeson, J. F. 957
Glick, Claris 2189
Goddard, Harold C. 1995
Godwin, Parke 60, 193, 958,
　1528
Goldsmith, Ulrich K. 959
Goldstein, Neal L. 960
Gollancz, Sir I. (ed.) 61,
　433-435, 479
Goodacre, Edward B. 815,
　874a, 961
Gordon, George 436, 2276,
　3366
Gorton, Mary Jane (ed., illus.)
　62
Gosse, Edmund 437, 962
Gower, John 964
Grant, J. E. 878, 965, 1695,
　1889
Granville, Barker, H. 1996,

1997, 2277, 2446, 2450, 2451
Graves, Robert 438-441, 634, 637, 966, 1826, 1831, 1890, 1892, 1909
Gray, Arthur 442, 1946
Gray, Cecil G. 930a, 967, 1079
Gray, Henry David 381, 382, 443, 874b, 968-970, 1194, 1251
Grebanies, Bernard 971, 1456, 1579
Green, A. Wigfall 972, 973, 1136, 2133
Greene, D.J. (ed.) 444
Greenwood, Sir G.G. 445, 446, 874a, 975
Greg, W.W. 2134, 2135, 2190, 2191, 2197, 2198, 2393-2396, 2447
Groos, K. 976, 1165
Grundry, W.G.C. 979
Grundry, Joan 978, 1457, 1539
Gundoff, F. 977
Gwynn, Frederick U. 1891

Hadow, W.H. (ed.) 4, 194
Haines, C.M. 447
Haines, C.R. 980
Hall, A. 981, 1138
Hall, Vernon, Jr. 448
Hallam, Henry 449
Haller, William 2069
Halliday, Frank Ernest 450, 1947-1949, 2448
Hamer, D. 982, 1851
Hamer, E.H. (ed.) 451, 452
Hamilton, Guy (tr.) 1950
Hankins, John E. 453
Harbage, Alfred (ed.) 34, 35, 63, 454-456, 874b, 986, 1773, 1806, 1998, 2136, 2192-2195, 2278, 2328
Hardison, O.B., Jr. 2137, 2449, 2501
Harris, Frank 457-459, 874a, 1458, 1529, 1566
Harris, Frederick James 460
Harrison, George B. (ed.) 64-68, 102, 103, 406, 461, 987, 1459-1461, 1539, 1549, 1579, 1765, 1999-2002, 2196, 2446, 2450
Harrison, John Smith 462

Harrower, John (ed.) 69
Hart, Alfred 2397
Hart, Thomas R. 1462, 1549
Harvey, G. 988
Harvey, W. 989
Harwood, Henry H. 195
Hasler, Jörg 1463, 1539
Havens, Raymond Dexter 463
Hawkes, Terence 2329
Hax, Samuel 990
Hayashi, Tetsumaro 991, 1464, 1553
Haydn, Hiram 2070
Hayes, Ann L. 992
Hazlitt, William Carew 464
Helton, Tinsley (ed.) 2071
Hemingway, S.B. 993, 1020a, 1598
Hendricks, W.O. 994, 1628
Henman, C. 1465, 1559
Henslow, Philip 2197
Henze, R. 1466, 1530
Herbert, T. Walter 998-1000, 1603, 1636, 1850
Herbert, William 1001, 1002
Herford, C.H. 465, 1003
Herrnstein, Barbara (ed.) 70, 196, 297, 303, 316, 369, 386, 414, 439, 449, 466, 471, 476, 495, 505, 533, 568, 584, 614, 635, 695, 745, 1530, 1892, 1893
Heuer, Hermann 197, 1467, 1579
Hews, Will 1004
Highet, Gilbert 467, 468
Hill, Charles J. (ed.) 71, 96
Hillebrand, H.N. 2199
Hinman, Charlton 1006, 1348, 2398, 2399
Hodges, C. Walter 2200, 2201
Hoffman, Banesh 1007
Hogan, Charles Beecher 2202
Hogrefe, Pearl 2138
Hogrogian, Nonny 72
Holgate, W. 1005
Holland, Vyvyan (ed.) 198
Holloway, John 2330
Holzapfel, Rudolph M. 73, 199, 469, 1008, 1531, 1587
Holzer, G. 1009, 1692
Holzknecht, Karl J. 1951

Honigmann, E.A.J. 2400
Hoopes, Robert 2072
Hope-Wallace, Philip 1010
Horace 1011
Hosley, Richard (ed.) 470, 2203-2205
Hotson, Leslie 200, 201, 471-473, 874b, 1012-1018, 1532-1535, 1774, 1807, 1813, 1894, 1895, 1952-1954, 2206, 2207
Hubler, Edward (ed.) 74-76, 100, 165, 186, 202-204, 255, 267, 474-478, 1008, 1019, 1020, 1430a, 1468-1470, 1531, 1536-1543, 1579
Hudson, Henry N. (ed.) 37, 77, 78, 479, 480
Hughes, Philip 2073
Hughes, Will 1020a
Huizinga, J. 2074
Hunt, F.C. 1021-1023, 1148a
Hunt, T.W. 1024
Hunter, G.K. 2279, 1025
Hunter, Robert G. 2280, 2349
Hussey, R. 964, 1026, 1678
Hutchinson, J. 1027, 1028
Huttar, Charles A. 1029, 1866
Hutton, James 1030, 1879
Hux, Samuel 1031, 1845
Hyde, H. Montgomery 1471, 1569

Ibbs, E.A. (illus.) 79
Inge, William Ralph 481
Ingram, W.G. (ed.) 80, 81, 482, 623
Iorio, Adrian J. (illus.) 82
Irvine, Helen D. (tr.) 483

Jackson, Edith A. 205
Jaggard, William 484
Jakobson, Roman 485, 493
James, George 486
Jenkins, Elizabeth 2003
Jenkins, Harold 2296
Jennett, Sean (ed.) 83
Jente, Richard 487
Jewkes, W.T. 2401
Jiriczek, O. 1472, 1522
Johannes, J.G. 206, 207
John, Lisle Cecil 488, 1837
Johnson, B.S. 1473, 1539
Johnson, C.F. 489, 490

Johnson, Charles M.W. 491, 1032, 1827, 1828, 1902, 1916
Johnston, G.B. 842, 995, 1033, 1207
Jones, Gwyn (ed.) 84
Jones, H.F. 492
Jones, L.G. 493
Jonson, Ben 1034
Jonson, G.C.A. 1035-1037
Jorgensen, Paul A. 2297
Jorgensen, Virginia 1038, 1737
Joseph, B.L. 2208-2210
Joseph, Sister Miriam 3367
Joyce, James 1039
Judges, A.V. (ed.) 2004
Jusserand, Jean Adrian 494

Kallsen, T.J. 1041, 1647
Kaplin, Milton 1042
Kastner, L.G. 1043
Kaufmann, U. Milo 1474, 1549
Kaula, David 1044
Keats, John 495, 1045
Keen, A. 1955
Keen, Francis 496
Keller, W. 1349, 1475, 1568
Kellett, E.E. 497
Kellner, Loon 498, 1691
Kelso, Ruth 2005
Kent, Sydney 208
Keogh, J.G. 1048, 1701
Ker, William Paton 361, 499
Kermode, John Frank 500, 1049, 2350
Kern, F.A. 1050
Kernan, Alvin B. (ed.) 501
Kernodle, G.R. 2211
King, Arthur H. 996, 1051
Kingsmile, H. 1138, 1476, 1525
Kirchbaum, Leo 2402
Kirk, Richard Ray 1606, 1898
Kirov, Todor T. 997, 1052, 1391
Kitchin, Laurence 2212, 2213
Kittredge, George L. (ed.) 85, 86, 112, 113, 502-504, 627, 2075
Klein, David 1053
Knappen, M.M. 2076

Knight, George Wilson 209,
210, 505-509, 874b, 1054-
1059, 1476a, 1544-1546, 2214,
2331, 2351
Knights, Lionel Charles 284,
510-514, 1060, 1061, 1476a,
1545, 1629, 1630, 1649, 1650,
1742, 1743, 1801, 1803, 1804,
1883, 1914, 2077, 2298
Kobayashi, Minoru 1062, 1218
Kocher, P. H. 2078
Kock, G. A. 1063, 1631
Kökeritz, Helge 2368, 2403,
2415, 2452, 2453
Kolve, V. A. 2139
Krämer, Ilse (tr.) 87
Krenzer, James R. 1632, 1702,
1751, 1867
Krieger, Murray 211, 515, 516,
1064, 1547-1552
Kristeller, Paul O. 517

LaMar, Virginia A. (ed.) 55,
88, 153, 518, 748
Lamson, Roy 1672
Landry, Hilton 212, 519, 1065-
1067, 1117, 1236, 1477, 1478,
1550, 1553-1555, 1644, 1655,
1665, 1669, 1690, 1693, 1744,
1793, 1802, 1808, 1835, 1903,
1917
Lanier, Sidney 213, 220, 520
Lanz, Henry 521
Larbaud, V. 1068, 1778
Latham, M. W. 2079
Law, Robert A. 826, 1069, 1611,
1643
Lawlor, John 2332
Lawrence, Basil Edwin 523
Lawrence, W. J. 1479, 1480,
1523, 1570, 2215-2219, 2313
Lawrence, W. W. 2281, 2315
Lea, K. M. 2140
Lee, Sir Sidney 524-529, 804a,
2006, 1070-1072, 1847, 1857,
1956
Leech, Clifford 2299, 2333, 2334
Legonis, Emile 358, 483, 530
Leigh, M. 950, 1073
Leishman, J. B. 215, 392, 430,
531, 532, 1556-1558
Leisi, Ernest 1074, 1868
Leith, A. A. 1075, 1853

Lerner, Laurence 1481, 1482,
1550, 1554
Leven, R. 1076
Lever, J. W. 533, 534, 851,
1077, 1078, 1483, 1539,
1838
Leveson, Sir Richard 1079
Levin, Harry 1484, 1550
Levin, Richard 920, 1080-
1085, 1679, 1686, 1752,
1829, 1881, 1886, 1896
LeWinter, Oswald (ed.) 535
Lewis, Clive Staple 398, 539,
603, 741, 2007, 2080
Lewis, Michael 874b, 1086
Leys, M. D. R. 2008, 2012
Liddell, Mark H. 538, 1087
Liggins, E. M. 539, 602
Linthicum, Marie C. 2220,
2454
Lloyd, Roger 1088
Loane, G. G. 1089, 1090,
1720, 1758, 1848
Lockwood, L. E. 216
Lodge, Thomas 1091
Loewenberg, J. 1092
Long, Mason 540
Long, P. W. 1093
Looney, J. T. 541
Loughlin, R. C. 1039
Loughlin, Richard L. 1094,
1137
Lounsburg, Thomas R. 2404
Louthan, Doniphan 1095, 1096,
1784
Lovejoy, A. D. 2081
Lovett, David 542
Lowers, James K. 217
Lubbock, R. 1955, 1957
Lucas, F. L. 2141
Luce, Morton 543, 544
Lüdeke, H. 1485, 1540
Lumiansky, R. M. 545, 1099,
1703, 1904, 1918
Lundquist, Carole 1100, 1687
Lynch, Arthur 804a, 1101-
1103, 1425

Mabie, H. W. (ed.) 92
MacCallum, Sir Mungo W.
2405
McClumpha, C. F. 1097, 1104-
1106, 1135, 1260, 1486, 1528

McClure, N. E. (ed.) 2009
MacCracken, Henry Noble 548
McCurdy, H. G. 1958
McCutcheon, Roger P. 1606, 1898
McFarland, Thomas 2335
McGuinness, Kevin 1107
Machiavelli, Niccolo 2439, 2456, 2479
Mack, Maynard 1897
Mackail, John William 549-551, 1108
Mackenzie, A. C. 1109, 1754
Mackenzie, Agnes Mure 552
Mackenzie, Barbara A. (ed.) 93, 218, 1559
Mackenzie, W. R. 2142
MacLeish, Archibald 553, 1110, 1794, 1795
McMahan, Anna B. 219, 554
McManaway, J. G. (ed.) 1487, 1561, 2369, 3371
McNeal, Thomas H. 923, 974, 1034, 1111, 1112, 1820, 1839
McPeek, J. A. S. 555
Macphail, A. 1113
Madariaga, S. de 781, 984, 1114, 1196
Madden, Dodgson H. 556
Mahony, P. 1115, 1610
Mahood, M. M. 557, 1116, 1589, 1645, 1814, 2370, 3372
Main, C. F. 94, 558, 559, 666, 1296, 1633, 1688, 1910
Maine, G. T. (ed.) 56
M., J. 546, 547
Malone, Edmund 1117
Malone, Kemp (ed.) 220
Malue, H. W. 1119
Manheim, Ralph (tr.) 2221, 2225
Mann, Thomas 885
Marder, Louis 560, 2222, 1119, 1120
Margeson, J. M. R. 2143
Marlowe, Christopher 2457
Marlowe, Phil 1121, 1138
Marriott, Sir John A. R. 2300
Marshall, W. 1488, 1520
Martin, L. C. (ed.) 2457
Martin, Philip 1122
Massey, Gerald 221-222
Masson, David I. (ed.) 561, 1123

Matthew, Frank 562
Matthews, G. M. 1124, 1125, 1328
Mattingly, Garrett 874b, 1126, 1766
Maxwell, J. C. 872, 1127, 1869, 2301
May, Louis F., Jr. 1128, 1761
May, Thomas 1129
Mayhew, A. L. (ed.) 2371, 2458, 3460
Mazzeo, J. A. 2082
Meader, William G. 2282
Meeks, L. H. 1130
Meller, Margrit 1131
Meyer, A. O. 2010
Michael, Laurence 1012, 1133, 1134, 1767, 1894
Miles, Josephine 564
Miller, E. H. 2011
Miller, Frank (tr.) 2459
Miller, Walter (tr.) 2460
Millett, Fred B. 1681
Mills, Laurens Joseph 565
Milstead, John (ed.) 346, 566
Milton, John 1136, 1137
Mincoff, M. 1489, 1580
Mitchell, R. J. 2012
Mizener, Arthur 567, 568, 828, 1140-1142, 1812
Mommsen, T. E. 2428, 2461
Monro, John (ed.) 569
Montgomery, Robert L. 1143
Moore, Carlisle 570, 1144, 1697, 1704, 1905, 1919
Moore, H. 989, 1145, 1251
More, Paul Elmer 571
Morgan, A. 1146
Morgan, Paul 1147
Morley, Christopher (ed.) 95, 1148
Morris, C. 2083
Morton, David 572
Motter, T. H. V. 2144
Moulton, Richard Green 2013
Muir, Kenneth 223, 573, 574, 587, 1148a, 1150, 1150a, 1151, 1394, 1422, 1560, 2283, 2336, 2337, 2352, 2462, 2463, 2467
Munro, John 874a, 1152, 2433, 2464

Murray, Howard 1153
Murray, J. T. 2223
Murray, R. H. 2084
Murry, John Middleton 575-
577, 852, 887, 1089, 1154-
1158, 1251, 1768, 1769,
1805
Mutschmann, M. 1148a, 1159

Nagler, A. M. 2221, 2224,
2225
Naylor, Edward W. 578, 1599,
1821, 2226
Neale, J. E. 2085-2087
Nearing, Homer, Jr. 1160,
1490, 1555, 1624
Needham, F. 1162, 1251
Neilson, William Allan (ed.) 71,
96, 578, 2465, 2497
Nejgebauer, A. 1163, 1164
Ness, F. W. 2372
Nethercot, Arthur H. 580
Netto, I. 976, 1165
Nevinson, J. L. 1167
Newbolt, Henry 224
Newcomer, A. G. 1001, 1168,
1223
Newdigate, B. H. 1169, 1251,
1425
Nicholson, F. C. 1173
Nickalls, B. 813, 1174, 1425
Nicoll, Allardyce (ed.) 1175,
1491, 1564, 2014, 2015, 2227-
2230
Nicoll, Josephine C. 581
Nisbet, Ulric 225
Noble, Richmond 582, 2231
Nolan, Edward F. 583, 1176,
1705, 1906, 1920
Norton, Thomas (tr.) 2466
Nosworthy, J. M. 1013, 1138,
1177, 1178, 1775, 1809, 1815,
2410
Nowottny, M. T. 1179
Nowottny, Winifred 584, 585,
1180, 1181, 1492, 1565, 1582,
1583, 1588, 1590, 1591, 1593,
1594, 1893
Noyes, Alfred 580, 1182
Nungezer, Edwin 2232

O'Dea, Raymond 1183
Odell, George C. D. 2233

O'Flanagan, J. I. 226
Ogle, M. B. 1184, 1185
Olfson, L. 1186, 1187
Oliphant, E. H. C. 1188
O'Loughlin, Sean 574, 587,
2467
O'Neal, Cothbum 227
Ong, Walter J. 1189
Onions, C. T. (ed.) 2006,
2016, 2373, 2468
Orange, Linwood E. 1190,
1619
Ord, Hubert W. 228, 588,
854, 1191, 1192, 1251
Ornstein, Robert (ed.) 2314
Osterberg, V. 904, 1195
Ovid 1197, 2459, 2469
Owen, D. E. 588
Owst, G. R. 2145

Palk, R. 1198, 1199, 1235
Palmer, D. J. 1493, 1540
Palmer, George Herbert 229
Palmer, H. E. 887, 1494,
1526
Palmer, John 2284, 2302
Paret, M. 1495, 1529
Parish, Verna N. 1200
Parker, David 1201
Parrott, Thomas Marc (ed.)
74, 99, 100, 101, 2285,
2470
Parry, Sir Charles H. H. 590,
1777
Parson, Howard 1202, 1870
Partridge, A. C. 2411
Partridge, Eric 2374, 2471
Pearson, A. F. S. 2088
Pearson, Hesketh (ed.) 591
Pearson, Lu Emily 592
Pegis, Anton G. (ed.) 2472
Pember, Francis William 593
Pemberton, Henry, Jr. 594,
1205
Pembroke, Earl of 1206
Penrose, Boies 2089
Pepper, Stephen C. 1634,
1891, 1912
Percy, Henry 1207
Perrett, Arthur J. 874b, 1209
Perrine, Lawrence 1210, 1261
Peterson, Douglas L. 595,
1211, 1416, 1830

Pettet, Ernest C. 1212, 2146,
2286, 2353
Phelps, W. L. 1213
Phialas, Peter G. 2287
Phillips, Gerald W. (ed.)
105, 106, 230, 231, 596,
597, 598
Pillai, V. K. A. 599
Pineton, Clara Longworth 45,
107, 179, 232-234, 396, 600,
601, 879, 1214, 1524, 1561,
1939, 1959
Piper, H. W. 539, 602, 1215,
1216, 1637, 1899
Pirkhofer, Anton M. 1217, 1586
Plato 2435, 2473
Platt, Arthur 905, 1219
Poel, William 2234
Pohl, Frederick J. 1138, 1220,
1221
Poirier, Michael 1496-1499,
1551, 1558, 1571, 1580
Pollard, A. F. 1222, 3476, 3479
Pollard, Alfred William 604,
1960, 2412-2414, 2474, 2475
Pollen, J. H. 2090
Pooler, C. Knox (ed.) 108, 235
Popovic, Vladeta 605
Porter, C. 1001, 1168, 1223,
1224
Pott, C. M. 1225
Potter, James L. 236
Powell, C. L. 2017
Powicke, F. M. 2091
Pratt, Marjory Bates 237
Praz, Mario 606, 1500, 1559
Price, Thomas Randall 607
Prince, Frank Templeton 238,
608, 609, 1276, 1501, 1565
Proser, Matthew N. 2338
Prosser, Eleanor 2147
Prouty, Charles Tyler (ed.)
2403, 2415
Puknat, S. B. 885, 1230, 1231
Puknat, Z. M. 1230
Purdum, R. 1232, 1822

Quennell, Peter 1961, 2018
Quiller-Couch, Sir Arthur T.
610
Quinn, Edward G. (ed.) 1933,
1962, 2432, 2476

Raab, Felix 2092
Raby, F. J. E. 1233
Radley, Virginia L. 1234,
1243, 1780, 1900
Ralli, Augustus 612
Rank, Otto 288, 613
Ransom, John Crowe 239,
614-617, 911, 1236-1239,
1642, 1673, 1674, 1707,
1770
Rattrag, R. F. 1004, 1240
Raymond, George L. 618
Raysor, F. M. (ed.) 619
Raysor, Thomas Middleton
(ed.) 370, 620, 621
Read, C. J. 2093-2095
Redding, David C. 1234, 1241,
1700, 1900
Redfern, Joan (tr.) 627
Redgrave, G. R. 2475, 2477
Redin, Mats 1242
Redpath, Theodore (ed.) 80,
81, 109, 482, 623, 1247,
3480
Reed, A. W. 2148
Reed, Edward B. (ed.) 110,
159, 624
Reed, Victor B. (ed.) 111,
150, 240, 270, 433, 440,
477, 491, 506, 510, 519,
545, 567, 570, 583, 616,
625, 636, 684, 715, 739,
1562, 1571, 1901-1908
Reese, M. M. 1964, 2288,
2303
Reeves, James 625, 1682
Reichert, John F. 917, 1244,
1613
Rendall, Gerald Henry
241, 242, 1148a, 1245,
2375
Rewcastle, G. 1246
Reynolds, G. F. 2235
Ribner, Irving (ed.) 112, 113,
627, 2149, 2304
Ricci, Luigi (tr.) 2456, 2479
Rice, E. F., Jr. 2096
Rice, Sir Robert 628
Richards, I. A. 627, 629-633
Richmond, H. M. 1248, 1841
Richmond, O. 1249, 1729
Rickert, R. T. (ed.) 2131,
2150

Ricks, Christopher 1502, 1580
Riding, Laura 438, 625, 634-637, 966, 1826, 1831, 1890, 1892, 1909
Ridler, Anne Bradley (ed.) 638, 2020
Ridley, Maurice Roy (ed.) 98, 114, 639
Rinaker, Clarissa 1250
Robbins, R. H. A. 1252, 1823
Robertson, Jean G. 244, 640
Robertson, John M. 245, 246, 641-643, 1563, 1564
Robinson, H. S. 644
Rodin, M. 1253, 1425
Roe, J. E. 645, 1254, 1255
Rogers, E. C. 1256, 1840, 1842
Rolfe, William James 1257, 1965
Rolle, Dietrich 952, 1258, 1259, 1745, 1888
Rollins, Hyder E. (ed.) 44, 115, 116, 247, 646, 647, 2480
Ronsard, Pierre 1262
Root, R. K. 648
Rosen, William 2339
Rosenberg, Marvin 2236
Rosenthal, M. Louis 1708, 1911
Ross, William 248, 649
Ross, W. D. (ed.) 2427, 2481
Rossiter, A. P. 2151
Rostenberg, Leona 1263, 1264, 1388
Rouse, William Henry Denham (ed.) 650
Rowse, Alfred Leslie (ed.) 117, 651-654, 1265-1270, 1966, 2021, 2097, 2482
Rubow, P. V. 1271, 1272
Rusden, G. W. 655
Ruthven, K. K. 1273, 1843
Rutter, Joseph 1274
Rylands, George Humphrey W. 656, 2376

St. Clair, F. Y. 1275
St. Lys, O. (tr.) 1276
Saintsbury, George 657
Salle, J. C. 1277, 1620
Salter, F. M. 2152
Salyer, Sandford 1503, 1541
Sampson, J. 1278, 1652, 1749
Sanderlin, George 1279

Sanders, Gerald De Witt 2022
Sanders, Norman 1040, 1132, 1280
Santayana, George 376, 658, 659, 1871
Sarrazin, G. (tr., ed.) 2483
Saunders, J. W. 2237
Schaar, Claes 249, 250, 660-662, 1281-1284, 1565, 1661, 1709, 1723, 1736
Schanzer, Ernest 2315
Schelling, Felix E. 663, 2305
Schmidt, Alexander 2483, 2484
Schmidtchen, P. W. 1286
Schoen-Rene, Otto E. 1285
Schoff, F. G. 1287
Schroeter, James 1288, 1710
Schuckling, Levin L. 664
Schultz, John H. 1289
Schwartz, D. 1290
Scotland, Catherine W. 874b, 1086, 1291
Scott, David 874a, 919, 1292
Scott-Espiner, Janet G. 1293 1294, 1294a
Seib, Kenneth 1295, 1711
Sellery, G. C. 2098
Sells, A. L. 665
Seltzer, Daniel 2238
Sen Gupta, S. C. 2289, 2306
Seng, Peter J. 558, 559, 666, 1296, 1633, 1910
Seymour, H. 1297
Seymour-Smith, Martin (ed.) 118, 119, 1298, 1299, 1854
Shaaber, Matthias A. 667
Shackford, Martha Hall 668, 1300
Shanks, Edward 669
Sharp, Frank C. 670
Sharp, (Mrs.) W. 671
Sharp, William 671, 672
Sharpe, R. B. 2239
Shattuck, C. H. 2240
Shaw, George Bernard 251, 874a, 1320, 1321, 1566
Sherbo, Arthur 444, 673
Sherzer, Jane 1322
Shield, H. A. 1323, 1324, 1595, 1600
Shikoda, Mitsuo 1325
Shilleto, A. R. (ed.) 2485
Shipley, Joseph T. 252

Shipwith, G. H. 1326
Shirley, F. A. 2241
Shore, William T. 674
Shroeder, J. W. 2416
Sidebotham, H. (tr.) 1327
Sidney, Sir Philip 326, 2016,
  2444
Siegel, Paul N. 675, 1328, 1329,
  1330
Silver, Frederick 253
Silverstein, Norman 1331
Simon, Henry W. (ed.) 124, 676
Simpson, Percy 2377, 2486
Simpson, Richard 254
Singh, S. 1332
Sipe, Dorothy L. 677
Sisson, Charles J. (ed.) 52, 53,
  90, 125-127, 522, 678, 679,
  1967, 2340, 2417, 2487
Sitwell, Edith 680
Skeat, W. W. 2371, 2378, 2458,
  2488
Skinner, B. F. 1333, 1334
Smart, J. S. 1925, 1968
Smeaton, William H. O. 681
Smedley, W. T. 1335
Smith, A. J. M. 1911
Smith, Barbara H. (ed.) 128
Smith, D. Nichol (ed.) 682, 683,
  2024
Smith, G. C. M. 1336, 1337,
  1663, 1748
Smith, Gordon Ross 684, 1338,
  1852, 1907, 1921, 2489
Smith, Hallett 685, 807, 1129,
  1609, 1339, 1507, 1555, 1609,
  1667, 1712, 1746, 1796, 1832,
  1874
Smith, Irwin 2242, 2243
Smith, J. C. (ed.) 1340, 2490
Smith, Logan Pearsall 686
Smith, Sir Thomas 2046, 2099
Smith, William George 2491
Snider, Denton J. 687, 1969
Somervell, R. U. 1341
Southam, B. C. 1347, 1872
Southampton, Earl of 1348, 1349,
  1421
Southern, Richard 2244, 2245
Speaght, William 2246
Spencer, Hazelton 688, 1970,
  2025, 2247
Spencer, Terence John B. 2341,
  2343

Spencer, Theodore J. B. 689,
  1350, 2026, 2100
Spender, Stephen 255
Spenser, Edmund 2438, 2490,
  2492
Spitzer, Leo 1351
Spivack, Bernard 2153
Sprague, Arthur Colby 2248-
  2250, 2307, 2436, 2493
Spurgeon, Caroline F. E. 690,
  691
Squire, John C. 692, 2494
Spurrier, Steven (illus.) 138,
  1567
Stabler, A. P. 1352
Stageberg, Norman C. 1912
Stainer, C. L. 1353, 1717
Stalker, Archibald 256, 693
Standen, Gilbert 694
Starnes, D. T. 1354, 1675
Stauffer, D. A. 1355, 1873
Steadman, John M. 784, 929,
  1356, 1357, 1844, 1855
Steeholm, Hardy 2027
Steeholm, Cara 2027
Steele, Mary S. 2251
Stephen, Pepper 1882
Stevens, George 695
Stevens, John 2028
Stevenson, Charles L. 696
Stirling, Brents 257, 324, 470,
  697, 698, 1358-1361, 1778,
  1818, 2342
Stockholm, J. M. 2252
Stoffel, C. O. 699, 721
Stoll, E. E. 700, 1362, 1363,
  2290
Stone, Reynolds (illus.) 139
Stone, Walter B. 1364, 1771,
  1895
Stopes, Charlotte C. 701-703,
  1138, 1365, 1366, 1425,
  1568, 1971
Stotsenburg, John Hawley 704
Stow, John 2029
Stowe, A. R. M. 2030
Strachey, C. 930a, 1251, 1367,
  1368, 1425, 1730
Strachey, Giles Lytton 705
Strachey, John St. Loe 706,
  1369
Strathmann, Ernest A. 1507,
  1541
Stroll, Elmer Edgar 2031

Stronach, G. 1370
Strong, J. R. 258
Strong, L. A. G. 140, 707
Stroup, Thomas B. 1098, 1371, 1798
Sturtz, S. V. 1262, 1372, 1725
Suckling, Sir John 2496
Suddard, Sarah J. M. 708, 1670
Sykes, C. 1373
Sypher, Wylie 1374

Talbert, E. W. 2154, 2308
Tannenbaum, Samuel A. 1315-1317, 1614, 2379
Tate, Allen 1378
Tawney, R. H. 2101
Tayler, E. W. 2102
Taylor, A. E. 2495
Taylor, Dick, Jr. 315, 356, 448, 709, 1379, 1380, 1425
Taylor, George Coffin 470, 710
Taylor, Henry Osborn 711, 2103
Terry, Ellen 712
Thaler, Alwin 713, 2253
Theobald, B. G. 259
Thomas, Karl F. 1833, 1834
Thomas, Walter (ed.) 143
Thomas, Wright 1713, 1884
Thompson, A. H. (ed.) 714, 2496
Thompson, E. N. S. 2155, 2254
Thompson, Karl F. 715, 1385, 1908, 1922
Thompson, Patricia 717, 874b, 1386, 1753
Thomson, James A. K. 716
Thomson, Walter (ed.) 143, 260, 1570
Thonon, Robert 1387, 1762
Thorndike, A. H. 2156, 2255, 2465, 2497
Thorn-Dury, George 718
Thornton, Gregory 719
Thorpe, Thomas 1388
Thurston, Herbert 1138, 1389
Tiddy, R. J. E. 2157
Tilley, Morris P. 2498, 2499
Tillyard, Eustace M. W. 2032, 2104, 2291, 2292, 2309, 2316, 2354
Titherley, Arthur W. 144, 261, 1390
Toliver, Harold E. 1392
Tonog Lanua, Francisco G. 985, 1393

Toole, William B. 2317
Traversi, D. A. 720, 2033, 2293, 2310, 2343, 2355
Trevelyan, G. M. 2034
Trewin, J. C. 2256
Tucker, T. G. (ed.) 145
Turner, L. M. 1138, 1395
Tyler, Thomas 262

Unwin, G. 2035
Ure, Peter 2318

Vaganay, Hughes 1294a
Van Dam, V. A. 699, 721
Van Doren, Mark 722, 1680, 1696, 1972, 2036
Venezky, Alice S. 2257, 2259
Venton, W. B. 264
Vietor, Wilhelm 2380, 2500
Violi, Unicio J. 263
Viswanathan, K. 925, 1397
Vizetelly, Ernest Alfred 723

Walker, Alice 2418, 2419
Wallace, C. W. 1973, 2258
Walley, George 1668
Walsh, C. M. (ed.) 149
Walton, J. K. 1511, 1580
Ward, B. A. 159
Ward, B. R. 265, 266, 724, 1138, 1398-1400
Warnke, Frank J. 2449, 2501
Warren, Clyde T. 366, 725, 859, 1401, 1658, 1913
Warren, Robert Penn 1914
Warren, Roger 1402
Wassal, G. 726, 727, 1683, 1738
Watkins, Ronald 2259
Watkins, W. B. C. 728
Watson, Curtis Brown 729, 2105
Watson, Ernest Bradlee 2260
Watson, Wilfred 874a, 1403
Webster, Margaret 2261, 2262
Weinberger, J. 730
Weisinger, Herbert 2344
Wells, Henry Willis 731, 887, 1020a, 1404, 1405
Welsford, Enid 2158, 2263
Wendell, Barrett 732, 733
Westfall, Alfred van Rensselaer 734
Wheeler, Charles B. 801, 1406

Whitaker, Virgil K. 735, 1512, 1517, 2037, 2345
Whitcomb, I. P. 1407
White, Edward Joseph 736
White, Henry Kesley 737
White, Robert L. 1408, 1714
Whorlow, H. 1409, 1657
Wickham, Glynne 2264
Wilde, Oscar 198, 267, 268, 591, 738, 1569
Wilder, C. F. 1410
Wilkie, K. E. 1411
Wilkins, Ernest H. 1412, 1413
Wilkinson, L. P. 1011, 1414, 1756
Willcock, Gladys D. 2381
Willen, Gerald (ed.) 111, 150, 240, 270, 333, 440, 477, 491, 506, 510, 519, 545, 567, 570, 583, 616, 636, 684, 715, 739, 1562, 1571, 1915-1922
Williams, Franklin B., Jr. 1415
Williams, Frayne 740
Williams, Philip 1513, 1543
Willoughby, Edwin E. (ed.) 2382, 2420
Wilson, Frank P. (ed.) 741, 742, 2038, 2106, 2311
Wilson, Harold S. 2265, 2346
Wilson, John Dover (ed.) 97, 151, 269, 743, 744, 1562, 1573-1580, 1974, 2039, 2040, 2294, 2421, 2422
Wilson, Katherine M. 1410, 1418
Wilson, Sir Thomas 1417
Wimsatt, W. K. 1514, 1552
Winifred, Lynskey 1715
Winny, James 271
Winters, Yvor 280, 745, 746, 1418, 1719
Withers, C. (ed.) 152
Withington, Robert 2266
Woodward, P. 1419
Wordsworth, William 46
Wright, Louis B. (ed.) 55, 88, 153, 518, 748, 1420, 2041, 2042
Wright, T. 2383, 2502
Wright, W. Aldis (ed.) 749
Wriothesley, Henry 1421
Wyatt, Thomas 1422
Wyld, H. C. 2403
Wyndham, George (ed.) 750

Yates, Frances A. 751, 1423, 2267
Yeatman, John P. 752
Yolland, Arthur 1424
Young, Frances Berkeley 753
Young, Sir George 754
Young, H. McClure 272
Young, Karl 2159

Zahniser, Howard 1635
Zeeveld, W. G. 2107
Zeydel, Edwin H. 1426
Zilboorg, Gregory 2043